Personal Effectiveness

Titles in the Institute of Managment Series
NVQ Level 3
The Competent First-Line Manager
Shields

Certificate (NVQ Level 4)
Management Task (second edition)
Dixon

Managing Financial Resources (second edition)
Broadbent and Cullen

Managing Information (second edition)

Managing People (second edition)
Thomson

Meeting Customer Needs (second edition)
Smith

Personal Effectiveness (second edition)
Murdock and Scutt

Diploma (NVQ Level 5)
Developing Human Resources
Thomson and Mabey

Managerial Finance
Parkinson

Managing an Effective Operation
Fowler and Graves

Managing Klowledge
Wilson

Managing in the Public Sector
Blundell and Murdock

Managing Quality
Wilson, McBride and Bell

Managing Schools
Whitaker

Managing in the Single European Market
Brown

Marketing
Lancaster and Reynolds

Tutor Support
*NVQ Handbook: practical guide-
lines for providers and assessors*
Walton

Personal Effectiveness

Second edition

Alexander Murdock and Carol N. Scutt

*Published in association with
the Institute of Management*

To Lara and Lars

Butterworth-Heinemann
Linacre House, Jordan Hill, Oxford OX2 8DP
225 Wildwood Avenue, Woburn, MA 01801-2041
A division of Reed Educational and Professional Publishing Ltd

 A member of the Reed Elsevier plc group

OXFORD   AUCKLAND   BOSTON
JOHANNESBURG   MELBOURNE   NEW DELHI

First published 1993
Reprinted 1994, 1995
Second edition 1997
Reprinted 1999, 2001, 2002

British Library Cataloguing in Publication Data
A catalogue record for this book is available from the British Library

ISBN 0 7506 3393 X

For more information on all Butterworth-Heinemann
publications please visit our website at www.bh.com

FOR EVERY TITLE THAT WE PUBLISH, BUTTERWORTH-HEINEMANN
WILL PAY FOR BTCV TO PLANT AND CARE FOR A TREE.

Typeset by Avocet Typeset, Brill, Aylesbury, Bucks
Printed and bound in Great Britain by Biddles Ltd
www.biddles.co.uk

Contents

Series adviser's preface

This book is one of a series designed for people wanting to develop their capabilities as managers. You might think that there isn't anything very new in that. In one way you would be right. The fact that very many people want to learn to become better managers is not new, and for many years a wide range of approaches to such learning and development has been available. These have included courses leading to formal qualifications, organizationally-based management development programmes and a whole variety of self-study materials. A copious literature, extending from academic textbooks to sometimes idiosyncratic prescriptions from successful managers and consultants, has existed to aid – or perhaps confuse – the potential seeker after managerial truth and enlightenment.

So what is new about this series? In fact, a great deal – marking in some ways a revolution in our thinking both about the art of managing and also the process of developing managers.

Where did it all begin? Like most revolutions, although there may be a single, identifiable act that precipitated the uprising, the roots of discontent are many and long-established. The debate about the performance of British managers, the way managers are educated and trained, and the extent to which shortcomings in both these areas have contributed to our economic decline, has been running for several decades.

Until recently, this debate had been marked by periods of frenetic activity – stimulated by some report or enquiry and perhaps ending in some new initiatives or policy changes – followed by relatively long periods of comparative clam. But the underlying causes for concern persisted. Basically, the majority of managers in the UK appeared to have little or no training for their role, certainly far less than their counterparts in our major competitor nations. And there was concern about the nature, style and appropriateness of the management education and training that was available.

The catalyst for this latest revolution came in late 1986 and early 1987, when three major reports reopened the whole issue. The 1987 reports were *The Making of British Managers* by John Constable and Robert McCormick, carried out for the British Institute of Management and the CBI, and *The Making of Managers* by Charles Handy, carried out for the (then) Manpower Services Commission, National Economic Development Office and British Institute of Management. The 1986 report, which often receives less recognition than it deserves as a key contribution to the recent changes, was *Management Training: context and process* by Iain Mangham and Mick Silver, carried out for the Economic and Social Research Council and the Department of Trade and Industry.

It is not the place to review in detail what the reports said. Indeed, they and their consequences are discussed in several places in this series of books. But essentially they confirmed that:

- British managers were undertrained by comparison with their counterparts internationally.
- The majority of employers invested far too little in training and developing their managers.
- Many employers found it difficult to specify with any degree of detail just what it was that they required successful managers to be able to do.

The Constable/McCormick and Handy reports advanced various recommendations for addressing these problems, involving an expansion of management education and development, a reformed structure of qualifications and a commitment from employers to a code of practice for management development. While this analysis was not new, and had echoes of much that had been said in earlier debates, this time a few leading individuals determined that the response should be both radical and permanent. The response was coordinated by the newly-established Council for Management Education and Development (now the National Forum for Management Education and Development (NFMED)) under the energetic and visionary leadership of Bob (now Sir Bob) Reid formerly of Shell UK and the British Railways Board.

Under the umbrella of NFMED a series of employer-led working parties tackled the problem of defining what it was that managers should be able to do, and how this differed for people at different levels in their organizations; how this satisfactory ability to perform might be verified; and how an appropriate structure of management qualifications could be put in place. This work drew upon the methods used to specify vocational standards in industry and commerce, and led to the development and introduction of competence-based management standards and qualifications. In this context, competence is defined as the ability to perform the activities within an occupation or function to the standards expected in employment.

It is this competence-based approach that is new in our thinking about the manager's capabilities. It is also what is new about this series of books, in that they are designed to support both this new structure of management standards, and of development activities based on it. The series was originally commissioned to support the Institute of Management's Certificate and Diploma qualifications, which were one of the first to be based on the new standards. However, these books are equally appropriate to any university, college or indeed company course leading to a certificate in management or diploma in management studies.

The standards were specified through an extensive process of consultation with a large number of managers in organizations of many different types and sizes. They are therefore employment based and employer-supported. And they fill the gap that Mangham and Silver identified – now we do have a language to describe what it is employers want their managers to be able to do – at least in part.

If you are engaged in any form of management development leading to a certificate or diploma qualification conforming to the national management standards, then you are probably already familiar with most of the key ideas on which the standards are based. To achieve their key purpose, which is defined as achieving the organization's objectives and continuously improving its performance, managers need to perform four key roles: managing operations, managing finance, managing people and managing information. Each of these key roles has a sub-structure of units and elements, each with associated performance and assessment criteria.

The reason for the qualification 'in part' is that organizations are different, and jobs within them are different. Thus the generic management standards probably do not cover all the management competences that you need to possess in your job. There are almost certainly additional things, specific to your own situation in your own organization, that you need to be able to do. The standards are necessary, but almost certainly not sufficient. Only you, in discussion with your boss, will be able to decide what other capabilities you need to possess. But the standards are a place to start, a basis on which to build. Once you have demonstrated your proficiency against the standards, it will stand you in good stead as you progress through your organization or change jobs.

So how do the new standards change the process by which you develop yourself as a manager? They change the process of development, or of gaining a management qualification, quite a lot. It is no longer a question of acquiring information and facts, perhaps by being 'taught' in some classroom environment, and then being tested to see what you can recall. It involves demonstrating, in a quite specific way, that you can do certain things to a particular standard of performance. And because of this, it puts a much greater onus on you to manage your own development, to decide how you can demonstrate any particular competence, what evidence you need to present, and how you can collect it. Of course, there will always be people to advise and guide you in this, if you need help.

But there is another dimension, and it is to this that this series of books is addressed. While the standards stress ability to perform, they do not ignore the traditional knowledge base that has been associated with 'management studies'. Rather, they set this in a different context. The standards are supported by 'underpinning knowledge and understanding' which has three components:

- Purpose and context, which is knowledge and understanding of the manager's objectives, and of the relevant organizational and environmental influences, opportunities and values.
- Principles and methods, which is knowledge and understanding of the theories, models, principles, methods and

techniques that provide the basis of competent managerial performance.

■ Data, which is knowledge and understanding of specific facts likely to be important to meeting the standards.

Possession of the relevant knowledge and understanding underpinning the standards is needed to support competent managerial performance as specified in the standards. It also has an important role in supporting the transferability of management capabilities. It helps to ensure that you have done more than learned 'the way we do things around here' in your own organization. It indicates a recognition of the wider things which underpin competence, and that you will be able to change jobs or organizations and still be able to perform effectively.

These books cover the knowledge and understanding underpinning the management standards, most specifically in the category of principles and methods. But their coverage is not limited to the minimum required by the standards, and extends in both depth and breadth in many areas. The authors have tried to approach these underlying principles and methods in a practical way. They use many short cases and examples which we hope will demonstrate how, in practice, the principles and methods, and knowledge of purpose and context plus data, support the ability to perform as required by the management standards. In particular we hope that this type of presentation will enable you to identify and learn from similar examples in your own managerial work.

You will already have noticed that one consequence of this new focus on the standards is that the traditional 'functional' packages of knowledge and theory do not appear. The standard textbook titles such as 'quantitative methods', 'production management', 'organizational behaviour' etc. disappear. Instead, principles and methods have been collected together in clusters that more closely match the key roles within the standards. You will also find a small degree of overlap in some of the volumes, because some principles and methods support several of the individual units within the standards. We hope you will find this useful reinforcement.

Having described the positive aspects of standards-based management development, it would be wrong to finish without a few cautionary remarks. The developments described above may seem simple, logical and uncontroversial. It did not always seem that way in the years of work which led up to the introduction of the standards. To revert to the revolution analogy, the process has been marked by ideological conflict and battles over sovereignty and territory. It has sometimes been unclear which side various parties are on – and indeed how many sides there are! The revolution, if well advanced, is not at an end. Guerrilla warfare continues in parts of the territory.

Perhaps the best way of describing this is to say that, while competence-based standards are widely recognized as at least a major part of the answer to improving managerial performance, they are not the whole answer. There is still some debate about the way competences are defined, and whether those in the standards are the most appropriate on which to base assessment of managerial performance. There are other models of management competences than those in the standards.

There is also a danger in separating management performance into a set of discrete components. The whole is, and needs to be, more than the sum of the parts. Just like bowling an off-break in cricket, practising a golf swing or forehand drive in tennis, you have to combine all the separate movements into a smooth, flowing action. How you combine the competences, and build on them, will mark your own individual style as a manager.

We should also be careful not to see the standards as set in stone. They determine what today's managers need to be able to do. As the arena in which managers operate changes, then so will the standards. The lesson for all of us as managers is that we need to go on learning and developing, acquiring new skills or refining existing ones. Obtaining your certificate or diploma is like passing a mile post, not crossing the finishing line.

All the changes and developments of recent years have brought management qualifications, and the processes by which they are gained, much closer to your job as a manager. We hope these books support this process by providing bridges between your own experience and the underlying principles and methods which will help you to demonstrate your competence. Already, there is a lot of evidence that managers enjoy the challenge of demonstrating competence, and find immediate benefits in their jobs from the programmes based on these new-style qualifications. We hope you do too. Good luck in your career development.

Paul Jervis

Foreword

Professor Tom Cannon, the Chief Executive of MCI, Lead Body for Occupational Standards in Managerial Competence, introduces the reader to MCI and the role of *Personal Effectiveness* in the gaining of competence.

MCI is the national body responsible for the creation, development and promotion of standards in managerial competence. We have spent the last three years reviewing the general standards based on several years of their practical application in all industries where individuals have management responsibility. This review, which incorporates recommendations made by independent studies such as the two major pieces of research by Gordon Beaumont and Sir Ron Dearing, has resulted, among other things, in the identification of the need for a separate *core* of standards of competence at all levels of management, together with the availability of suites of optional units to cover the specific and diverse responsibilities of individual managers.

The emphasis of these responsibilities might lean towards the need for options in, for example: personnel functions such as recruitment and selection, or staff appraisal; specific functions of managing quality or energy; the growing managerial function of managing projects. As well as the various suites of options which will be available at the different levels, there will also be more specialized units such as standards for management consultants, standards for managing projects and modules in *continuing professional development* (CPD) developed around the management standards themselves.

Whichever bias your role as a manager may have, and whatever approach you may wish to take in order to develop your particular needs towards competence, the crucial development needs for any manager relate to their *behaviour* in that role; their *personal effectiveness* or *personal competency* in ensuring that objectives are met.

The authors of this book are attempting to address these *personal competency* requirements. While their main audience will be those who are new to management roles, it is also understood that all individuals are naturally more competent in some behaviours than others and that a certain amount of continuous development is required by all managers. The book should, therefore, be of value to those who are concentrating on their *continuing professional development* and they may care to revisit the areas more directly associated with their personal needs, no matter what their level of responsibility or experience in management. The authors help by providing ideas for further reading, experiment and exploration.

As with many academic texts, the authors do not necessarily expect that everyone will follow the chapters sequentially from start to finish; every individual will have his or her own interests to pursue as appropriate. If you are following an academic course of study, course tutors are likely to direct you to specific chapters at appropriate points throughout your course attendance. This is a good approach and will help you to focus on specific issues as needed. If you are using the text for your own interests or in association with distance learning, an equally beneficial approach is for you to dip in and out of the book as you like.

At the end of the day, though, it is not appropriate for managers to dis-aggregate their thinking and behaviour in this way, and you will need to draw your learning and development together so that your *spontaneous behaviour* in performing in your job is more *informed* than before; in other words, you will know why you are behaving in particular ways instead of just what you are doing. The aim must ultimately be for you to fulfil your role *holistically* by bringing together the more disparate work and behaviour of others into the management of your role in meeting your organization's mission and achieving strategic objectives.

With this in mind, I, and my team at MCI, would like to wish you well with your ventures into managerial theory, best practice and behaviour and trust this book goes some way towards helping you to succeed in your aspirations and ambitions.

Tom Cannon

Russell Square, London. March 1997

Glossary of terms

Adviser   In the context of NVQ, SVQ, or crediting occupational competence purposes, an adviser is a person specially trained and accredited to help in the process of development and in the compilation of evidence for assessment.

Approved Centre   An organisation which has been approved by an awarding body to deliver assessment to NVQs/SVQs.

Assessment   The process by which a manager is judged as competent (or not yet competent) against the Management Standards.

Assessment Contract   This is a document summarizing the units and elements for which a manager will be seeking credit and the date by which they undertake to present their completed portfolio (or sections of it). It is signed by the manager and the Crediting Competence adviser.

Assessor   The person who undertakes the formal evaluation and assessment of a manager's evidence for the purpose of judging whether he or she is competent. The assessor requires EOSC Units D32 and D33 and must be able to accurately interpret the Management Standards, against the manager's job, to the level being assessed.

Authenticity   Concerns whether evidence in your portfolio is genuinely the result of your own work (if it is the result of group work you will need to directly identify your role).

Award   In the N/SVQ context, an award is another name for a qualification.

Awarding Body   A body which develops and awards the qualifications based on Occupational Standards.

Business Links   Business Links are contracted to Training and Enterprise Councils (TECs) to provide business support services in a local area. There could be a number of outlets working to the hub of the Business Link. Formed from partnerships often involving services from local enterprise agencies, chambers of commerce, local authorities and transferred activities from TECs.

Business School projects   This project has two strands, both of which involve funding work with business schools. One strand is supporting Business Schools to introduce management programmes based on the MCI Management Standards. The second strand is looking at the demand for competence-based management, particularly within small and medium-sized enterprises (SMEs), and mechanisms for meeting that demand.

Career Profile   The Career Profile enables you to list your experiences, responsibilities, accomplishments, training, education and voluntary activities which will help you identify your competences.

Competence   The ability to perform in the workplace to the standards required in employment.

Competency   The personal behaviour (note *competency* applies to behavioural skills, while *competence* applies to functional performance) required in order to achieve competence. The MCI Personal Competency Model defines this behaviour under various categories.

Context   Another word for situation. A competent manager or supervisor must be able to show that they are competent in a variety of contexts. See **Transferability**.

Continuing Professional Development (CPD)   MCI is currently developing a suite of CPD Modules which can be used in association with the Management Standards, to help managers take responsibility for their own learning and continue their development through planned activities (real and simulated) which are clearly defined and have measurable outcomes.

Credit   It is possible for individuals to gain one credit per unit of competence towards a full qualification. For management, there are between eight and ten units per level of qualification.

Element of Competence   Describes what a manager is expected to be able to do within one aspect of their role.

Evidence   Material which directly or indirectly proves individuals' competence. This material might include documents, video recordings, audio recordings, photographs, published material, etc.

External Verifier   A person appointed by the awarding body to provide independent verification on the quality of assessments and internal quality assurance arrangements at centres. The External Verifier requires EOSC units D35, D32 and D33.

Generic   This is a term used for all MCI Standards, meaning that they apply to all managers, or potential managers, from any sector or industry.

Internal Verifier   A person within the approved centre with responsibility for ensuring quality of assessment within a centre. The Internal Verifier requires EOSC Units D34, D32 and D33.

Key roles   Different areas in which a manager operates within their role.

Key Purpose (of management)   To achieve the organization's objectives and continuously improve its performance.

Knowledge and understanding   The knowledge and understanding which underpins competent performance.

Lead Body   Government-designated body representative of an occupational sector, or cross-sectoral roles, responsible for setting and maintaining National Standards within those occupations.

Management Standards   The National Standards of performance for managers and supervisors, developed by MCI under contract from the DfEE as part of the national standards programme.

Management Standards Review   The MCI Standards which form part of the VQ framework (Levels 3, 4 and 5) have been under review for the last two years. The final stages of the review, which will include recommendations from the Dearing Post 16 and Beaumont 100 VQ reviews, are due to be completed, with the standards published, April 1997.

MCI   The Management Charter Initiative is an employer-led organization whose mission is to promote management development, particularly competence-based management development, for the benefit of both individuals and organizations. MCI is the operating arm of a charity, the National Forum for Management Education and Development, and seeks to increase the quality, quantity, relevance and accessibility of management development. MCI operates from Central London with about thirty full-time staff. MCI Wales now has an office in Cardiff.

Mentor   A person who assists a manager to develop and grow personally, often a more experienced manager.

National Standard   Statement of what is expected in terms of competent performance in employment.

NCVQ   National Council for Vocational Qualifications – the accrediting body for all NVQs in England, Wales and Northern Ireland.

National Training Organization (NTO)   During 1996/7, OSCs, ITOs and Lead Bodies (and others who can meet the criteria, must bid for NTO status. The Government is hoping to rationalize the scope and number of such organizations.

NVQ   National Vocational Qualification.

Performance Criteria   The outcomes which a manager has to achieve in order to demonstrate competent performance.

Personal Competency   The Personal Competency Model serves to identify the personal qualities, skills and attributes which are associated with effective management behaviour.

Portfolio   An individual manager's package of information and evidence necessary to support his/her claim to competence. A portfolio may contain, as well as documentary evidence, photographs, video recordings, audio recordings, published material, etc.

SCOTVEC   Scottish Vocational Education Council – Scottish accrediting body for VQS. SCOTVEC is also the Awarding Body for SVQs in Scotland. There are some UK based Awarding Bodies who also award SVQs.

SVQ   Scottish Vocational Qualification.

TDLB   The Training and Development Lead Body. Originally the body responsible for the development of national standards for trainers, assessors and advisers. The TDLB no longer exists. The body now responsible for all national standards in personnel, training and development is the EOSC.

Total Quality Management   Provides internal and external customers with products and services that fully satisfy mutually agreed requirements, at the lowest cost.

Transferability   The ability to perform competently in various contexts/situations.

Unit of Competence   A grouping of Elements of Competence, covering part of a manager's role. This is the level at which assessment for NVQs/SVQs takes place and is the smallest part of a set of standards which can be awarded separate certification.

Introduction

ABOUT THIS BOOK

This book aims at introducing the manager to the idea of managerial *competence* (effective performance) and the techniques and approach required in personal *competency* (behaviour and skills) in order to achieve effective performance.

- It identifies the personal effectiveness skills involved in the gaining of competence.
- It identifies the central role of communication in all aspects of personal effectiveness.
- It shows the relationship to the Management Charter Initiative's (MCI) units of managerial *competence* and personal *competency* required to perform at the first levels of management, including those managers who, for example, may also be studying for the Certificate in Management which is based upon the MCI Units of Competence, as well as the continuing development of experienced managers.

BACKGROUND TO THE MCI UNITS OF COMPETENCE

As the result of various research carried out in the 1980s by such leading authorities in the field of managerial competence as Charles B. Handy, The National Forum for Management Education and Development was established to identify the competences required by British management and to obtain employer commitment to the development of their managers. The National Forum, of which MCI is the operating arm, is the industry lead body recognized by the Department for Education and Employment for the development of competence-based standards in the area of management.

Recruitment of employers, academic institutions and private agencies has been achieved through approaches by, and public relations exercises launched through, the Confederation of British Industry (CBI), British Institute of Management (BIM) (now known as the Institute of Management - IM) and other National Forum members and founder members of the MCI. MCI developed the four levels of managerial standards of competence (supervisory, first line, middle and senior management) between 1989 and 1995. These standards have been thoroughly reviewed by MCI (between 1994 and 1997) to ensure the most effective grouping of core and optional standards at National Vocational Qualification and Scottish Vocational Qualification (NVQ/SVQ) levels 3, 4 and 5.

MCI, in association with other bodies, is currently preparing proposals to the Department of Education and Employment (DfEE) to become a National

Training Organization (NTO). NTOs will be responsible for a wider range of training and development issues than the current Lead Body arrangements allow, including the preparation of more specific guidelines for the input of knowledge and understanding, relevant practical experience, and more detailed assessment and verification guidelines.

The rationale behind the introduction of NTOs is also to allow various organizations, such as the many Lead Bodies currently involved in the development and promotion of occupational standards, to use the opportunity to form partnerships together and rationalize their work to provide more consistency and better coordination across a range of occupational competences. This outcome is the result of some of the many recommendations made in the reports by Gordon Beaumont and Sir Ron Dearing, who have been researching the effectiveness of the Vocational Qualification system and the education of young people sixteen years and above, respectively.

WHAT IS PERSONAL EFFECTIVENESS?

Personal effectiveness is herein defined as a distinct set of behavioural competencies (as opposed to competences which define the performance of functions), which are a group of skills embedded within all work-related activities. Personal effectiveness relates to the behavioural aspects of the MCI Standards of Managerial Competence as identified holistically in the MCI Integrated Model of Personal Competency (as defined below).

Each *Unit of Managerial Competence* (which includes the relevant standard to be achieved in the form of a specific set of performance criteria and the knowledge specification against which individuals can develop) also provides the performance and knowledge evidence requirements and guidance for individual assessment for the award of National or Scottish Vocational Qualifications (N/SVQs). Every unit also has an identified set of *key behaviours* without which a manager will not be able to achieve competence. Key behaviours *are* the personal competencies needed by managers in order to develop effective performance. It is these key behaviours which this book attempts to help managers to build and apply appropriately.

THE IMPORTANCE OF DEVELOPING SELF-KNOWLEDGE

In order to achieve personal competency it is necessary for you, as the manager, to understand your own strengths, and maximize them, and to also identify your own weaknesses and learn how to overcome them. By taking responsibility for your own learning through self-development, you should be able to improve your own opportunities and prospects, as well as build the ability to facilitate the identification of the strengths and weaknesses of others. This, in turn, will provide you with the opportunity to agree with others how to address their own self-development needs, through formal reviews, daily interaction and informal feedback, advice and guidance.

Therefore, this book's ethos is about managers developing self-knowledge and applying it to their behaviour, both in relation to their own job performance and in managing others. By *managing others*, the authors are referring both to those managers who have direct line responsibility for their own staff and to those *working with and through people* who are not necessarily their direct responsibility. Each chapter makes its own contribution to this self-knowledge ethos, and readers are invited to approach any of them, in any order, according to their immediate needs, as well as their future development plans.

IDEAS FOR FURTHER READING

At the end of each chapter you will be given suggestions for further reading, several of which will be repeated. If your access to further texts is limited for any reason, the following titles should provide you with sufficient information and ideas to further your own development:

Handy, Charles B. (1985) *Understanding Organizations*, 3rd edn, Penguin Books, London.
Hannagan, Tim (1995), *Management Concepts and Practices*, Pitman Publishing, London.
Mullins, Laurie J. (1993), *Management and Organizational Behaviour*, Pitman Publishing, London.
Honey, P. and Mumford, A. (1990), *The Manual of Learning Opportunities*, Peter Honey, Maidenhead.
Pedler, Mike and Boydell, Tom (1985), *Managing Yourself*, Fontana, London.
Pedler, Mike, Burgoyne, John and Boydell, Tom (1986), *A Manager's Guide to Self-Development*, McGraw Hill, Maidenhead.

THE UNITS OF COMPETENCE AND THE MCI PERSONAL COMPETENCY MODEL

The revised MCI Managerial Standards of Competence, the overview of which identifies how they fit into the N/SVQ structure and which is supplied at the end of this introduction, were published in total at the end of April 1997, and are available from any of the management Awarding Bodies or directly from MCI. The MCI Integrated *Model of Personal Competency* identifies the behaviours and skills necessary for you to develop, before you are able to prove competence in the functions, identified in each of the key roles within the overview mentioned above. While each chapter attempts to separate out the various behaviours and skills for ease of learning and development, it must be understood that all these behaviours and skills are necessary for managers to apply across all the units of competence, at different times and under varying circumstances.

An overview of the MCI Integrated Model of Personal Competency

Acting Assertively
Acting Strategically
Behaving Ethically
Building Teams
- Managing others
- Relating to others

Communicating
Focusing on results
- Planning and prioritising
- Striving for excellence

Influencing Others
Managing Self
- Controlling emotions and stress
- Managing personal learning and development

Searching for Information
Thinking and Decision Making
- Analysing
- Conceptualizing
- Taking decisions

The chapters in this book address each of these ten areas of personal competency, although not necessarily in the same order. The titles and detailed behavioural *outcomes* within each of the Personal Competencies, as shown above, do not always reflect those used in the chapters, although the relationships should be easily identifiable from the chapter decscriptions below. The *outcomes* used in each of the chapters are there for learning and development purposes and can be seen as *objectives* to be achieved following input received, exercises undertaken, case studies followed or on-the-job learning and observational outputs etc.

Chapter 1 looks at the need for managers to develop their ability in *Building Teams.*

Managers who build effective teams encourage team effort, build cohesion and maintain motivation.

There are two major behaviours addressed in this chapter, the first of which looks at competency needed in *Relating and showing sensitivity to others*. This involves the manager developing skills and behaviour so that he or she:

- Actively builds effective working relationships with others
- Makes time available to support others in assuming responsibility in and for their work
- Encourages and stimulates others to make the best use of their abilities
- Evaluates and enhances people's capability to do the job, taking the necessary action to ensure they receive the appropriate training and development as needed

- Provides constructive feedback which is designed to improve people's future performance
- Shows respect for the views and actions of others
- Shows sensitivity to the needs and feelings of others
- Uses power and authority in a fair and equitable manner.

The second set of behaviours addresses the important competency of *Managing and obtaining the commitment of others*. This involves the manager developing behaviours which guarantees that he or she:

- Keeps others informed about plans and progress
- Clearly identifies what is required of and by others
- Invites others to contribute to the planning and organizing of work
- Agrees and sets objectives which are both achievable and challenging
- Checks individuals' understanding and commitment to a specific course of action
- Uses a variety of techniques to promote good morale and individuals' productivity
- Protects others and their work against negative impacts
- Identifies and resolves causes of conflict or resistance – between individuals, groups, or those between individuals or groups and the organization
- Communicates a vision which generates excitement, enthusiasm and commitment.

Chapter 2 helps individual managers to develop their *Communication and Presentation* skills.

Managers with skills in communication and presentation are able to share information, ideas and arguments with a variety of audiences.

This involves the manager in performing in such a way that he or she:

- Listens actively, asks questions, clarifies points and rephrases others' statements to check mutual understanding
- Adopts personal communication and presentation styles appropriate to listeners and situations, including selecting an appropriate time and place for the event
- Uses a variety of media and communication aids to reinforce points and maintain interest
- Presents difficult ideas, concepts and problems in a way which promotes understanding

- Confirms listeners' understanding through questioning and interpretation of non-verbal signals
- Encourages listeners to ask questions or rephrase statements to clarify their understanding
- Modifies communication and presentation in response to expectations, responses and feedback from listeners as necessary.

Chapter 3 addresses the more controversial topic of *Ethical Perspective.*

Managers with an ethical perspective identify concerns and resolve complex dilemmas in an open reasoned manner.

This chapter invites the manager to develop behaviours which demonstrate that he or she:

- Complies with legislation, industry regulation, professional and organizational codes
- Shows integrity and fairness in decision making
- Sets objectives and creates cultures which are ethical
- Identifies the interests of stakeholders and their implications for the organization and individuals
- Clearly identifies and raises ethical concerns relevant to the organization
- Works towards resolution of ethical dilemmas based on reasoned approaches
- Understands and resists personal pressures which encourage non-ethical behaviour
- Understands and resists apparent pressures from organizational systems to achieve results by any means.

Chapter 4 identifies the need for all managers to *Focus on Results.*

Managers who focus on results are proactive and take responsibility for getting things done.

There are two major sets of behaviour addressed in this chapter, the first of which identifies that when a manager is *Planning and prioritizing objectives,* behaviour is developed which shows that he or she:

- Maintains a focus on objectives
- Tackles problems or takes advantage of opportunities as they arise
- Prioritizes objectives and schedules work to make best use of time and resources
- Sets objectives in uncertain and complex situations
- Focuses personal attention on specific details that are critical to the success of a key event.

The second set of behaviours contained in this chapter concentrates on the manager *Showing commitment to excellence*. In showing such concern, it is believed by management gurus that the individual manager:

- Actively seeks to do things better
- Uses change as an opportunity for improvement
- Establishes and communicates high expectations of performance, including setting an example to others
- Sets goals that are demanding of self and others
- Monitors quality of work and progress against plans
- Continually strives to identify and minimize barriers to excellence.

Chapter 5 focuses on the need for the manager to develop skills in *Influencing Others*.

> Managers who are able to influence the behaviour of others plan their approaches and communicate clearly using a variety of techniques.

This requires development of behaviour by the manager (keeping ethical considerations in mind at all times) whereby he or she:

- Develops and uses contacts to trade information and obtain support and the necessary resources
- Creates and prepares strategies for influencing others
- Presents himself or herself positively to others
- Uses a variety of techniques, as appropriate to the audience and circumstances, to influence others
- Understands the culture of the organization and acts to work within it or influence its change or development

Chapter 6 is about *Information Search*, a skill often underestimated by managers and left to others to perform, but which is, nonetheless, an exceptionally important managerial skill.

> Managers with information search skills gather many different kinds of information, using a variety of means, develop important working relationships and produce better decisions as a result.

In developing this skill, the manager:

- Establishes information networks to search for and gather relevant information
- Actively encourages the free exchange of information
- Makes best use of existing sources of information

- Seeks information from multiple sources
- Challenges the validity and reliability of sources of information
- Pushes for concrete information in ambiguous situations.

Chapter 7 highlights the need for the manager to develop *Self-confidence and Personal Drive*.

> Managers with self-confidence and personal drive show resilience and determination to succeed in the face of pressure and difficulties.

In demonstrating this behaviour, the manager:

- Takes a leading role in initiating action and making decisions
- Takes personal responsibility for making things happen
- Takes control of situations and events
- Acts in an assured and unhesitating manner when faced with a challenge
- Says no to unreasonable requests
- States his or her own position and views clearly in conflict situations
- Maintains beliefs, commitment and effort in spite of setbacks or opposition.

Chapter 8 is about *Self-management* and the belief that in order to manage others and/or tasks, a manager must first manage him/herself.

> Managers skilled in managing themselves show adaptability to the changing world, taking advantage of new ways of doing things.

Again, there are two major sets of behaviour highlighted in this chapter, the first concentrating on the importance of the individual manager's *Self-control*, whereby he or she focuses on his or her own stress management and:

- Gives a consistent and stable performance
- Takes action to reduce the causes of stress
- Accepts personal comments or criticism without becoming defensive or offensive
- Remains calm in difficult or uncertain situations
- Handles others' emotions without becoming personally involved in them.

The second behavioural set focuses on *Managing personal learning and development*. In this situation, the manager:

- Takes responsibility for meeting his or her own learning and development needs
- Seeks feedback on performance to identify his or her own strengths and weaknesses
- Learns from his or her own mistakes and those of others
- Changes behaviour where needed as a result of feedback
- Reflects systematically on own performance and modifies behaviour accordingly
- Develops self to meet the competence demand of changing situations
- Transfers learning from one situation to another.

Chapter 9 is about the manager's *Strategic Perspective*.

> Managers with a strategic perspective identify the way forward in a complex environment, referring constantly to a longer-term vision for the organization.

In order to demonstrate effective behaviour here the manager:

- Displays understanding of how the different parts of the organization and its environment fit together
- Works towards a clearly defined vision of the future
- Clearly relates goals and actions to the strategic aims of the business
- Takes opportunities when they arise to achieve longer-term aims or needs of the organization.

Chapter 10 focuses on the largest responsibility of managers and the most difficult managerial behaviour to assess as a process; *Thinking and Decision Making*. It is only possible to assess the process in terms of the outcomes achieved.

> Managers displaying thinking and decision-making skills analyse and make deductions from information in order to form judgements and take decisions.

There are three major sets of behaviour to this chapter, commencing with the manager's ability in *Analysing*. When analysing, the manager:

- Breaks situations down into simple tasks and activities
- Identifies a range of elements in and perspectives on a situation
- Identifies implications, consequences or causal relationships in a situation

■ Uses a range of ideas to explain the actions, needs and motives of others.

The second behavioural set focuses on the manager's need for *Conceptualizing* in order to make decisions. In this process, the manager:

■ Uses his or her own experience and evidence from others to identify problems and understand situations
■ Identifies patterns or meaning from events and data which are not obviously related
■ Builds a total and valid picture (or concept) from restricted or incomplete data (which happens to be most of the time).

The third set of behaviours addresses a manager's *Judgement and decision-making* abilities. When forming judgements and making decisions, the manager:

■ Produces a variety of solutions before taking a decision
■ Balances intuition with logic in decision making
■ Reconciles and makes use of a variety of perspectives when making sense of a situation
■ Produces his or her own ideas from experience and practice
■ Takes the experience and practice of others into account
■ Takes decisions which are realistic for the situation
■ Focuses on facts, problems and solutions when handling an emotional situation (not personalities)
■ Takes decisions in uncertain situations, or based on restricted information when necessary.

ACTION PLANNING

A book of this nature can only get you started on the way to being more effective as a manager. If you are using this book as part of a distance-learning or taught course, then you will have undertaken a range of assessed tasks. It is helpful to review your progress by considering what is involved in and learned through doing those tasks. This section will help you to:

■ Identify aspects of ongoing learning
■ Learn how to learn from non-success and its importance
■ Review the MCI competences and provide yourself with specially developed questions to review your own situation
■ Develop a model to plan for your development of increased effectiveness in areas of managerial and personal effectiveness
■ Understand the sort of Managerial Competence Questions used by trained MCI assessors and advisers by providing you with a typical *checklist,*

■   Plan your personal development and change requirements

THE IMPORTANCE OF ONGOING LEARNING

The learning cycle (Figure I.1) is a critical concept for people who wish to continue to make progress in their managerial development. This learning cycle is an ongoing process. Experience forms the basis for reviewing, drawing conclusions and planning. Experience can arise just as easily from lack of success as from succeeding in activities.

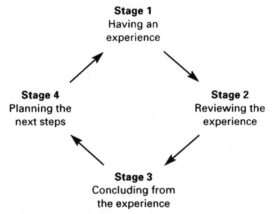

Figure I.1   The Kolb Learning Cycle

Failure is a word which has an unfortunate negative meaning associated with it. Who would wish to have the word applied to them? However, failure nearly always brings with it the opportunity to learn. It is only when failure is not used for learning that there is really true failure.

Roget's Thesaurus offers as an alternative to 'failure' the words ' cessation', ' discontinuance' or 'stall'. These words imply that some expected event or progress has not taken place. If a domestic appliance such as a vacuum cleaner stopped working, then most intelligent people would consider some obvious reasons before calling in an expensive technician or throwing the appliance away. By finding out why the cleaner did not work you would gain knowledge which you could apply to other electrical appliances in your house.

Similarly when, as a manager, you find that something you set out to accomplish does not work out as planned, you have an opportunity to learn why this should be. The opportunity is to learn not only how you might have set about it differently but also how you might act in future situations. It is called learning from experience.

There is a perception of experience which is familiar to all who have to plough through piles of curricula vitae or application forms. This phrase 'I have X years of experience' often appears. The question which might go through the reader's mind is: 'X years of experience, or one year's experience repeated X times?' How much has the person learned from that experience?

Personal Effectiveness is not simply acquired from reading a book or carrying out book-based activities. It is something derived from the thoughtful and informed *application* of learning and experience, in the workplace.

APPLICATION OF LEARNING

The Managerial Competence and Personal Competency identified by the MCI will have considerable relevance for you as a manager. Furthermore, these competences and competencies, respectively, have acquired wide acceptance as a basis for many management qualifications.

We would suggest that you take the MCI competences as a basis and add or amend them as necessary. The recently revised standards, with their core and optional competences at the three Vocational Qualification (VQ) levels, or alternatively from the integrated model (detailed at the end of this chapter), will be readily applicable to your work situation.

You will need to plan how you can put into practice the knowledge base which this book offers in the area of personal effectiveness, and the development of the personal competencies. The opportunities to do this are probably far greater than you might think.

- The obvious opportunities of your current job which you are currently using
- The obvious opportunities of your current job which you are *not* currently using but which you could use if, for example, you managed your time better
- Whatever aspects of your manager's job which he or she may be persuaded to let you undertake
- The opportunities presented by jobs which colleagues undertake, in which you may be able to negotiate time to spend learning yourself
- The opportunities offered by your workplace to become involved in the organization and management of social, sports, trade union and welfare activities
- The range of non-work involvements and activities which you are currently undertaking, e.g. sports, leisure, religious interests, etc.
- The range of non-work involvements and activities which you are *not* currently undertaking, as above, for example, but which you could undertake if, for instance, you managed your time better
- The family-based activities which you are currently undertaking (problem solving, planning, organizing, etc.)
- The family-based activities which you are *not* currently undertaking (problem solving, planning, organizing, etc.) but which you could undertake if, for example, you managed your time better.

A PRACTICAL EXAMPLE

One of the MCI units of managerial competence is:

- C12   Lead the work of teams and individuals to achieve their objectives (*optional* for those managers interested in achieving a VQ Level 4)

You will see from the overview at the end of the chapter that the unit has three elements, each of which may need separate development planning in order for you to achieve competence. Against each element is identified the *key behaviours* of:

- Acting absorbitively
- Building teams
- Communicating
- Thinking and taking decisions

It is these types of key behaviours or *personal competencies* which this book seeks to help you develop or improve.

It is possible that some readers of this book may not have the opportunity to do all the elements in their current job. Perhaps you do not manage a team of staff with whom you can plan work, assess performance and provide feedback. This difficulty has been identified and incorporated into the new Vocational Qualification framework. However, it is recommended that managers, or potential managers, take all the opportunities they can in order to develop as many of the competences, and thereby the competencies, as possible.

Figure I.2 overleaf takes you through a flow chart which enables you to consider how you can develop, or improve, a management skill or competence. The first question(s) you should ask yourself is: 'Is it a part of my job?' or more broadly 'Is it conceivable that I should do it at some point in my job?'

Though you may not manage staff as part of your normal activities, perhaps the opportunity arises to take the responsibility from time to time. Most organizations involve staff in project teams or working parties. Coordination of such activities is not automatically associated with seniority. Sometimes it rests with the person who shows willingness to do it.

Management skills are acquired through practice and the application of learning. Taking advantage of suitable opportunities is crucial. A person who does not reach beyond proficiency in their current job is, in effect, making a statement that they do not seek to progress further.

Let us suppose that the particular competence is one which currently is not part of your job, taking a fairly broad definition. The next question you might put to yourself is: 'Is it likely to become a part of my job (in the future)?' This might involve a bit of crystal ball gazing. At the time of writing many organizations are 'downsizing', which is *management speak* for reducing staff and layers of management. This exercise almost inevitably brings new responsibilities to bear on those staff who remain. There is an awareness that the environment is constantly changing for many organizations. Their staff need to be focused on innovation and develop new skills. So it is quite possible that the skills your job does not require now may be essential for your job next year – if your job is to remain yours!

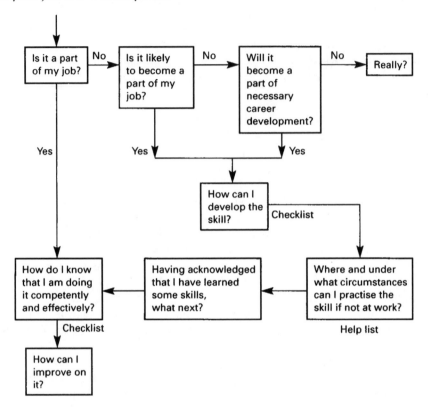

Figure I.2   The acquisition of competence

Let us assume that the particular managerial competence or personal competency is one which you cannot see as applicable for your job now or in the foreseeable future. The next question to ask yourself is: 'Does it represent a skill that I might need for my own future career development?'

Now before answering that question it may be worth pausing and considering the views of Charles Handy, a respected management writer who spends a lot of his time analysing what the future might hold for the world of work and organizations. He believes that in the future it is not employment that will be important but rather *employability*. The possession of a job will not count for much unless the person has *saleable* skills, since security of employment is becoming a thing of the past. Indeed we would argue that security of employment *is* already a thing of the past.

```
┌─────────────────────────────────────────────────────────────────┐
│                  Management competence help list                 │
│          A   Work related                  C   Leisure activities │
├─────────────────────────────────────────────────────────────────┤
│   1   Subordinate feedback          1   Team memberships          │
│   2   Colleague feedback            2   Committee involvements     │
│   3   Line manager feedback         3   Obtaining resources       │
│   4   Customer feedback             4   Using resources           │
│   5   Team meetings                 5   Decision-making           │
│   6   Liaison work                  6   Problem-solving           │
│   7   Staff supervision             7   Evaluation                │
│   8   Report writing                8                             │
│   9   Verbal reports                9                             │
│  10   Interviewing                                                │
│  11   Progress chasing                  D   Home/family           │
│  12   Planning                      1   Decision-making           │
│  13   Negotiating                   2   Problem-solving           │
│  14   Quality checking              3   Negotiating               │
│  15   Standard setting              4   Obtaining resources       │
│  16   Advice provision              5   Using resources           │
│  17   Using resources               6                             │
│  18   Decision-making               7                             │
│  19   Problem-solving               8                             │
│  20   Evaluation                                                  │
│  21                                                               │
│  22                                                               │
│          B   Work info. sources         E   Self help and learning│
│   1   Staff manual                  1   Coach/mentor              │
│   2   Annual reports                2   Management course material│
│   3   Business plans                3   Fellow course participants│
│   4   Job descriptions/specs        4   Short courses             │
│   5   Finance procedures            5   Management tutors         │
│   6   Personnel procedures          6   Library resources         │
│   7   Review documents              7                             │
│   8   Meeting minutes               8                             │
│   9   Computer database             9                             │
│  10   Information leaflets                                        │
│  11   Working party reports                                       │
│  12   Company newsletters etc.                                    │
└─────────────────────────────────────────────────────────────────┘
```

Figure I.3   Help list. Based on a model provided by Richard Hooper of the London Borough of Enfield

So the question revolves around whether possessing the competence is something which improves your attraction to employers. The question thus becomes: 'How can I develop the skill or competence?'

The help list (Figure I.3) is a simple checklist which you can use and add to. It sets out a number of possible sources for the development of a desired skill or competence. Some of these are related to work activities (Section A). These are ongoing things which you may be doing which enable you to practise the particular skill within the work setting itself. The list allows you to add to it where you feel appropriate. Often there is a need to acquire more information to establish what the desired skill is and where it might be found within the organization. We have listed some information sources available within most organizations.

In some cases you may desire to develop a competence but you cannot locate any possibility to do it within your current work situation. Perhaps you do not have the necessary responsibility and your own manager is unable or unwilling to delegate to you. How do you seek and use the opportunity to experience using the competence? There are essentially three areas of possibility:

1   You may find the opportunity within your actual or potential leisure pursuits. Many candidates and students have found that the experience of organizing and managing a sports or social club at work, school or college has made a major positive impression on employers.

2   In your home life you may find that you can develop and practise competence. 'Sound management of the economy', as Margaret (now Baroness) Thatcher used to say, 'is all about good housekeeping'. Time management, priority setting, problem solving and decision making are all activities that most people have to handle in everyday life.

3   Finally there is the possibility of self-help and learning through study. Some skills can be acquired through 'simulation'. That is how people learn first aid. Handling disciplinary situations is best practised in the classroom before trying it out in the *real world*. However, well-planned training courses can often provide a realistic experience for candidates and students.

CHECKLIST OF QUESTIONS to ask as you work through the MCI Personal Competency Model

The following integrated checklist is provided to help your *Action Planning*. It will give you an overall idea of the kinds of issues which might occur throughout your period of management development. Each chapter will provide you with those questions that can be most effectively adapted to the situations under discussion. In some cases they have been tailored specifically and occasionally added to.

Who or where are your largest customer bases (customers may be internal or external to the organization)?
How do you find out about your customers' needs?
How do you make customers aware that your products/services are available?
How effective are the communication mechanisms that you use?
What would you do if there was a low take-up of the products/services you provide?
How do you currently coordinate your activities in order to develop your product/service provision?

How are organizational performance standards determined and by whom?
How do you ensure that these performance standards are being met?
How do you measure these standards?
How do you deal with any customer complaints?
How do you handle health and safety issues at your workplace?
How appropriate is your location for the product/service you provide?
Which outside agencies do you currently liaise with?
Are there any joint working arrangements in your product/service provision (this may apply across teams, or between organizations)?
What are these and for what purposes do the arrangements exist?
What actions would you/have you taken with others at times of particular difficulty or change?
Which methods do you use to analyse facts and figures for your job purposes?
How do you present these facts and figures to others for decision-making purposes?
How effective are your analytical and mathematical skills in convincing others?
Were the outcomes of these presentations appropriate for the decision-making purposes?
How might you improve your analytical and mathematical skills?
How do you liaise with others at off-site locations?
How is information fed back into the decision-making process?
What, if any, interdepartmental group activities do you participate in?
What are the main purposes of these groups?
How would you identify your own development needs within the job role?
How would you meet the needs you had identified?
How do you evaluate your progress?
What are the main working relationships you maintain?
How do you/would you maximize productive relationships and networks?
How do you/would you promote equal opportunities within and between those with whom you relate?
What are the key elements, in your opinion, in promoting effective working relationships?
What do you see as your strengths in establishing good working relationships and which aspects would you want to develop further?
How would you/do you go about establishing and developing working relationships with others, both internal and external to the organization?
How easy/difficult do you find asking support of or taking problems to others?
How might this be improved?
How easy/difficult do you think others find asking you for support or in bringing their problems to you?
How could it be improved?
What support would you/do you give to others in their relations with others outside the organization (or department)?
How could these relationships be improved?
What formal and informal actions would you/have you taken to actively promote effective working relationships and prevent their breakdown?

How do you/would you deal with conflict in your relationships or in the relationships of others arising from:

- Differences of opinion on courses of action?
- Personal animosity?
- Moral dilemmas (between individuals or individuals and the organization)?
- Racism?
- Sexism?
- Other discriminatory behaviour?
- Non-compliance with organizational rules, norms or values?

What do you see as *counselling* in the workplace?

What is the purpose and what are the limitations of workplace counselling?

What is your role as counsellor – both formally and informally?

What are the key elements of effective workplace counselling?

Who are the parties involved in starting and inducting those for whom you will be responsible?

How effective is this process, the people involved, and how might you improve it?

How do you determine the training and development needs of yourself and others?

What activities do you use for the development of others (formal and informal)?

How do you plan these activities?

How do you review progress and evaluate the outcomes of training and development?

Have you taken any steps to improve equality of opportunity in the development of others?

What were the outcomes?

Have there been any specific incidences which have caused you concern for the equality of opportunities in the development of all?

How do you set work objectives (or participate in setting them) for yourself and others?

How do you review and update these objectives?

Identify an objective you have had to meet and specify how you planned the work activities to meet this objective.

How did you decide which method would work best?

How do you decide how to allocate work to others?

What would you say is your leadership style?

What are the effects of your style on others? For example, are you, do you think, making the most use of the skills available to you (yours and others)?

How does this tie in with the overall work objectives set?

How do you evaluate your own performance against your work objectives?

How do you evaluate the performance of others against their objectives?

What methods do you use to give feedback to others about their performance?

Can you pinpoint anything which you consider particularly important when giving feedback?

How do you address equal opportunities issues into this aspect of your work?
What information do you need to do your job and for what purposes?
Do you have any problems obtaining this information?
To whom do you supply information?
How much time do you spend in:

- Gathering information?
- Analysing information?
- Providing information?

How do you go about gathering, analysing and providing information?
Can these methods be improved?
How do you currently store and receive information?
How often do you hold meetings (formal and informal), briefings and group discussions?
For what purposes do you hold meetings etc.?
Do your meetings always (often, sometimes, rarely) :

- Start on time?
- Finish on time?
- Achieve their objectives?

Do you always have the necessary information in advance of the meetings?
Do you always supply the necessary information in advance of the meetings?
Are you confident about:

- Chairing meetings?
- Contributing to the purpose of meetings?
- Taking minutes?

Would you say your meetings are always

- Well prepared?
- Well administered?
- Well controlled?

Are the people at your meetings there because they:

- Have a part to play?
- Have an interest?
- Have been sent?

What are the meetings' follow-up processes?
Do your meetings result in positive action?
Have you attended committees in your current role and prepared reports for these committees?

Questions devised by, and adapted from, the Crediting Competence Team at South Bank University and reproduced with permission.

YOUR FIRST ACTION PLAN

1   Determine whether each of the MCI Managerial Competences and the related Personal Competencies are relevant to your present job.

2   If they are not relevant now, how might they become rele-

vant in the future?

3   Are there any competences not encapsulated by the MCI Standards of Competence or Personal Competency which you believe should be included?

4   Make notes regarding your own learning preferences (private study, trial and error, practice, reflecting on events etc.) and the opportunities you have taken in the past. How might you improve them/develop them in the future?

5   Discuss your skills and behaviour with others internal and external to the organization as appropriate. How effective are you now? How might you improve them, in general terms, in the future?

EXAMPLES OF MCI UNITS OF COMPETENCE

Those who are either relatively new to management, or are aspiring to become managers, should aim to achieve competence in all the following units. This book aims to help you to develop your *behavioural* skills, as identified in the *Personal Competency Model*, as discussed earlier in this introduction and which are required for you to be *competent* in all of the managerial *functions*, as identified in the following summary. It does not specify which units would be appropriate to any particular qualification. Qualifications are likely to present students and candidates with the need to address a core of competences and to select some options from a specific group of units.

The following is an example qualification:

Unit title	*Element titles*	
A3 Manage activities to meet customer requirements	A3.1	Implement plans to meet customer requirements
	A3.2	Maintain healthy, safe and productive work conditions
	A3.3	Ensure activities meet customer requirements
A4 Contribute to improvements at work	A4.1	Support improvements in activities
	A4.2	Recommend improvements to organizational plans
F4 Implement quality assurance systems	F4.1	Establish quality assurance systems
	F4.2	Maintain quality assurance systems
	F4.3	Recommend improvements to quality assurance systems
B2 Manage the use of physical resources	B2.1	Secure resources for activities

	B2.2	Use resources effectively for activities
B3 Manage the use of financial resources	B3.1	Make recommendations for expenditure
	B3.2	Control expenditure against budgets
C2 Develop own resources	C2.1	Develop oneself to improve performance
	C2.2	Manage own time and resources to meet objectives
C5 Develop productive working relationships	C5.1	Develop the trust and support of colleagues and team members
	C5.2	Develop the trust and support of one's immediate manager
	C5.3	Minimize interpersonal conflict
C8 Select personnel for activities	C8.1	Establish personnel requirements for activities
	C8.2	Select personnel against team and organizational requirements
C10 Develop teams and individuals to enhance performance	C10.1	Identify the development needs of teams and individuals
	C10.2	Plan the development of teams and individuals
	C10.3	Develop teams to improve performance
	C10.4	Support individual learning and development
	C10.5	Assess the development of teams and individuals
	C10.6	Improve the development of teams and individuals
C12 Lead the work of teams and individuals to achieve their objectives	C12.1	Plan the work of teams and individuals
	C12.2	Assess the work of teams and individuals
	C12.3	Provide feedback to teams and individuals
D2 Facilitate meetings	D2.1	Participate in group discussions or meetings
	D2.2	Lead group discussions or meetings

D4 Provide information to support
    decision making

D4.1   Obtain information for
       decision making
D4.2   Record and store
       information for decision
       making
D4.3   Analyse information to
       support decision making
D4.4   Advise and inform others

FURTHER READING

MCI Integrated Management Standards; April 1997, National Forum for Management Education and Development, London. The Integrated Standards are recommended for general Management Development purposes. (Four publications – one for each of the Key Roles: A – *Managing Activities*; B – *Managing Resources*; C – *Managing People*; D – *Managing Information*.) Part of a set of seven key roles. Others in the series: *Managing Quality*; *Managing Energy*; and *Managing Profits*.

MCI Management Standards; June 1997, National Forum for Management Education and Development, London. These are recommended according to the Management *level* in which you may need to gain a qualification. For example, the Level 4 Standards will be appropriate if wish to gain either an N/SVQ Level 4 or a Certificate in Management and the Level 5 standards for an N/SVQ Level 5 or a Diploma in Management Studies (DMS).

1 Building teams

Managers who build effective teams encourage team effort, build cohesion and maintain motivation.

INTRODUCING THE RELATIONSHIP BETWEEN THE MCI PERSONAL COMPETENCY MODEL AND BUILDING TEAMS

The MCI Integrated *Model of Personal Competency* identifies the behaviours and skills necessary for you to develop, before you are able to prove competence in any managerial function. This chapter attempts to deal with the various behaviours and skills necessary for you to apply across all managerial functions, transferring your learning to different occasions, at different times and under varying circumstances (contexts), consistently. The outcomes below, as identified within this section of the model, should be borne in mind while you work through this chapter.

Outcomes required in building teams:

There are two major areas of behaviour required of managers when building teams, the first of which looks at competency needed in *Relating and showing sensitivity to others*, the outcomes of which are that the manager:

- Actively builds effective working relationships with others
- Makes time available to support others in assuming responsibility in and for their work
- Encourages and stimulates others to make the best use of their abilities
- Evaluates and enhances people's capability to do the job, taking the necessary action to ensure they receive the appropriate training and development as needed
- Provides constructive feedback which is designed to improve people's future performance
- Shows respect for the views and actions of others
- Shows sensitivity to the needs and feelings of others
- Uses power and authority in a fair and equitable manner.

The second set of behaviours addresses the important competency of *Managing and obtaining the commitment of others*. This involves the manager developing behaviours which guarantee that he or she:

- Keeps others informed about plans and progress
- Clearly identifies what is required of and by others
- Invites others to contribute to the planning and organizing of work
- Agrees and sets objectives which are both achievable and challenging
- Checks individuals' understanding and commitment to a specific course of action
- Uses a variety of techniques to promote good morale and individuals' productivity
- Protects others and their work against negative impacts
- Identifies and resolves causes of conflict or resistance – between individuals, groups, or those between individuals or groups and the organization
- Communicates a vision which generates excitement, enthusiasm and commitment.

INTRODUCTION

You may have heard the term 'One can choose one's friends, but not one's relatives'. We have all had experiences in private life surrounding the issues of developing relationships with parents, grandparents, siblings, our own children and so on. These relationships develop informally and are more or less effective depending upon how the individuals within the *role set* behave towards each other. Interrelations within a group may vary between being positive and constructive and negative and destructive, depending upon situations, circumstances and the predominant motivation within the group.

Each individual within the role set has a contribution to make towards the overall *culture* of the group, which may be positive or negative. If the contribution is unacceptable to the group, and unless the individual is especially *powerful and influential*, the prevailing culture will override any apparent opposition to the *health* of the group. In some cases, where the individual is seen by the rest of the group as being particularly obstructive, the culture can even destroy that person's individuality if he or she is not prepared to conform. In the extreme, the individual may even need to leave the group altogether. This can happen, of course, during adolescence when young people attempt to establish their individuality and sometimes demonstrate their opposition to the prevailing family culture. The family may tolerate this period of maturation, occasionally it will not; note the increasing incidence of teenage homelessness.

The workplace is the same. Here again we are unable to choose those with whom we *work*. Sometimes, as managers, we have some control over whom we recruit, but our effectiveness as interviewers and ultimate selectors of personnel will determine how appropriate these final choices will be. We are, whatever these choices, presented with a group of people with whom we must interrelate and try to influence their interrelationships with each other.

Once more, the effectiveness of these interrelationships begins with us as individuals within a working group who require mutual trust, support, respect and cooperation between all individuals within the role set, in order to achieve group objectives. This can be seen as a role of *informal* leadership, which can be held by different people at different times, depending upon the circumstances, or *formal* leadership where a given person assumes the responsibility.

LEADERSHIP

As a definition for leadership, one could state that it is a dynamic process whereby one individual provides the *wherewithal* for those he or she is leading, to influence each other to contribute voluntarily to the achievement of group tasks in a given situation.

An ongoing debate among practitioners is whether leadership can be separated from the role of management. It is obvious that there are effective leaders who do not necessarily have the authority of management; it is therefore impossible for them to implement certain activities without referring to the relevant authority. The question which remains then is 'Can a manager be effective without also being an effective leader?' It may be possible for a manager to *delegate* certain aspects of the leadership role, but this still requires the manager to *lead* those to whom he or she delegates.

To meet the objectives of *relating and showing sensitivity to others* and *managing and obtaining the commitment of others* leaders must first endow the trust, support, respect and cooperation onto others within the role set, in order to fulfil the group objectives, which will then provide a *mutually enabling* culture. People who feel trusted will then trust in return. It is sometimes difficult for managers to see how they can *release control* in this way and maintain what they perceive to be the vital prerogative of management: to *manage*.

The role of leaders

John Adair (1985) separated the functions of a leader into three common organizational needs: those of the group; those of the individual; and those of the task as shown in Figure 1.1. This model could be developed to show that a leader's function is to provide the key role in identifying organizational objectives, which defines the needs of the task(s) to be performed and then link them to the individual departments or units of operation, at the same time linking individual and group needs to those of the whole.

Difficulties arise where the individual and group objectives do not match those of the organization. It is inevitable that these *objectives* will not coincide completely as individuals and groups bring their own particular needs to the workplace. The leader then has the *task* of balancing all these needs and creating synergy between them (where measured outcomes are more than the sum of all the parts) in order to optimize the outcomes.

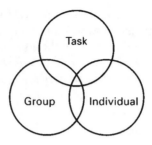

Figure 1.1   Action-centred leadership model (Adair, 1985)

Types of leadership

There are various views of what constitutes *type* in terms of leadership. *Types* of leadership is a separate category to *styles* of leadership, which will be discussed separately. Individual styles may be applied within any of the following examples of types of leadership:

- *Charismatic*, based upon the personality of a leader; such a leader would be trusted, respected, seen as someone with power based on the effects of achievements gained through their style, knowledge, influence and so on. An example of a *charismatic* leader might be Richard Branson.
- *Traditional*, based upon birthright; such a leader might, for instance, have inherited a business or title from his or her family. Robert Maxwell's sons, and indeed Her Majesty the Queen herself, may be seen as traditional leaders
- *Situational*, based on being in the right place at the right time; such leaders may acquire their position through, for example, the death of the current leader and their deputy would naturally pick up the title – Vice President Lyndon Johnson, for instance, following the death of President John F. Kennedy.
- *Appointed*, based on bureaucratic authority; such leaders are appointed through climbing through the ranks to achieve higher authority. This approach can be particularly witnessed in the public domain, where public appointments are based on bureaucratic progression.
- *Functional*, based on behaviour or actions expected; these leaders are only appointed on the basis of the needs of the function itself. For example, an individual who may have all the leadership skills required to perform the job is unlikely to be appointed unless they also have had extensive experience in the function itself (e.g. accounts, sales, personnel, operations, etc.).

What makes you a leader?

Anyone can become a leader if he or she can persuade others to follow. People follow for a variety of reasons, for example:

- The fear of criticism and/or punishment
- The need to obey rules and procedures
- Respect for a leader because he or she happens to be the leader
- The leader has gained credibility over time
- and so on.

These reasons for *following* a leader are not mutually exclusive. For example, followers may both respect their leader and fear the consequences of disobedience. Where respect for a leader exists because he or she happens to be the leader the continuation of such respect is likely to be more reliant upon effective systems and procedures. Where a leader is followed for fear of their criticism and/or punishment, flexible approaches, creative thinking and effective interpersonal communication are required in order to overcome such fear. Current researchers in organizational behaviour identify a preference among managers and staff alike, for the *respect and trust model of leadership*.

Leadership of working teams

If the formally recognized leader is to become the genuinely accepted leader of his or her working team, that *acceptance* must be earned. Leaders constantly find themselves in competition with informal leaders who can exercise certain powers (length of service; the ear of a director; champion of the workers and so on) and it would, therefore, be unwise for the formal leader to rely on the negative forces of fear and convention. In the long run, a team's respect and trust are likely to produce more effective results.

The formal leader's aim is not to depose the informal leaders but more positively to gain the support of the informal groupings in order to meet organizational objectives. Informal leaders will cause fewer problems if the leader shows that he or she merits respect and proves capable of being trusted. The leader must be prepared to commit time and personal effort in achieving satisfactory results from this approach.

Leadership styles

When a problem or demand occurs on which teams or individuals have to act, the leader is often presented with the dilemma of the choice of leadership style. Should the approach be authoritarian (at one extreme) or would the democratic involvement of the team be more appropriate (at the other)? The choice is not simple; in any given situation a wide range of approaches present themselves. According to Tennenbaum and Schmidt (1958) these include:

■ The leader gives the orders – the feelings and opinions of the team may or may not be taken into consideration, but they are expected to obey.

■ The leader 'sells' his or her decisions – as well as giving the orders, the group is persuaded to accept them and the leader recognizes that there may be resistance.

■ The leader explains his or her decisions – the group is given the opportunity to discuss the leader's intentions and thinking, allowing the exploration of the implications of decisions and to develop the instructions for implementation more fully.

■ The leader's decisions are open to change – still taking the initial decision, the leader is prepared to hear other ideas and modify/change the decision before taking further action.

■ The leader chooses between the ideas of individuals within the group(s) – having defined the problem or need, the leader allows group members to suggest ways of tackling it, providing the leader with a range of alternatives, who then selects the most promising.

■ The leader states the problem and the group decides – the leader still defines the problem and then states parameters within which the decisions must be made, but the group decides together what should be done.

■ The leader defines the limits within which the group has total freedom – within the specified limits, the group defines and analyses problems as the individuals perceive them and decides together what should be done. The leader commits in advance to help implement whatever the group decides (see Figure 1.2).

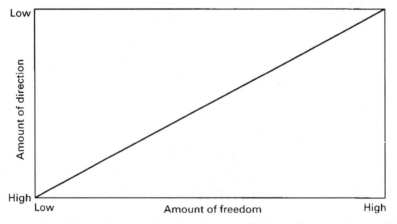

Tells . . . Sells . . . Explains . . . Adapts . . . Chooses . . . Defines problem . . . Defines Parameters

Figure 1.2   Leadership styles (derived from the Tannenbaum and Schmidt, 1985, model)

The forces behind leaders making the choice

- Forces within the leader – the leader's own beliefs and inclinations. Some people are more comfortable as directive leaders. They may argue that they are paid to take responsibility for taking decisions and producing results.
- The leader's confidence in the workgroup – A leader's view of the individuals in their work group is coloured by the amount of trust endowed upon people in general. This varies considerably between leaders which in turn affects their willingness to accept people's competence and good intentions.
- The leader's tolerance of uncertainty – Where leaders involve others, it is implicit that outcomes are less predictable than their own decision taking. Where some leaders have low tolerance of such uncertainty, others thrive on it as a challenge.

Forces within the workgroups

- The strength of their need for independence – Where some individuals want to take responsibility for their own behaviour, seeing it as a challenge and tribute to their competence, the self-confidence of others may not yet be sufficiently developed to accept responsibility; they may need to know that someone else is accountable. Their defence may be that they see delegation as *buck passing*.
- Tolerance of uncertainty – While some people prefer clear-cut directives, others prefer to accept the risks of greater self-direction.
- Expectations about leadership style – Those used to strong directives may perceive involvement as a threat; those used to involvement will resent authoritarian decision takers.
- Pressure of time – While often less a pressure than perceived by either leaders or their followers, the idea of time pressure is perhaps the greatest pressure of all. The more urgent the need for action, the more difficult it is for leaders to involve others and for others to accept involvement.

Making the right choices

There is no one best style for all situations and the able leader is not likely to be consistently autocratic or consistently democratic. Style will depend upon the situation, the problem and the individuals involved. Based upon each issue or situation, an able leader accurately assesses his or her own needs, as well as those of others in the organization likely to be affected by his or her methods of leadership; senior management, colleagues, own staff, people in other departments and so on. An able leader also takes into account individuals' readiness for growth and development. If direction is appropriate, the leader directs; if involvement is relevant, the leader involves.

When assessing and measuring the effectiveness of decisions made by individuals, it is important to remember that it is not the number of decisions they help make, but the significance of each decision made! It is also necessary to remember that, whatever the level of involvement of individuals in the decision making process, the leader must accept the positive and negative outcomes of all decisions made. Delegation is not passing on the responsibility and accountability of achieving the organization's/department's objectives, but sharing responsibility for the actions employed in attaining them.

To reiterate the question posed at the beginning of this section: 'Can leadership be divorced from the role of management?' What do you think?

EXERCISE

One does not necessarily require the title of *manager* in order to manage, and the less obvious the process of management is, the more effective it appears be; a debate which is likely to continue between practitioners for some time yet:

An interesting exercise might be for you and a group of your colleagues to discuss this issue along with the implications for the varying styles of leadership in different organizations in general, focusing on your own organization's overall leadership style in particular. In discussion, you should consider aspects of:

- Building relationships
- Time needed to support others
- Making use of others' abilities
- Evaluating and enhancing others' abilities
- Providing feedback
- Showing respect and sensitivity to others' needs, feelings, views and actions.

THE NATURE OF POWER

This section is based upon the concepts developed by Charles B. Handy in his book *Understanding Organizations* (3rd edition, 1985). In defining power, it can be said that it relates to the capacity to affect the behaviour of others or the actual ability to do something. In defining authority in relation to power it can be termed as the 'status' which legitimizes the use of power. Influence is the application and the effect of power and authority (see also Chapter 5).

Power/authority applies not only in hierarchies but also in different ways in all work and social environments. Everyone is influenced by external power sources in some way. For example:

- When a baby cries it may be *demanding* its food
- Governments *demand* taxes
- The organization *demands* that work be done
- A friend *seeks* a favour.

All four instances exert some kind of power over the individual. Charles Handy distinguishes between power and influence. He says that the difference lies in the fact that *influence is an active process* and that *power is a resource providing the ability to influence*. Recourse to any source of power is likely to provoke different kinds of response in those over whom it is exercised.

Power as a source of influence

Sources of power:

Physical power – A superior physical force using coercion to *make* people work; e.g. the bully, a tyrant or a commander in the armed forces, (threats are often sufficient). This is seen as the power of the last resort.

Resource power – Possession of a valued reward is often a useful basis for influence. It is calculating, and in order to be effective:

- There must be control of the resources and
- Those resources must be desired by the potential recipient (links to the *expectancy* theory of motivation)

Conflicts of power occur where physical power in the form of, for instance, laws affecting picketing, industrial action, etc. resulting in imprisonment for those convicted of infringement of these laws, versus resource power in the form of trade unions' ability to withdraw labour.

Bureaucratization of power reduces individual power. For example, in the public sector the individual power of a manager to reward by increasing pay or promotion, etc. is reduced by corporate procedures and so on.

Position power – This is present as the result of legal or legitimate power that comes as a result of the role or position of the individual in the organization. For example, the role of manager allows him or her to give orders to staff. Power tends to reside in the position rather than the individual. This normally has to be supported by physical and/or resource power; in other words, the organization must back the manager or control the resources, otherwise the manager's influence will fail.

Position power gives the occupant potential control over some invisible assets:

- Information
- Right of access to a variety of networks
- The right to organize

Expert power – This form of power is vested in someone because of their acknowledged expertise. In meritocratic tradition people do not resent being influenced by *experts*. It is often linked to occupations such as doctors, lawyers, economists, etc. As a power base, expert power requires no sanctions, but if expertise is questioned, it may be necessary for the holder to fall back onto other sources of power.

Personal power – or referent/charismatic power resides in the person and his or her personality. It can be enhanced by position or expert power, success and self-confidence, but it can be seen to fade when an individual leaves a particular post or a group or suffers defeat or failure. It is less resented than other power sources and comes from those over whom it is exercised. It is tied to the individual rather than the position. It operates mostly in informal power structures.

Negative or reflective power – If power is used in the agreed constituency, i.e. in its appropriate domain, it can be regarded as legitimate. If used contrary to accepted practice or outside the appropriate domain, power is regarded as disruptive and illegitimate, i.e. negative. Managers and all employees have the latent power to disrupt or stop work, distort, filter and confuse information. It is often practised at times of low morale, irritation or stress and so on.

Relativity of power

The power of person 'A' must have salience for person 'B' or it is ineffective. Bribes may sway some people but repulse others; prestige and threats may bring about similar reactions. The effective amount of power that anyone has will constantly ebb and flow as the constituency in which it is exercised changes its membership.

Balance of power

There is a power equation; power is seldom one-sided – even a prisoner can *hit back*. Negative power is often practised at work, for example the power to disrupt production. One type of power can offset another; for example, money can overrule loyalty.

Domain of power

Few sources of power are universally valid over all constituencies. Some people wish to extend their domain or scope of power and diminish the domain of others. For example, one manager may wish to exert control and influence over a particular department or project at the expense of another manager's control and influence. Legitimate power or influence means that managers' domains of power are prescribed and recognized by others; the conditions under which and over whom it can be exercised have been laid down.

It is not always necessary to officially sanction such power; custom is a strong legitimizer, since power is often regarded as legitimate until challenged. Once challenged, the power may not necessarily be destroyed but simply restricted. For example, the computer expert, once an unquestioned organizational genius, has seen his or her domain progressively restricted over recent years, although their expertise is seldom called into question.

A recent discussion between one of the authors of this book and a residential care manager identified a member of staff in this home, in post for twenty years, as having 'more power over some individuals' than the manager herself. This is a kind of 'time-served' legitimized power where an individual literally overpowers younger and perceived weaker staff members. The manager was presented with some difficulty over this situation, because it had been allowed to grow over the years and made it impossible to implement any sanctions. The woman's power and influence had become the *custom* which met the expectations of the wider group. It was believed that this power would be eroded by the different expectations of new staff members.

EXERCISE

Try analysing the kinds of *power* which are used by individuals and groups within your organization. How effective are they in achieving organizational objectives? How might these people improve their effectiveness?

CREATING EFFECTIVE WORKGROUPS

Effective team working

In order to create effective teamwork, individuals should be encouraged to:

- Be open and honest in their dealings with others in the group
- Use mistakes; eliminate fear of punishment, rejection, etc.
- Use competition and conflict to reach agreements and avoid the unhealthy aspects of extreme competition and conflict
- Use relationships to build support and trust; no-one should feel isolated or threatened by their choice of behaviour, etc.
- Ensure activities are productive and stimulating; sessions without objectives will be frustrating and time-wasting

- Provide the wherewithal for all to own the group's decisions; everyone must be involved in the processes contributing to them in their own unique ways
- Enable the group to take risks, depending upon circumstances and situations
- Recognize, acknowledge and compliment personal development
- Have clear and agreed objectives and roles.

Key factors in group behaviour

Development

Group development is concerned with the processes it undergoes. In general, when a group *forms* it is concerned with establishing the tasks it needs to perform, the rules associated with their activities and so on. Unfortunately, very few groups concentrate on the processes they go through at this early stage, which means that much is left unsaid and unresolved until issues and/or personality difficulties emerge at a later date.

The next stage in the development cycle is where individuals explore the possibilities between them, generally known as *storming*, followed by establishing the *norms* relevant to the activities of the group; where individuals agree the way they will make and implement decisions. The group then begins to *perform* and get things done.

Size and cohesiveness

The size of the group influences its behaviour; a group with more that twelve individuals will lose cohesiveness and sub-groups will begin to form in order to develop closer working relationships. As implied, the cohesiveness of groups (or the attractiveness of the group to individual members) is inversely correlated to the size of the group.

Group norms

As norms are established for the overall behaviour of the group, any deviance, or the joining of a new member, will result in group pressures affecting their performance and behaviour, with the expectation that individuals will conform. Leaders are likely to bring relevant individuals to the group in order to optimize the group's effectiveness and limit unhealthy conflicts and competition.

However, if the leader is looking for changes or to break up any 'groupthink' (Janis, 1972) which may have developed (the denial of important or essential information or evidence which threatens the normal thinking and behaviour of the group and which is therefore manipulated or ignored), the leader may wish to bring in someone who is able to resist the pressures to conform. Such individuals will gradually gain credibility through whatever strengths they happen to possess and will eventually influence the original group away from its accepted norms.

Leadership is discussed elsewhere in this chapter in some detail, but it must be remembered that without effective leadership which adopts the styles necessary to motivate and develop the group, the group is unlikely ever to become effective.

Individual role identity

Every member of a workgroup has something specific to offer; some will coordinate the activities and ideas of others; some prefer to come up with all the ideas, but have little patience for honing them to implementation; some will reflect on their own and others' actions and decisions and analyse their usefulness, etc. Others will analyse current situations and determine the logic of plans and ideas; others have contacts outside the immediate group and are good at finding out things and obtaining information and additional resources. Still others like to get jobs completed and move onto the next challenge and so on.

All membership has its purpose; each will exhibit mixtures of introversion and extroversion in varying degrees according to the occasion, circumstance and need. Each individual must be motivated, according to their various needs and expectations, through encouragement and recognition, without the fear of threat or recrimination and be dealt with sensitively by leaders who are aware.

HOW MOTIVATION AND DELEGATION AFFECT TEAM BUILDING AND VICE VERSA

Motivation

It is essential to recognize the importance of purpose, self-management and challenge for other people. Motivation might not readily spring to mind as involving communication skills. However, if viewed as a means of communicating shared interests and needs, it can be seen that in order to do this we also need to, once again, communicate individual and organizational needs, expressed objectives, targets and plans. It is only when there is a coincidence between these organizational and individual issues that motivation can be achieved.

From the various researches carried out; from Maslow's (1943) hierarchy of needs, through Hertzberg's (1959) hygiene and motivational needs (two factor theory) and onto Vroom's (1964) expectancy theory (after Porter and Lawler) and then to Alderfer's (1972) ERG theory (existence, relatedness and growth), it is clear that people are motivated in various ways and by various means including; financial gain, status, recognition, achievement, responsibility as well as freedom and interest, etc. We can also make certain general points about the characteristics positively associated with people who are highly motivated. These would include:

- *Purpose* – People who are highly motivated tend to be results or goal oriented. This would involve a large amount of commitment which then increases work performance.
- *Self-management* – People seek to have a level of control over their own lives. Highly motivated people seem to desire and to have a large measure of self-determination over their lives. This includes the ability to make their own decisions; possessing a certain level of autonomy.
- *Challenge* – Highly motivated people have a desire to improve and test themselves against the highest possible standards.

It can be added that people are also seen as social animals who voluntarily integrate their own goals with those of groups/organizations with which they work (or leave if they cannot).

It is interesting to note that externally imposed incentives and controls, favoured by the 'rule them with fear' school, are inefficient as well as undesirable. This is why organizational development theory now favours the moves in management style from:

- Individual to shared responsibility
- Autocratic to collaborative approaches
- Power relationships to empowerment of others

In order to look at the question of how we can better motivate other people we need to bear in mind not only these general points but also the extremely important principle of being able to identify the needs and goals of those we seek to motivate. In order to do this, we need to become good listeners.

Figure 1.3   A perception-based model of motivation

What has been discovered from what the wealth of motivation theory tells us is that if we increase effort by facilitating the motivation of others we raise performance. From the individuals' standpoint, of course, if they perceive that the outcomes are worthy of their effort they will be willing to make the effort in order to perform and achieve the desired outcomes. The performance has to be focused, however, and must satisfy both organizational and personal needs. How do we do this?

- Tie effort to performance.
- Link performance to desired outcomes.

- Look at the value of work, i.e. we must assess how much this goal is valued by the person we are trying to motivate.

The needs of individuals may be developmental; starting with small gains or focused rewards progressing to the higher needs (to use Maslow's terminology) of recognition and self-actualization (fulfilment); or move backwards and forwards along a continuum of needs depending upon occasions and circumstances. Managers need to keep up to date with peoples' changing needs and circumstances. Personal situations also affect individuals' motivation and their needs of the time.

Where individuals carry out limited duties, regardless of how intellectually demanding of them they may be, if they operate in isolation and with little support people are likely to become tired and bored and feel unvalued. Such individuals can become more insular over time and keep all forms of communication with others to the barest minimum.

Personal effectiveness skills required in order to help motivate others

- Be an active listener
- Applaud, compliment and reward
- Give considered answers
- Consult and take account of what people say
- Seek out their needs
- Give responsibility and the necessary authority
- Offer challenge

Showing appreciation

Showing appreciation for work done by others is key to the development of good working relationships as well as building assertive behaviour. Some managers appear to think it is *soft* and non-assertive to thank others for what they have done. This is simply not so; the approach will build self-confidence, trust and mutual support between team members.

Making apologies

Likewise, apologizing when you are wrong will gain credibility and support from others. False apologies and empty promises will have the reverse effect, but to admit mistakes takes courage initially, which will be eventually rewarded by positive responses from others.

Delegation

It is necessary to identify appropriate reasons for delegating tasks and to match the skills involved in performing tasks with those assuming responsibility. If managing is about 'achieving results through people', then all managers should delegate. We know that managers in successful companies delegate tasks and responsibilities right down the line; yet delegation is often dealt with badly, if at all!

Some people may see delegation more as a job task that a personal skill, yet there is a personal effectiveness dimension to delegating. Many of the problems associated with poor delegation are either failure to communicate, or inability to do it properly. The following attitudes are all too typical of some managers:

- 'I would rather do it myself'
- 'They'll only do it all wrong'
- 'I'll have to watch them like a hawk'
- 'I tried delegating once; it was more trouble than it was worth!'
- 'I don't want them to do my job for me!'

There are three *reasons* for delegating:

- To free time for yourself
- As a training or development exercise
- For motivational purposes

Delegated tasks usually fail for one of the following reasons:

- Wrong reason for delegating
- Wrong task(s) delegated
- Task(s) delegated to the wrong person
- Factor 'X'

Delegation works in a management context that is increasingly emphasizing the notions of empowerment and shared responsibility. So sharing and delegating both tasks and responsibility, with the necessary authority, is becoming the norm. However, the three reasons are very different and when a task is delegated, one should be clear about the motives for doing so.

Freeing time for yourself. For a manager, this is a perfectly legitimate reason to delegate. However, it is worth asking yourself if you always delegate only menial tasks and tricky assignments and whether you keep certain tasks for yourself as 'hobbies'.

Training and development exercises. This is an excellent way to develop skills and confidence in your staff. However, if it is a training exercise, the skills to be learned and practised should be clearly spelled out.

Motivation. The importance of self-management and challenge in this context has already been discussed.

Delegating the wrong task and/or to the wrong person

Many more delegation exercises would be more successful if the tasks were matched more carefully to the person. The following six rules should be followed for successful delegation:

1 *Clarity*   The purpose should be spelled out.
2 *Matching delegates to task*   The skills required should be carefully considered. The level of the task should be challenging, but appropriate.
3 *Discussion*   The task, from the purpose through to the fulfilment, should be talked through.
4 *Resources*   Sufficient resources, particularly time, should be made available.
5 *Monitoring*   The rewards should be discussed and progress should be regularly checked.
6 *Review*   Achievement should be checked against objectives.

Factor 'X' – the unpredictable element.

There is little control possible over factor 'X'. This means that even where we have been careful to identify our purpose in delegating tasks and responsibility, and even where we have followed the six rules, things can still go wrong. However, a crucial issue is to determine what should be done to be realistic and accept that sometimes things do go wrong – the element of risk!

It is important to allow failure; progress can only be made if we accept occasional failures. It should be a part of the review process to try to identify why things may have gone wrong and to learn the lessons without blaming anyone.

EXERCISE

From the previous discussions relating to team building, including motivation and delegation, determine from your own team interaction at work whether improvements can be made in the commitment to achieve organizational outcomes.

PREPARING FOR ACTION PLANNING

Remember the checklist of questions identified in the *Introduction* to this book? Try them again to identify your further development needs. We have reproduced those most appropriate to this chapter to help you.

How are organizational performance standards determined and by whom?

How do you ensure that these performance standards are being met?

How do you measure these standards?

How do you handle health and safety issues at your workplace?

Which outside agencies do you currently liaise with?

Are there any joint working arrangements in your product/service (this may apply across teams, or between organizations)?

What are these and for what purposes do the arrangements exist?

What actions would you/have you taken with others at times of particular difficulty or change?

How do you liaise with others at off-site locations?

How is information fed back into the decision-making process?

What, if any, interdepartmental group activities do you participate in?

What are the main purposes of these groups?

What are the main working relationships you maintain?

How do you/would you maximize productive relationships and networks?

How do you/would you promote equal opportunities within and between those with whom you relate?

What are the key elements, in your opinion, in promoting effective working relationships?

What do you see as your strengths in establishing good working relationships and which aspects would you want to develop further?

How would you/do you go about establishing and developing working relationships with others, both internal and external to the organization?

How easy/difficult do you find asking support of or taking problems to others?

How might this be improved?

How easy/difficult do you think others find asking you for support or in bringing their problems to you?

How could it be improved?

What support would you/do you give to others in their relations with others outside the organization (or department)?

How could these relationships be improved?

What formal and informal actions would you/have you taken to actively promote effective working relationships and prevent their breakdown?

How do you/would you deal with conflict in your relationships or in the relationships of others arising from:

- Differences of opinion on courses of action?
- Personal animosity?
- Moral dilemmas (between individuals or individu-
  als and the organization)?
- Racism?
- Sexism?
- Other discriminatory behaviour?
- Non-compliance with organizational rules, norms
  or values?

What do you see as *counselling* in the workplace?

What is the purpose and what are the limitations of workplace counselling?

What is your role as counsellor – both formally and informally?

What are the key elements of effective workplace counselling?

Who are the parties involved in starting and inducting
those for whom you will be responsible?

How effective is this process, the people involved, and how
might you improve it?

How do you determine the training and development needs
of yourself and others?

What activities do you use for the development of others
(formal and informal)?

How do you plan these activities?

How do you review progress and evaluate the outcomes of
training and development?

Have you taken any steps to improve equality of opportunity in the development of others?

What were the outcomes?

Have there been any specific incidences which have caused
you concern for the equality of opportunities in the development of all?

How do you set work objectives (or participate in setting
them) for yourself and others?

How do you review and update these objectives?

Identify an objective you have had to meet and specify how
you planned the work activities to meet this objective.

How did you decide which method would work best?

How do you decide how to allocate work to others?

What would say is your leadership style?

What are the effects of your style on others? For example,
are you, do you think, making the most use of the skills
available to you (yours and others)?

How does this tie in with the overall work objectives set?

How do you evaluate the performance of others (and your own) against their objectives?

What methods do you use to give feedback to others about their performance?

Can you pinpoint anything which you consider particularly important when giving feedback?

How often do you hold meetings (formal and informal), briefings and group discussions?

For what purposes do you hold meetings etc.?

Do your meetings always (often, sometimes, rarely):

- Start on time?
- Finish on time?
- Achieve their objectives?

Do you always have the necessary information in advance of the meetings?

Do you always supply the necessary information in advance of the meetings?

Are you confident about:

- Chairing meetings?
- Contributing to the purpose of meetings?
- Taking minutes?

Would you say your meetings are always

- Well prepared?
- Well administered?
- Well controlled?

Are the people at your meetings there because they:

- Have a part to play?
- Have an interest?
- Have been sent?

What are the meetings' follow-up processes?

Do your meetings result in positive action?

How might your information provision and running of meetings influence effective team building?

Questions adapted from those devised by the Crediting Competence Team at South Bank University and reproduced with permission.

ACTION PLANNING

Analyse your own behaviour in terms of strengths (positive outcomes) and weaknesses (negative effects), in dealing with actual work-based occurrences with regards to the various relationship situations discussed in this chapter.

Decide how you might deal with them differently in the future and what your immediate training requirements are and future development needs.

Discuss them with your immediate manager and negotiate how you might address them.

FURTHER READING

Hannagan, Tim (1995), *Management Concepts and Practices*, Pitman Publishing, London.

Handy, Charles B. (1985), *Understanding Organizations*, 3rd edn, Penguin Books, London.

Mullins, Laurie J. (1993), *Management and Organizational Behaviour*, Pitman Publishing, London.

Nicholson, John (1992), *How Do You Manage?*, BBC Books, London.

Parsloe, Eric (1992), *Coaching, Mentoring and Assessing – A Practical Guide to Developing Competence*, Kogan Page, London.

2 Communication and presentation

Managers with skills in communication and presentation are able to share information, ideas and arguments with a variety of audiences.

INTRODUCING THE RELATIONSHIP BETWEEN THE MCI PERSONAL COMPETENCY MODEL AND COMMUNICATION AND PRESENTATION

The MCI Integrated *Model of Personal Competency* identifies the behaviours and skills necessary for you to develop before you are able to prove competence in any managerial function. This chapter attempts to deal with the various behaviours and skills necessary for you to apply across all managerial functions, transferring your learning to different occasions, at different times and under varying circumstances (contexts), consistently. The outcomes below, as identified within this section of the model, should be borne in mind while you work through this chapter.

Outcomes required in communication and presentation

When developing communication and presentation skills, appropriate to various audiences and circumstances, there is a complex set of personal effectiveness behaviours required, the outcomes of which are that the manager:

- Listens actively, asks questions, clarifies points and rephrases others' statements to check mutual understanding
- Adopts personal communication and presentation styles appropriate to listeners and situations, including selecting an appropriate time and place for the event
- Uses a variety of media and communication aids to reinforce points and maintain interest

- Presents difficult ideas, concepts and problems in a way which promotes understanding
- Confirms listeners' understanding through questioning and interpretation of non-verbal signals
- Encourages listeners to ask questions or rephrase statements to clarify their understanding
- Modifies communication and presentation in response to expectations, responses and feedback from listeners as necessary.

INTRODUCTION TO COMMUNICATION

These outcomes may all seem obvious; that we all instinctively know this. Unfortunately, we can see everywhere, all the time, how misunderstandings can occur between individuals and resentments build because people are not communicating effectively with each other. If this can happen between two people in private, causing apparently irrational and immature behaviour leading to negative results, it takes little imagination to understand how people become irrational towards each other in organizations, within nations and between nations; war being the worst of all possible outcomes.

The nature of interpersonal communication

Definition: The exchange of information, verbally and through bodily expression, between two or more people in order to influence the occurrence of action, ideas or thoughts; at work, in leisure or community pursuits, or in individuals' domestic lives.

We communicate with each other, whether we wish to or not, in order to:

- Inform
- Instruct
- Motivate
- Persuade
- Encourage
- Negotiate
- Understand the views and ideas of others
- Listen because we like to and want to learn
- Seek, receive and give counselling, information, advice, decisions and so on.

Types of information we wish to communicate to, and receive from others, can be categorized as:

- Knowledge
- Data

- Attitude
- Intention
- Emotion

Interpersonal communication can hover between being easy, good, happy and positive, and being difficult, not so good, unhappy and negative. Communication, and thereby relationships themselves, often break down as the result of not *talking* to each other.

Verbal and non-verbal components to communication

We need to recognize the many forms of verbal and non-verbal communication and to *actively* listen to others. What we say, what we do, and even our refusal to talk, all communicate messages to those with whom we interact. Yet, however well we think we communicate, there are problems.

These problems, which are often caused by gaps in our communicating ability, are nearly always unintentional and they point to the difference between the intended message and the message received. Even with verbal communication, the words we use do not contain the whole of the message. Various commentators agree that a message is made up of 7 per cent words, 38 per cent voice tonality and 55 per cent body language!

The receipt of any piece of communication, then, is based on individuals' impressions of that which is being communicated. These impressions are complex agglomerations which are the result of more than the obvious components that are being communicated. Any discussion of what communication is must therefore comprise more than a systematic analysis. It should also involve an understanding of the individual differences and expectations of those with whom we interrelate and whose perceptions are often based more on emotion, prejudice, guesswork, and so on.

First impressions

We also judge people based on very little evidence. It is quite well known in the selling business, for instance, that first impressions are extremely important. Various commentators have suggested that we make our minds up when we are interviewing in the first ten seconds, two minutes, or five minutes. Is it possible to elicit (or project) enough information in that time to give someone a rounded picture of character, personality and abilities?

On what information are such judgements made? Are they likely to be correct? Whatever the answers to these questions, researchers into the subject suggest, quite rightly, that we should maximize our opportunities by positively trying to create a good first impression. Conversely, we should attempt to defer judgement when meeting others for the first time.

WHAT FACILITATES INTERPERSONAL COMMUNICATION?

Active listening

The *active listener* will deliberately start by *taking in* rather than *giving out* information. In order to be effective communicators, we need to know other people's interests, needs and so on. We therefore need to demonstrate to others that we are interested in what they are saying.

It is therefore necessary for us to create an environment in which others can be honest and give information freely. To do this, it is important that we confirm to them that we have heard and understood their message; that we are supportive and not standing in judgement of them. We can do this by providing encouragement and constructive feedback, rather than constantly probing, interpreting and evaluating what they have said.

To listen actively to another person we should:

- Establish rapport
- Make eye contact
- Match body language – by mirroring actions, posture, gestures
- Ask questions – to confirm, seek information and recognition
- Not interrupt or change the subject – active listening means letting the other person *set the agenda*
- Keep the focus on them, by using words such as *you* and *your* rather than *me* and *mine*
- Use names.

Body language and other non-verbal communication

Body language is what usually springs to mind when we talk about clues to non-verbal, interpersonal communication. Body language will be discussed here in the normally accepted definition of the phrase, plus one or two other points for consideration which might not spring to mind so readily.

Characteristics

These include facial expressions:

- Gaze and eye contact; bodily posture
- Gestures and use of hands in adding to, or contradicting, the spoken word
- Proximity (some cultures expect to be in closer proximity when in discussion than others)
- Personal appearance (we are what we wear): are we really telling people something about ourselves by the clothes we choose to wear?

Body language is important and it constitutes an integral part of the information which people consciously or unconsciously use to assess others. The interview is a situation in which this *activity* is particularly focused.

Important behaviours one might expect to see in others, and indeed portray oneself, at an interview, would include:

- *Appearance* appropriate to the context of the interview (one would not normally expect to wear jeans to a selection interview, or a formal review meeting or by contrast, to turn up wearing a pin-striped suit for an informal counselling session at a job centre).
- *Eye contact* to avoid eye contact implies dishonesty, even though this is not always true (e.g. shyness, feelings of threat, etc.), therefore ensure eyes are levelled at the other person's eyes without staring or gazing for too long (this can seem like threatening behaviour) – above all, *smile*.
- *The body* including the position of the feet
- *Stance* The body should be pointed towards the other person to encourage mutual interest and respect. To turn away implies disinterest, impatience or lack of time. Leaning towards the other person in a relaxed non-fidgeting way shows friendliness
- *Sit comfortably* The legs should either be side by side or loosely crossed to express comfort and a relaxed attitude. Unnecessary hand movements are best avoided. (Other than gestures which add to the positive meaning you are expressing, hand movements can be a distraction and even put across different messages to your words and facial expressions!)
- *Show interest and enthusiasm* this will encourage the other person to relax, even to enjoy the session/interview by the warmth generated under these conditions
- *Listen and respond to what is said* Too often 'interviewers' are guilty of thinking far too much about the next questions they want to ask, they actually forget to listen to the answers to the current questions! Not only will the *interviewees* stop making efforts when it is realized that they are not being listened to, the interviewers also look rather foolish if they then ask questions which have already been answered!
- *Nod head to show understanding* hold upright, straight and level (to hold the head forward and high denotes aggression, to hold it forward and rigid denotes anxiety)
- *Hold hands open and outstretched* hold them away from the face and offer a firm handshake (pointed fingers and

raised hands indicate aggression; clenched fists and folded arms defensiveness)
- *Steady voice*   shows confidence and soft, pleasant tones indicates friendliness.

Verbal communication

Characteristics

Verbal communication, both face to face (including meetings) and on the telephone, involves conversations; listening skills; and talking. All these are supported by body language – even while talking on the telephone one can hear when someone is smiling or frowning by their tone of voice!

It is very important for managers to develop their conversational skills and to present ideas and opinions verbally. Demands upon verbal articulation will increase as areas of responsibility widen both informally in general conversations and formally in planned and prepared presentations.

Speech is also used by people to communicate emotions and their innermost feelings. It is possible to communicate all these needs by using a variety of elements of speech which can be controlled and used to good effect. Such elements would include:

- Voice *tone*
- Speech *emphasis*
- Speech *content*
- Use of *figurative* language
- *Humour* in speech
- *Speed* of speech
- *Pronunciation* used
- *Pitch* of voice
- *Inferred* speech

Creating the environment

Some would say that a climate of independence within workgroups such that people do not feel threatened by the existence of other groups is important in facilitating interpersonal communication. It is vital to make all information available within and between groups to facilitate good working relationships and by being aware of what others are doing.

If people are aware that they need to know what is happening in other areas of the organization for their own understanding and development (they will then know where to send enquiries and enquiries about their own work will be passed onto them in return), they will look out for and enjoy being able to pass on and receive information. Typically, if this kind of interaction is not encouraged, although people will still talk to each other, such talk is likely to be unproductive, creating cliques which have a tendency to gossip, start rumours and hold grumbling sessions about *the management*, other individuals and other groups.

Flexibility of staff to work in various capacities within and between departments might also be said to help effective communication. People become less *attached* to their assigned roles (which can make them insular) and more inclined to develop an organizational approach, thus creating greater and more effective channels within which to demonstrate their skills and abilities.

THE CENTRAL ROLE OF COMMUNICATION IN THESE ACTIVITIES

Why are good workplace communications important?

- It is a two-way process between people at all levels, within all functions and disciplines; it takes place upwards, downwards and sideways.
- It ensures efficiency and success.
- Managers have a responsibility to communicate.
- It creates trust between people, especially when systems and procedures are being developed.
- It facilitates job satisfaction.
- It is vital in specific arrangements or agreements between management and employees, e.g. consultation, negotiation, etc.
- It reduces misunderstandings.
- It involves people – staff want to know:
  - What is happening and why
  - The way their jobs can contribute to organizational prosperity and effectiveness
  - The future prospects of the organization.
- There are legal obligations in organizations with union recognition.
- Employees are able to contribute.

Who is responsible for communications?

Communication involves everyone, but management is primarily responsible which should ensure:

- A positive lead from the *top*
- That policy is put into practice
- That practice is properly maintained
- That policy and practice are regularly reviewed
- That adequate facilities and opportunities exist
- That adequate feedback is obtained
- The chain of communication is clearly understood by those involved and to keep the chain as short as possible

The larger the organization, the more likely specialist functions (e.g. personnel as well as line managers) will take an active interest in employee communications – possibly involving direct responsibility.

The process of workplace communications

The means of workplace communication (which includes the medium used) can be various. For most purposes they include:

- Spoken; may also include non-verbal aspects
- Written; correspondence, report writing, written proposals and so on
- Representational; often to external organizations, but also to other departments, teams, etc.
- Communication with self; thinking
- Team briefing, etc.

Effective workplace communication is:

- Clear, concise and easily understood; presented objectively
- Presented in a manageable form to avoid rejection
- Regular and systematic
- As relevant, local and timely as possible
- Open to questions being asked and answered.

Maintaining effective communication will require:

- Monitoring
- Reviewing
- Communicators knowing their roles
- Appropriate information being available
- Information reaching all who need or want it
- Information not being unnecessarily restricted
- Communication bringing desired benefits
- Practice in matching policy

This will depend upon:

- Appropriate training
- The extent of employee cooperation
- The quality of management decision making
- The level of involvement by senior managers
- Absenteeism and labour turnover
- The employee relations climate.

Communication is one of the key skills for the competent manager. A commonly agreed definition of management is *achieving results through people*. In order to do this we need to practise the whole range of management competences and fulfil a variety of roles. These are all predicated on our ability to communicate with our colleagues at work (and sometimes with ourselves).

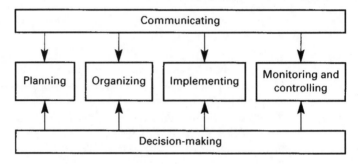

Figure 2.1   The management context

If we examine the management sequence illustrated in Figure 2.1, it becomes clear that communicating is involved at every stage of the process. It is therefore a critical component of almost every management skill. In this sense it can also be defined as a dimension of personal effectiveness (see Figure 2.2).

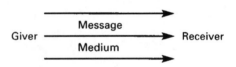

Figure 2.2   The components of communication

WHAT IMPEDES INTERPERSONAL COMMUNICATION?

According to the Open University (1990), in their *Effective Manager* course material, there are nine barriers to effective communication:

1   Uncertainty of message; when we are simply not sure what to say, or how to say it.
2   Faulty presentation; this might occur by choosing the wrong medium (for example, a memo when a face-to-face discussion would be more appropriate).
3   Limited capacity of target; or where the receivers of the message are not trained to interpret the information (e.g. financial statements) and they feel threatened by being presented material with which they are not equipped to deal. Information thus provided is likely to be rejected or only selectively absorbed by the receivers.

4   Unstated assumptions; where sender and receiver are unaware that they each have different assumptions about aspects of the message.

5   Incompatible viewpoints; failure to communicate because the sender and receiver of messages view circumstances from a completely different perspective. For example, managers may view the introduction of a new computer system as providing opportunities for improving performance and saving people from the boredom of routine tasks, while others may see the introduction of information technology as a means of downsizing.

6   Deception; where the sender deliberately withholds certain aspects of information.

7   Interference; noisy telephone lines; the phone ringing while we are trying to write a complex letter; an emergency occurring in the office while we are trying to negotiate with a client, etc.

8   Lack of channels; where people who possess information with which others might usefully benefit, and vice versa, but who are unaware of the needs of each other because there are no formal channels allowing such exchanges of information.

9   Cumulative distorted communication – 'Chinese whispers'; The longer the chain of people receiving and passing the information, the more distorted the message will be by the time it reaches the last in the chain.

If individuals and groups are encouraged to consider each other as 'customers' just like any other customers, they will have no reason or inclination to build resentments. They will begin to understand that everyone, including themselves, need positive and friendly interaction in order to do their jobs to the best of their ability.

Conflicting views can present problems. Often we spend so much time thinking about what we want to express ourselves, we do not listen to what other people are trying to say. It is a hard, but very important lesson if we can listen to others while remembering the main points of our own arguments; sometimes these become modified when listening to other viewpoints.

EXERCISE

Who has the responsibility for communicating within your organization? Analyse the effectiveness of the various modes of communication and determine how *you* might improve them.

IMPERSONAL COMMUNICATION

The written word, including reports and letters, effective reading and taking notes; meetings; public presentations; exhibitions and conferences; electronic communication: computerized information – internal, external (locally, nationally, internationally); electronic mail, facsimile, etc. are all examples of the impersonal communication with which managers must deal effectively and efficiently.

Use of business English

Written communication

Good writing involves not one skill, but many. Writing skill is a continuum that ranges from basic information provided in notes and memos to highly complex communication transmitted through reports. Each medium we use requires different skills and for most of us there is also a requirement for a technical or conceptual component.

The first principle in the use of business English is to *Keep it Short and Simple* (the KISS approach). It is very tempting for managers and professionals to use jargon common to their organizations or professions. It would cause offence and be considered rude if used when the recipients are not familiar with it. The same would apply if a manager talks *down* to their correspondees; assuming them to be unable to comprehend the nature of the ideas they are trying to transmit.

A balance must then be maintained between an acceptable, non-turgid, non-academic style of writing, free of any jargon, and a language which is common within and between English-speaking organizations. Indeed the style of this book is intended to be easily readable, unambiguous and understandable!

It is important to decide the purpose, target audience and format. This will provide the requirements for the content. Clear thinking is also required in both written and oral presentation. If you understand the issues and the rules for presenting them, you will be able to argue logically and to identify any problems in the arguments of others. The purpose could be to:

- Change behaviour or beliefs
- Answer a question
- Present facts
- Present results of an audit or similar activity
- Describe situations, events, or ideas
- Provide information
- Record past events
- Recommend
- Influence decision making
- Bring about action
- Persuade

(Adapted from Hardy, 1990)

Structure

Once the purpose of writing is defined, we then need to organize the important ideas into some sort of structure. We are lucky today; indeed as I am writing this section of the book and tap out the ideas onto my computer keyboard, with the word processing package I am using I can move whole sections around; break up sentences and reorder them; delete unwanted parts and add to ideas as I come back to them afresh, without wasting paper or time or running the risk of forgetting ideas as they come to me. I can suddenly move between chapters as ideas flow from one source into another area more suited to another chapter, and return again to add further thoughts. For me this is ideal; it is not however always possible to use a computer.

When it is not possible to use information technology to develop ideas for writing, it can be a good idea to mind-map ideas first (see Figure 2.3) rather like you might do when sitting an examination and you think through in advance how you might tackle the answer, linking your ideas with arrows. You will find, especially if you are a lateral thinker like me, that your completed map will be far from linear with main ideas and associated ideas circling and spiralling all over the page. However, it is possible, once you have completed this process, to order the ideas logically, making sections and subsections which also help to develop the ideas further.

Another way of developing from the sub-headings would be to list ideas in bullet point format for each section. Both these approaches are called *top down*. With reports, a good technique would then be to *top and tail* each section. That is, for each section, write a first sentence encapsulating the purpose or key point; then write a summary containing the conclusion, or key point. It then remains only to fill in the text contained in the mind map or bulleted list.

Whichever process you use, commencing all written communication by thinking about headings and sub-headings is a perfect means for developing your ideas and allowing them to flow easily. Sometimes you will add to them as you proceed, sometimes you will change or remove some of your original headings, but all will make writing easier to commence, develop and complete, whatever your purpose.

Good journalistic technique says that you should put the most important point first, and then any supporting information below it. Using this technique, the reader is then able to *cut off* the text at any point, as required, without missing the most important issue.

Logical reasoning

The logical form into which most arguments can be translated is known as a *syllogism* and consists of:

- A major premiss (or proposition); the statement of a general law or principle or fact

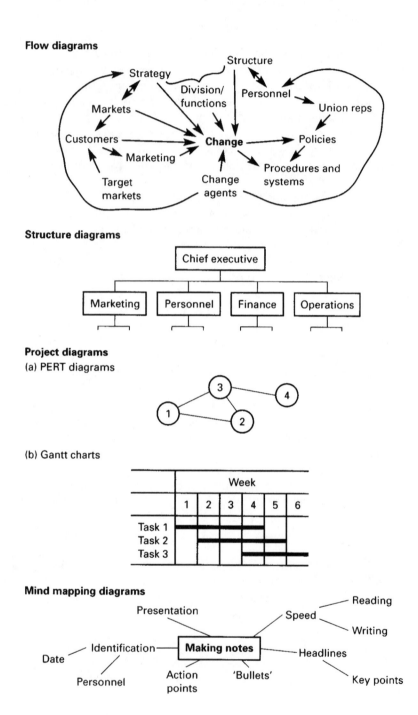

Figure 2.3   Diagrams used in visual presentations

- A minor premiss; connecting a particular case with the general law, principle or fact
- A conclusion; a new fact validly inferred from the two premisses.

Developing the theme

Serial arguments. These are commonly used in reports and technical papers where the *conclusion* of one argument becomes the *premiss* of the next. e.g.:

> If we develop managers to *delegate* effectively to their work-groups, individuals will become more *competent* in their jobs and be more *satisfied* with their performance, which will, *in turn*, allow their managers more time to *think* creatively, which will also, *in turn*, provide the basis for the learning organization to evolve and *develop new areas of strategic thinking* ...

and so on.

Lateral thinking. When we think laterally, we develop innovative solutions to problems by approaching them from entirely different directions. It is vital to write clearly and explain the rationale behind new ideas when writing. Where logical thinking is about linear, progressive, deductive approaches to problem solving, lateral thinking is about the use of unorthodox or apparently illogical methods of approaching the problem and is likely to need a certain amount of defending (especially where individuals' backgrounds are technical or scientific, i.e. use logical thinking!).

Writing style

The major objective here is to get over the key points in a way that is clear and effective. As already mentioned, this usually means the use of simple and clear language. Many people forget this, but the most difficult ideas can often be put over in a simple way, using straightforward language.

Correctness of language

Dictionaries record the accepted usage of words by the most educated people of the day, so that when we talk of correctness, in this context, we mean the speech or writing of formally educated people. However, it is necessary to use the rules as a guide rather than a rigid formula because English in all its forms is fluid and constantly changing. Without rules for language, however, there would be endless confusion of meaning.

Obstacles to thinking clearly

If you identify any obstacles which might be inhibiting your own clear think-ing, you can learn to overcome them. Such obstacles you might encounter are:

- *Language* can be an obstacle. Names used for things are rarely ambiguous, but more abstract terms can mean dif-ferent things to different people (e.g. *right* and *wrong*, *good* and *bad).*
- *Preconceived ideas.* Attitudes and opinions can be major obstacles to clear thinking. These are based upon our back-ground, education and experience and become our convic-tions. They are often just prejudices which prevent us from thinking clearly on certain subjects. They are strongly held beliefs which usually collapse if put to the test of logical reasoning. Prejudices should not be confused with criteria for judgement.
- *Self-interest.* Suspect your own opinions and those of others when it is obvious that the need to change them *appears* to threaten your own or others' security or happi-ness. This is not easy to do for yourself, but objective scrutiny of your own motives is very helpful for self-devel-opment as would be your facilitation of that of others.
- *Generalizations.* Be careful of sweeping statements in argu-ments which might hide the important issues. They are sometimes also based on prejudices. It is helpful to make general statements more precise by inserting words like *many, can, could, sometimes,* etc.

Attract and maintain the interest of the reader

Write to *express* yourself to, not to *impress* your reader. Inexperienced writers often try to impress others and while they might talk with their own voice, they will try to be someone else when they write. The use of unfamiliar words and meandering sentences will result in vague or even meaningless writing, which will irritate rather than communicate.

One of the advantages of the top-down approach discussed above (apart from helping us to structure the information and the logical flow) is that it focuses attention on the main points of the argument. At the same time it also helps to attract and maintain the interest of the reader. Some useful guidelines are:

- *Words*   As well as avoiding jargon as already mentioned, avoid the use of complicated words and phrases where simple ones will do.

- *Sentences*   The shorter your sentences, the better. It is not always possible, but if you aim for ten to twenty words a sentence, that makes your work very readable. *Punchy* statements are also more likely to be remembered.

- *Paragraphs*   Three to five sentences per paragraph also break up the words into manageable chunks and are best if they contain details of one idea or issue at a time. Words that are spread out between paragraphs with plenty of blank paper showing between them and between sections, encourage continued reading.

- Cramped paragraphs and lengthy sections are likely to bore readers and divert their attention to wondering how much longer they need to concentrate, rather than on how interesting or useful the information is.

- *Active verbs* give a stronger and clearer sense of meaning. Why say 'it is undergoing problems of a functional nature' when you really mean 'it doesn't work'?

- *Name it*   Why go all round the houses to say something which would be better understood if you just said it? Ask yourself the question – if someone said to you 'but what does that mean?' how would you tell them? If you rehearse a simple verbal explanation, it may help you to write it. In other words, many people would be much better writers if they *wrote like they spoke*!

- *Create mental pictures*   So many words are abstract and represent concepts rather than things. It is then much harder to say just what you mean. In shifting from thinking to communicating, place yourself in the position of the reader. If that person is an outsider or a newcomer, try to remember how little you knew before you learned the special knowledge you now have.

- *Assumptions*   Many people start with the 'but if's' before making the main point. This only obscures what they have to say. If you stick to the Point, Evidence, Conclusion style, you will avoid this.

- *Idea overload*   It is common for people to try to say two things in one sentence. This usually results in *neither* having the required impact. If you want to make two points, write two sentences. A slight variation on this theme is the *sentence within a sentence* (or in parentheses – brackets, commas, dashes – where the sentence is complete without it).

- *Common mistakes*   Search through some of your writing and check for the following: *This, it, they, you, we,* etc. – Is it obvious what or who is being referred to? Typographical errors may lead to confusion – check completed work.

- *Right first time*   Many people agonize over their written work precisely because it is not right first time. You need to realize that nobody gets it right first time. It is much better to write it and then revise it, especially if the material is complex.
- *Perfection in grammar, style, spelling*   People do get over-concerned about grammar, but if it sounds right, it is likely to be right. As a final check – read it aloud. Real howlers should stand out when you say it aloud. There is not a great deal you can do about spelling – except that you should be honest if you are not always accurate. In that case, use a spell-checker on your wordprocessor, or get someone to check it for you. Even when you would normally spell something correctly, it is easy not see your own mistakes, but for someone else it is likely to *stick out like a sore thumb*.
- *Punctuation*   Do not punctuate to observe some rule, do it because the sentence you are writing demands punctuation if it is to be understood. Punctuation enables the reader to read quickly and without ambiguity. Common sense and logic are the best guides to punctuation.
- *Fitness for purpose*   Match your style to the application. A company annual report has to be formal but most other documents do not. You can also use creative layout or other visual ideas.
- Above all, there is the need to know who your reader is. When writing to other managers, or sending them copies of letters you have sent to others, it is vital to be aware of the relevance of the information to them (and the language they use); it should be pertinent to their jobs, their professions or to their wider interests.

The large amounts of information received by managers means that anything which is not directly relevant will either be *binned* or, at best, *filed* unread. This is not only a waste of time and resources, it also impacts upon the wider environment and the unnecessary waste of paper.

The presentation and interpretation of data

Most written communication is presented in report form for management purposes. Simple methods should be used to display the data in a way which captures the essential aspects. In presenting any data it is important to use a neutral approach in your use of language, avoiding emotive words or statements, such as may be used by the popular press. Avoid language as a smokescreen to hide features of your study, for example obscure quotations, long and complicated sentences and excessive footnotes which can be distracting and even completely offputting for the reader.

Honesty is vitally important. Look for the strengths and weaknesses in the work of others you use (and discuss it) and also reveal in your report the strengths and weaknesses of your own work.

Types of report format

There are various types of report format. Some organizations require a lengthy and intricate approach to report writing; you must determine the *house style* as required. It is our intention here, however, to discuss concise and effective approaches to presenting findings in report format.

Reports are structured documents and are commonly organized in sections identifying:

- Title and author
- Intended readership
- A table of contents with actual headings and sub-headings to allow readers to determine the nature of the report
- Terms of reference: the authorisation and purpose of the report
- Summary of the main points of other sections, conclusions and any recommendations in order to tempt readers to delve into the detail within the report
- Background and history. Generally, it is necessary to devote a small section to the background of the report and the relevant history. This will usually identify the problem(s) or issue(s) requiring attention. It will also be useful if specific objectives for the investigation, or required outcomes are identified here
- Method of investigation:
  - Specific research will require the author to discuss alternatives and identify the preferred methods with full justification.
  - A general management report will require the investigator to identify which approach has been used.
  - Both types of report will need to include any constraints envisaged and how these may be overcome.
- General and specific findings of the investigation itself. This section will detail the circumstances and issues arising out of the investigation. This will be a factual account, reporting the findings in as subjective a manner as possible. If interviews have been carried out, these should be reported based upon the actual answers given to questions.
- When seeking information from others, particularly when researching attitudes and opinions, certain guarantees should be made. These might include:
  - All information obtained will be treated as strictly confi-

dential (i.e. names of respondents will not be used when discussing their responses if they do not wish them to be so)

- If interviews are carried out, the persons concerned will have the opportunity to see and verify the recorded statements
- Those participating will be entitled to a copy of the final report if they wish
- If the research is to be used by an academic institution for examination purposes, the question of subsequent publication will require the permission of participants.

■ Criteria for analysis, highlighting strengths, weaknesses, opportunities and threats

■ The analysis itself

■ Discussion

■ Conclusions drawn from the investigation. These will be based upon the actual analysis of the data collected with no new material included

■ Recommendations (where appropriate) based upon your enquiry or investigation. This is the *action centre* of the report and should meet the defined purpose of the report

■ Appendices: these are pieces of supplementary data not essential to the main findings, or updates of information which will eliminate the need for rewriting. They may include glossaries of technical terms and a list of abbreviations

■ Acknowledgements: thanks to people who helped prepare the report

■ Bibliography: sources of references used in the research

■ References: unpublished material not generally available, e.g. company papers.

Reviewing the report

Having written the report, leave it for a day or two before revising and editing it. This allows time to think about what has been written and how. New thoughts may emerge, their inclusion will improve the report. Type or print out the first draft when it will be easier to:

■ Read the material objectively

■ Assess the contents

■ Decide if it looks good

■ Review the language, logic and sequence of presentation

■ Determine whether the main body supports the recommendations

- Decide whether it is convincing
- Know if you are proud of it.

Graphic communication

Graphic communication is the use of visual techniques to aid communication. There are many ways in which the techniques of graphic communication can enhance your ability to communicate clearly and effectively. Among the many different types of graphic communication techniques are:

- Lettering and typography
- Illustration and design
- Graphic enhancement – signs and icons
- Maps and diagrams

Both lettering/typography and illustration/design are really specialist functions best left to professional designers. However, they are usefully discussed in the context of word processing and DTP (desk top publishing).

We live in a fairly rich visual culture, and in a technological and fast-changing world we are used to dealing with huge amounts of information. We learnt a long time ago that much information can be assimilated quickly, and that graphic design and logos can help to carry simple messages with great impact. Many companies also appreciate the importance of visibility, and pay hefty consultants fees to have their corporate logos designed. Of course, such devices can be used at a more modest level by all of us. We can incorporate icons or logograms into our documents and presentations to enhance the visual impact and the message.

Information technology

The use of desktop PC computers has opened up many more options for the graphic illustration of information. The main applications are:

- *Word processors* These offer the ability to manipulate numerical information – such as financial information or stock/production levels – on a grid. The most sophisticated ones offer the ability to illustrate the information in diagrams such as pie charts or bar charts.
- *DTP* Adds to word processors the ability to design pages, complete with illustrations. There have been many claims that the advent of DTP will turn us all into designers. Of course, this is not true. It may well not be an efficient use of your time to spend hours slaving over a hot computer to produce a perfect document. However, for the computer-literate, documents and OHPs can be produced with much higher quality if you can acquire the basic skills.

Statistical presentation

These forms of presentation are used almost exclusively for illustrating numerical data. They include pie charts, various types of bar chart and line graphs (Figure 2.4).

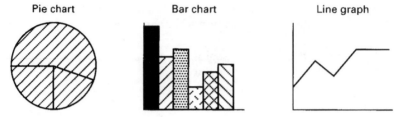

Figure 2.4   Statistical presentation

EXERCISE

Taking a report which you, or a colleague, has written recently, on the basis of the above discussion, rewrite it to be more attractive to the reader.

Visual/aural presentations

Making information visually attractive is particularly important when making presentations to colleagues or potential customers. As well as attention to the visual, this is an opportunity to use available technology to its full potential. When planning such a presentation, there are several elements to bear in mind:

- *Purpose*   We need to identify what the presentation is intended to do. It is necessary to ask two things here. What is the purpose for you? What is the purpose for your audience? There may be differences. This provides the focus, the structure and the style for the presentation.
- *Expectations*   Both your own and the audience's expectations need to be considered.
- *Objectives*   These too might differ between you and your audience.
- *Target audience*   We are likely to speak to colleagues in a different way from the way we do to potential customers. The nature of the audience will influence the level of formality. The size of the audience will influence the style.

■ *You – the speaker*   You must ask yourself three further questions:
Am I the right person to make this particular presentation to the audience?
What makes me a suitable person to do this?
Why will I be considered credible?

■ *Resources*   This will be decided to some extent by the nature of the target audience, by the available resources, and by the nature of the venue. For a small, informal group it may be appropriate to hand out copies of discussion documents. But it is possible, in most cases, to use an overhead projector or a flipchart. It can be very useful to hand out hard copies of the OHP slides for reference and note-taking.

■ Slides, video and audio facilities are also increasingly available at many venues for major presentations. Many chief executives of major organizations will expect to use a teleprompter for a major speech these days.

■ *When and where to present*   These may be crucial aspects for any presentation. There may be a need to coincide it with the launch of a product or service; the introduction of new legislation or professional/organizational codes; stages in business planning and so on.

■ *Timing*   As a general rule, the shorter, the better. Few people can concentrate for longer than about 20 minutes on a single speaker. However, sometimes it is necessary to speak for longer. In this case, try to enliven your presentation by breaking it up by adding an extra visual element, or by seeking the involvement of the audience. This interactive element always helps to interest the audience. It can be done by simply asking questions at regular intervals.

■ *Physical surroundings*   Consider the most appropriate place to present, the size of the audience and the seating arrangements in relation to whether everyone will be able to see, hear and take notes if they wish.

Once these basic planning factors have been analysed, you can then move on to the detailed construction of the presentation itself. In doing this you should pay attention to the following:

■ *Structure*   It should be broken down and organized into a coherent and logical structure – say what you are going to say; say it; summarize what you have said. Obviously the detailed structure is dependent on the application itself, but it should include:

- Purpose
- Overview
- Background/introduction
- The body of information (including claims and evidence, if appropriate)
- Summary

■ *Visual aid layout*   For example, it is often tempting to put too much information onto an OHP. It is better to limit text to a minimum. Headings are a must, and *bullet point* lists are very effective. It is useful to remember that people seem to be able to remember points more easily if they come in threes. When using an OHP it is very tempting to read the words on the slide. This is a mistake, and a lost opportunity – they can all read for themselves. You should use your commentary to amplify, emphasize or to digress.

■ *Visual*   Remember to use diagrams, charts, tables, icons, etc. where possible.

■ *Commentary/style*   You will need to make a choice of method of presentation before deciding how to remember the substance of it. You can read from a script, speak from prepared notes or speak without notes. The choice will depend on your skill and confidence.

■ *Interacting with an audience*   The rapport you create with your audience is a most important ingredient in ensuring that the message of any presentation gets across. This will depend upon you: looking and smiling at individuals (not the same ones all the time); maintaining good eye contact; asking questions where appropriate. It is also necessary to be: relaxed; well prepared; well rehearsed; appropriately dressed; confident; enthusiastic; audible; and clear. It can be effective if you make good use of humour. You must control the pace of your delivery, and you should never apologize for your presence or denigrate yourself. You should not distract the audience by your mannerisms or go on too long.

Creating a visual presentation is an ideal opportunity to use the facilities of the computer to help you create visual material of a high standard. Some people feel more at home by using traditional aids such as the white board, overhead projector, films/video films, slide projector and handouts.

However, too much visual material can cloud a point rather than illuminate it; the audience will concentrate more on the equipment itself and the techniques rather than on what you are saying. It is therefore vital to ensure that the use of any visual aids support, illustrate and reinforce points and they should be short, concise, simple and easy to see and hear.

EFFECTIVE READING

We all have to read – to keep informed, to keep up to date, and so on. But most of us could make our reading work much more efficiently for us.

- *Reduce your reading time*   This can be done by judicious scanning. Before even beginning to read, you should look at the contents to identify sections of importance (and of no importance). Then you should look at the subtitles only, again to identify sections of particular interest. Thus, before you begin reading you should know what you are looking for, and where in the document you are most likely to find it. When you do read, you should scan – do not expect to read every word. Most documents will contain only a few key ideas that you will wish to retain. The major task is to identify those.
- *Record what is important*   When you have identified those few key ideas, you need to be able to remember them or to mark them for future reference. One way to do this is to use a highlighter pen as you go along. Another is to write a very brief summary and attach it to the front page of the document. Action points should be marked in a different colour or a different style.

TAKING NOTES

Have you ever looked at the notes you have made of a meeting and wondered what on earth you have written? We often tend to take notes as a means of keeping ourselves occupied rather than with an eye for future use. We have all been guilty of reducing the effectiveness of our notes because we fail to record the most basic and often the most important information. Notes should always be dated, and should include the names of those present, if they relate to a meeting. A good habit to get into is to begin notes with a statement of their purpose – why you are recording this information, and what the record is to be used for. Other points to take account of are:

- *Be selective*   Notes should not be too long, and should contain only summary information which can be of potential use later on.
- *Organize*   The rules of any good writing apply. Information should be grouped, and organized into headings.
- *Presentation*   Again, diagrams can be useful ways of illustrating information or dynamic processes. Bullet-point lists, again, help to summarize and show information in digestible form.

- *Neatness* Reasonable writing, neatly presented, and without doodles helps the visual clarity of notes.
- *Action points*   These are among the most important items of information to record – whether they apply to you or others – yet they are often left out. Some visual device for recording action points can be helpful. Examples might include bracketing, use of coloured pens, or use of a special right-hand column.

Remember, we make notes in many circumstances and for many reasons. These techniques will help to improve the effectiveness of your note-taking.

MEETINGS

Purpose

Meetings should be useful ways to make things happen; to agree priorities, discuss and solve problems, identify new methods of working, agree and allocate responsibilities, follow up progress and so on. However, these purposes can be, and often are, abused. Some people simply insist upon meetings because they have always had them. Others use them as a method of checking individual performance assuming that group pressures will make people perform better. Others may use meetings as a method of group discipline.

We have all been to meetings that have been a waste of time for all concerned. Why does it seem so easy for so many meetings to turn out like this? Malcolm Peel (1988) has identified six deadly sins:

1   Unnecessary attendance
2   Lack of preparation
3   Bad tactics
4   Ineffective communication
5   Personality problems
6   Procedural problems

A meeting should have a clear purpose, and it should be known and agreed by all concerned. This not only helps to integrate and focus the activities of the meeting, it also serves as a way to measure its effectiveness.

Planning

A meeting should be properly planned and organized. Planning involves people, information and resources. The first and most obvious point is that a meeting cannot take place if any key contributors are not present. As well as being forewarned of meetings, participants should receive relevant information in good time before the meeting. If the purpose of the meeting is to discuss a report, no useful contributions can be made if the report is received cold for the first time at the meeting. Good organization will ensure that transport, rooms and other necessary facilities are available.

The conduct of the meeting will depend to some extent on the level of formality, and the nature of the meeting. A working meeting – for instance to produce a draft document, or to solve a technical problem – may take some considerable time. Usually, however, the shorter the meeting, the better, as long as the objective is achieved.

Elements of an efficient and productive meeting are:

- Purpose or objective known and shared by all
- Agenda set and followed
- Timetable set and agreed
- Notes/minutes recorded
- Input and involvement by all
- Outcomes discussed and decided
- Action points summarized at end

There are three essential categories of membership at any meeting:

1   *The chairperson*, who is responsible for calling the meeting in the first place as well as its purpose and the content of the agenda. This person must also, at the meeting itself, coordinate the issues, control participation and ensure optimum contributions from the relevant membership as well as handle any conflicts. Above all, the chairperson must not dominate the meeting; must seek clarification of any technical or other complex concepts; and should make personal notes of the proceedings.

2   *The secretary*, who is responsible for all arrangements before, during and after the meeting. This will include the provision of all the necessary documentation, other specific information required for the meeting, equipment, materials, any refreshments needed, and may also be required to take minutes unless another member is present for the purpose.

3   *The other members*, who should ensure adequate preparation for their contributions at the meeting. These will include the relevant experts required for the facts; someone who is able to identify compromise solutions; someone who is good at throwing up ideas (even if they are not all useful!); someone who can commit resources; and at least one person who is prepared to admit they do not understand, because most people are afraid to show their ignorance.

Construction of agenda

There are specific stages with coherent progression which must be addressed throughout the course of the meeting and the minutes will normally be recorded in order of discussion:

1. Apologies for absence
2. Minutes of previous meeting
3. Matters arising from previous minutes
4. List of new items in order of urgency or importance
5. Any other business
6. Date and time of next meeting

Recording of meetings

These should simply record the facts and any decisions taken and follow-up action required under each item. It is not necessary to record verbatim comments from each member other than where they directly refer to further action or further decisions required.

It is important to ensure that an accurate account of those attending the meeting be listed at the top of the minutes with relevant roles allocated alongside the names.

Item one should name those who should have attended the meeting but who have apologized, for urgent or important reasons, and who have been excused by the Chair.

All members should have had sufficient time before the meeting to read the minutes of previous meetings and make any necessary notes in order to raise queries. Item two then requires that the minutes are agreed by all members and then signed by the Chairperson and Secretary.

Ideally, an *Action Column* should be ruled up on the right-hand side of the minutes to identify the initials of those who have agreed at the meeting to follow up as necessary. Do not commit responsibilities to those absent from the meeting, unless they have previously agreed to be involved! This is a common mistake which can result in demotivation, inaction and compromised objectives.

Item three will deal with the matters arising from those minutes, which may be taken in a different order depending upon any newly agreed priorities identified at the meeting.

This will then be followed by item four which addresses all new issues to be dealt with by the meeting, in order of priority.

Item five covers any other business which may not be listed on the agenda and which has been identified by members as new, although perhaps not urgent, items for discussion.

The meeting members will then agree the time, date and place of any further meeting.

Techniques for effective communication at meetings

- *Kiss*   keep it short and simple as discussed earlier in this chapter. You must try to be clear and concise so that what you say is understood by everyone at the meeting.

- *Know your own subject*   be familiar with all the written material made available before the meeting, and therefore be confident that you will be able to deliver your information and answer likely questions without fear of being unprepared.

- *Listen*   avoid interrupting others midstream. Let them make their points, no matter how difficult it may be because you disagree, or are frightened you might forget what you want to say. Make your own notes, of course, so that you can come back to your points, but by listening to others without interruption it is possible to influence the discussion (or be positively influenced by the speaker) if the need continues. You will gain support and credibility as a good listener with the ability to acknowledge and apply what others think to your own thought development, without upsetting or embarrassing anyone. If you do not listen, not only the speaker but also others in the group are less likely to want to listen to you when it is your turn to speak.

- *Use humour*   this can be very helpful; it will relax everyone and help produce a conducive environment, especially where there are difficult problems to resolve or complex issues to debate. However, make sure it is relevant and that you do not become the scapegoat and ridiculed as the result of being known as a joker and never taken seriously.

- *Speak* when you have something constructive to add to, or ask about, the discussion and not just for the sake of being heard. A common mistake is for people to contribute to their own function or specialism and remain quiet during the discussion of issues outside their immediate control or interest. This makes them not only appear disinterested in the problems of others but that they are ignorant of them as well. Therefore, listen keenly to what is being said in all topics and allow your ideas to form accordingly. It can reveal to others where they have been less than efficient in transmitting information.

- *Compromise*   where necessary and if you are able; don't just *stick to your guns* as a matter of principle. Uncompromising attitudes, unless the implications are too great for those you are representing (when you should explain them very clearly to the rest of the meeting) will achieve nothing. It could also damage your reputation as a good manager with the ability to view situations from a wide perspective.

■ *When negotiating* identify those areas with which there is agreement and spell them out before making strong points over which you are seeking agreement, but may be difficult for other members to accept.

■ *Acknowlege the strengths and achievements* of others at the meeting, including those who are not present. This also has positive effects on others' views of your abilities and perceptions.

One of the managers interviewed for this book found staff meetings very traumatic when she first arrived in post because of one individual's attitude within the group. No-one wanted to discuss things because the person concerned was always on the defensive, making it impossible for others to air their views and opinions. The manager then concentrated on holding small group meetings to much greater effect; others found it easier to contribute and develop their self-confidence.

When she finally ran a full staff meeting, the manager had been able to facilitate the removal of the individual's defensiveness, who then had little to say beyond relevant issues, making a more constructive and positive meeting in all. The manager's main tip for effective meetings: 'Always plan and prepare thoroughly, or you will look stupid. Take it from one who knows!'

As a final comment on the art of communicating, the manager would add:

Remain focused on the end-product or outcome. Take time to read everything; policies, procedures, everything relevant. Past course materials make excellent reminders, especially if bad habits are creeping in. Keep up to date with things, it is no good having manuals of procedures and then allow the dust to settle on them. They have a purpose, so use them. Really understand the essence of their existence not just to act by the book, but to internalize their purpose and be party to their development.

EXERCISE

Ask a colleague to observe your behaviour at the next meeting you run. Ask for feedback on your effectiveness:

Was the agenda covered in time?
Did you contribute appropriately and effectively?
Did you make it possible for all attending to contribute?
Did you handle any disagreements and how effective was this handling?

Telephone technique

The telephone is often the first line of response to customers, or the public at large, for many organizations. But what sort of impression do your customers get from your organization? Try phoning your own organization from outside. What sort of response do you get? Is it prompt, helpful, informative, efficient?

It would be a pity to spend millions of pounds on a major media campaign to promote a product or service or a particular organization and have it spoilt because customers are treated badly by those answering the telephones.

Telephone checklist

How to use the telephone effectively:

- Ensure the equipment is appropriate for the size and purpose of your organization.
- Give technical training. All staff should be able to use all available facilities provided by your equipment.
- Structure jobs appropriately. Good support and guidance for all staff answering the telephone are essential in helping them to give effective customer service.
- Establish good discipline. Show how to deal with various types of enquiry, making and receiving personal calls, peak time procedures and so on.
- Provide behavioural training. Make sure that the people answering telephone calls use the voice you would like your customers to hear. All organizations have their own preferred ways for staff to behave when dealing with telephone enquiries.

PREPARING FOR ACTION PLANNING

Remember the checklist of questions identified in the Introduction to this book? We have reproduced those most suited to this chapter to help your preparation.

How do you find out about your customers' needs?
How do you make customers aware that your products/services are available?
How effective are the communication methods you use?
How do you deal with any customer complaints?
How do you handle health and safety issues at your workplace?
How appropriate is your location for the product/service you provide?

Which outside agencies do you currently liaise with?

What actions would you/have you taken with others at times of particular difficulty or change?

How do you present facts and figures to others for decision-making purposes?

How effective are your analytical and mathematical skills in convincing others?

Were the outcomes of these presentations appropriate for the decision-making purposes?

How might you improve your analytical and mathematical skills?

How do you liaise with others at off-site locations?

How is information fed back into the decision-making process?

What, if any, interdepartmental group activities do you participate in?

What are the main purposes of these groups?

What methods do you use to give feedback to others?

Can you pinpoint anything which you consider particularly important when giving feedback?

What information do you need to do your job and for what purposes?

Do you have any problems obtaining this information?

To whom do you supply information?

How often do you hold meetings (formal and informal), briefings and group discussions?

For what purposes do you hold meetings etc.?

Do your meetings always (often, sometimes, rarely):

- Start on time?
- Finish on time?
- Achieve their objectives?

Are you confident about:

- Chairing meetings?
- Contributing to the purpose of meetings?
- Taking minutes?

Would you say your meetings are always

- Well prepared?
- Well administered?
- Well controlled?

Are the people at your meetings there because they:

- Have a part to play?
- Have an interest?
- Have been sent?

What are the meetings' follow-up processes?

Do your meetings result in positive action?

Have you attended committees in your current role and prepared reports for these committees?

Questions adapted from those devised by the Crediting Competence Team at South Bank University and reproduced with permission.

ACTION PLANNING

Discuss your effectiveness as a 'person-to-person' communicator with your boss, your colleagues, subordinates, friends and relations.

Prompt their responses by asking about your behaviour under the various headings in this chapter and try to record them objectively (do not disagree with them, just think about what they have to say).

Were there any surprises? Were there areas of agreement between the various responses? If so, record your reactions and thoughts concerning them. What about the varying responses? Whom do you believe to be the most accurate in their observations of your behaviour and why? Be honest with yourself, this is all about self-development, not punishment for ineffective behaviour.

Do you have problems sifting through and reading all the material that lands upon your desk? Try out some of the simple rules discussed in this chapter and keep a log of the information you have gathered, recorded and stored.

Discuss with your boss the effectiveness of any reports you have submitted recently and make notes of any areas of development required. (Remember to assess your language – including use of jargon; any aids you have used to support your arguments – visual and otherwise; note-taking and other secondary information used in your reports.)

Discuss with those with whom you regularly 'meet' your effectiveness at meetings and group discussions. Detail your strengths and areas for development.

What are your particular strengths when dealing/liaising with people or agencies outside your own organization?

Would you say you had any particular difficulties?

What are your development needs in relation to the concepts and practicalities discussed in this chapter?

How do you intend to address them?

FURTHER READING

Cameron, Shelia and Pearce, Sue (1995), *The Management Studies Handbook*, Chapters 13–16, Pitman Publishing, London.

Hannagan, Tim (1995), *Management Concepts and Practices*, Pitman Publishing London.

Handy, Charles B (1985), *Understanding Organizations*, 3rd edn, Penguin Books, London.

Pease, Allan (1988), *Body Language: How to read others' thoughts by their gestures*, Sheldon Press, London.

3 Ethical perspective

Managers with an ethical perspective identify concerns and resolve complex dilemmas in an open reasoned manner.

INTRODUCING THE RELATIONSHIP BETWEEN THE MCI PERSONAL COMPETENCY MODEL AND AN ETHICAL PERSPECTIVE

The MCI Integrated *Model of Personal Competency* identifies the behaviours and skills necessary for you to develop before you are able to prove competence in any managerial function. This chapter attempts to deal with the various behaviours and skills necessary for you to apply across all managerial functions, transferring your learning to different occasions, at different times and under varying circumstances (contexts), consistently. The outcomes below, as identified within this section of the model, should be borne in mind while you work through this chapter.

Outcomes required in an ethical perspective

This chapter invites the manager to develop behaviours which demonstrate that he or she:

- Complies with legislation, industry regulation, professional and organizational codes
- Shows integrity and fairness in decision making
- Sets objectives and creates cultures which are ethical
- Identifies the interests of stakeholders and their implications for the organization and individuals
- Clearly identifies and raises ethical concerns relevant to the organization
- Works towards resolution of ethical dilemmas based on reasoned approaches
- Understands and resists personal pressures which encourage non-ethical behaviour
- Understands and resists apparent pressures from organizational systems to achieve results by any means.

The aims of this chapter are to introduce the reader to concepts of ethics that are relevant to the decisions that a manager has to confront. The chapter is not intended to turn the reader into an expert on moral theory. Neither will it transform an individual with fundamentally immoral or unethical beliefs into a fine, upstanding member of society. However, we hope that it will pose some questions which will encourage you to think about the ethical dimensions of your behaviour as a manager.

By the end of this chapter and in the particular learning exercises we hope that you will be able to:

- Appreciate the nature of ethical behaviour within organizations
- Understand the difference between absolute and relative ethical issues
- Distinguish between narrow and broad definitions of business ethics
- Be conscious of cultural and minority issues in ethical behaviour
- Identify sources of pressure to behave non-ethically
- Apply a stakeholder approach to ethical behaviour
- Recognize features of ethical codes, in particular the code put forward by the Institute of Management.

THE NATURE OF ETHICAL BEHAVIOUR

In September 1993 the Institute of Management conducted a major survey of its members on 'Ethics and the Professional Manager'. In the covering letter accompanying the survey questionnaire Roger Young the Director General of the Institute of Management observed that:

> Recent events have led to a growing interest in the ethical issues faced by managers as they balance the competing demands of those with a 'stake' in the organization. Yet despite this interest, there is little information about the experiences and opinions of managers themselves in relation to ethical and moral conflicts at work.

Roger Young then commented that 'There is clearly a close relationship between professional management and ethics'.

The survey represents an important source of managerial perception of what constitutes ethical behaviour in the UK. Previously much of the work on business ethics had been carried out in the United States. There business ethics had for a considerable time formed an essential part of both undergraduate and postgraduate business degrees. As we write it has still to make as significant an impression on equivalent courses in the UK.

The survey found that about nine out of ten responding reported that they adopted an ethical perspective towards management and were prepared to speak out about ethical issues in the workplace. However, the findings indicated that a significant proportion of managers in the sample said that there was an 'ethical mismatch' between their own views and those which they reported that their own organization held. Significantly, the survey findings also revealed that managers appeared to see various behaviours identified in the questionnaire as more of an ethical issue for organizations in general than for their own organization in particular.

Ethics as 'tiers of issues'

Matthews (1988) suggested that organizational ethics can be seen in terms of 'tiers'. These tiers or layers represent a graduation of importance. The 'tiers' can be represented as follows:

- *First-tier issues*   These are the most serious because they
  (a) Affect large numbers of people
  (b) Cause the greatest harm
  (c) Are on the verge of illegality
  The sort of things which would be considered first-tier issues would be the manufacture of unsafe products and generating large-scale industrial pollution.
- *Second-tier issues*   These we would describe as intermediate issues because they may affect a large number of people but are less serious in the amount of harm caused than first-tier issues. Examples of issues in this category would be the presence of monopolies, bribery and false advertising.
- *Third-tier issues*   These are distinguished by the following factors. They are:
  (a) Less likely to be life threatening
  (b) Likely to have implications for social responsibility
  The sort of issues which might figure here are such things as a lack of community involvement and a failure to make charitable donations.

Absolute and relative ethics

As well as the ethics as tiers we can also consider the question of absolute as opposed to relative ethics. In order to understand this we need to understand two kinds of reasoning which you might use to guide your behaviour.

Moral obligation reasoning

This is based on the moral thinking of a philosopher called Immanuel Kant. If you are interested in reading further on this then we give you references in the further reading at the end of the chapter.

Kant claimed that morality consists in doing your duty according to *a priori* principles. By this he meant that you did not look at the particular circumstance but instead considered what basic principle should guide your actions. So if lying is wrong then all lying is unethical and you cannot 'pick and choose' according to the circumstances.

Outcome reasoning

This is based on the writings of a philosopher called John Stuart Mill who talked about something he called 'utilitarianism'. In his view you can ethically defend carrying out actions which promote the greatest good of the greatest number of people. Therefore if telling a lie does this then telling a lie can be ethical.

Application of moral obligation versus outcome reasoning

- *Lying*   Moral obligation reasoning would not significantly distinguish between telling a lie to avert pain or to conceal an action. Outcome reasoning would accept lying to protect as acceptable or even ethically correct.
- *Corruption*   Moral obligation reasoning would deem all corruption as unethical if corruption was, in principle, unethical. Outcome reasoning would accept that paying bribes to achieve a good outcome (for example, getting food into famine areas) was ethical.

Both moral obligation reasoning (MOR) and outcome reasoning (OR) are relevant

An integrative model could offer the following criteria:

1   Utilitarian outcomes (MOR): The question would be 'does the behaviour produce the greatest good for the greatest number within the organization?'
2   Individual rights (OR): Does the behaviour respect the rights of all affected parties?
3   Distributive justice (OR): Does the behaviour treat people equitably?
4   Overwhelming factors(?): A decision may be ethical even when it results in some good and some bad when a person's behaviour uses questionable ends to achieve a positive end or when it is based upon inaccurate or incomplete information.

Relativism in ethical behaviour

There is a school of thought which asserts that behaviour is judged by the standard of the local environment. This is the 'when in Rome do as Romans do' principle. In the commercial sector this has been defined by the views of Milton Friedman and Albert Carr.

Friedman (1962, p.33) said:

> In a free economy there is one and only one social responsibility of business – to use its resources and engage in activities to increase its profits so long as it stays within the rules of the game, which is to say, engages in open and free competition, without deception or fraud.

Thus Friedman asserts that business to pursue any goal other than maximizing profit is tantamount to theft from the owners and thus could be viewed as immoral. Charitable intentions do not change this.

Carr contended that business people had to engage in bluff and deception as part of everyday business activity both within and outside their organizations. He claimed as long as 'he complies with the law of the land and avoids telling malicious lies he is ethical ... A good part of the time (he) is trying to do unto others as he hopes others will not do unto him.' Ethical behaviour can be self-serving since it involves avoiding antagonizing competitors, suppliers, etc. Carr argues that you can both appear ethical yet also bluff and deceive in order to gain an advantage. Elaine Sternberg (1994) sought to set out the rules of the game, including a ban on cheating. This includes a ban on 'losing deliberately'. Playing the game means playing to win. All activity within the game which is not devoted to winning is either not seriously playing or constitutes cheating.

Both Friedman and Carr are arguing that business (office) ethics are different from individual (domestic) ethics. Carr argues for the morality of the card game. Deliberate cheating is not acceptable but bluff, deceit and misrepresentation have a role. Friedman argues for a clear duty to pursue profit to the exclusion of all distraction.

Narrow versus broad ethics

Tom Sorell and John Hendry (1995) suggest the existence of two categories of narrow and broad business ethics. They define narrow ethics as 'when it only relates to those employed or directly concerned with the organization (such as shareholders or current customers)'. Broad ethics, on the other hand, acknowledges the responsibility of the organization to society at large.

Environmental issues mean that, increasingly, organizations accept the broader definition of business ethics. The interesting question this poses is whether this represents a conflict with Friedman's claim that the only morally acceptable behaviour is profit maximizing (within the constraints of the law!). The argument might be that if the customers of the organization are concerned with its stand on environmental and social matters then it is profit-maximizing behaviour to recognize this. Accordingly, the organization adopts a broader view of business ethics.

The public image of companies – and almost all organizations – has become more important in a time of mass communication. A broader concept of business ethics can influence the narrower concept. Thus the way a company treats staff may be influenced by the pressure of media and consequently of public opinion. The narrow code of business ethics (towards staff) can undergo a change as a result of this. For example, a practice of sacking employees before they acquire employment protection may be legal but if exposed in the media gives the company a bad image.

Similarly, narrow codes of ethics influencing how staff behave within the organization may impact upon the broader business ethics towards the environment. A professional such as a doctor or a scientist may feel constrained by a narrow code of ethics and reluctant to 'whistleblow' on a colleague whose behaviour is not acceptable within a broader code of ethics. Rather, the decision is to deprive the transgressor of 'peer respect' for his or her actions.

The latter parts of this chapter will concentrate upon, in turn, the concepts of narrow ethics as applied to stakeholders within or close to the organization and broader ethics as applied more to the community or society at large.

Cultural and minority issues in ethics

The United Kingdom is a multi-cultural and multi-racial society. One of the authors lives in a London borough which boasts over 125 different languages within its boundaries. Many organizations incorporate 'equal opportunity' statements into their recruitment material and include such statements on advertisements.

For many managers, especially those working in public sector settings, there is no need for a book such as this to remind them of their ethical responsibility to behave in a fair and even-handed fashion. Later in the chapter we make reference to the legislation governing discrimination and equal opportunity. Here we will draw attention to some of the issues associated with what is increasingly being called 'managing diversity'.

The evidence for the continued existence of discrimination in employment on the grounds of race, sex and national origin, etc. is compelling. Studies carried out before and after the passage of relevant legislation have demonstrated that racial discrimination continues to take place. Newell (1995), summarizing these studies, suggests that they showed that 90 per cent of white job applicants were successful as compared to 63 per cent of Asian and West Indian applicants *where the only significant difference was the race of the applicant* (authors' italics). Newell notes that discrimination is often hard to prove and that this may account for its continuance despite the fact that it is illegal and has been so for some time.

Where female employment is concerned there has been a pattern of increasing workforce participation. This is to some extent linked to the growth of the service sector at the expense of traditional manufacturing and also to expansion of part-time and temporary work. Studies have shown that women's careers are less likely to be continuous and that there will probably be periods 'out of the workforce' and part-time employment. This has been associated with what Newell calls 'horizontal' and 'vertical' segregation. The terms 'glass ceilings' and 'glass walls' convey a similar meaning.

Horizontal segregation (glass ceiling) is associated with the lack of women in managerial jobs compared to their proportion in the overall work-force. As you look higher up the organization ladder then the proportion of women declines even further. Some would argue that this is a consequence of his-toric patterns of male recruitment and that, in time, women will move through the organization and into more senior roles. However, others would say that there is direct and/or indirect discrimination which either discourages women from applying for promotion or works against their being offered promotion.

Horizontal discrimination (glass walls) operates to restrict women to particular roles or functions within an organization or occupation. Thus women tend to be employed by airlines more in customer service roles (flight attendant and check-in staff) than in equipment-related roles (pilot, engineer and maintenance staff). This is in part a leftover from an image of women as best suited to a 'caring' role. Possibly there is also a perception by some airlines that customers expect a male presence behind the controls.

General pressures to behave unethically

Before moving on to consider ethical behaviour within your organization let us pause and consider what pressures exist to behave unethically. We could start with a story, a version of which most readers will probably have heard.

> A person is asked by a colleague at a party whether they would take all their clothes off in public for £1 million. The person almost immediately replies that they would do it. The colleague then asks if they would do it for £1. The person refuses saying 'what sort of person do you think I am?' The colleague comments 'Well, you've already shown what sort of person you are – now all you're quibbling over is the price!'

You might want to bear this story in mind when you read about someone who behaves unethically for an apparently minor reward. The temptations in orga-nizations are relative. The minor functionary may allow you into the car park place (to which you are not entitled) for the promise of a drink. The senior manager in the same company would regard being offered a drink to behave unethically as an insult to his or her intelligence.

Temptation to act unethically is often linked to discretion. If a manager or official has a discretion over how to act and there is little immediate recourse by the client, customer or employee against the way the discretion is exercised then there is temptation.

The expectations of organizations can encourage people to cut corners. Where the organization wills the end and is indifferent to the means then this is a powerful incentive to engage in unethical behaviour in order to achieve what is perceived as a desirable outcome. This is the area of the rogue dealer such as Nick Leeson or the police officer who fabricates evidence in order to secure the conviction. Similarly, where the organization is focused upon the process rather than the outcome the employee is tempted into avoiding decisions and merely ensuring that their paperwork is in order. Thus there are circumstances where unethical practice takes place because a person is being denied a decision or resource which they have an ethical right to expect.

We would submit that where there is an organizational or managerial indifference to *either* ends or means then the conditions exist to promote unethical behaviour. Where there is an indifference to both ends and means then you have virtually an ethical vacuum!

ETHICAL BEHAVIOUR WITHIN THE ORGANIZATION

In a later chapter (Chapter 9) we look at the concept of stakeholders within an organization. Here we will be addressing ethics as defined more narrowly by stakeholders within the organization itself. You, yourself, as an employee are such a stakeholder. Therefore, like it or not, your behaviour will have an impact within the organization.

We will raise here a number of questions about ethical behaviour. In some cases we can offer answers. Organizations are seeking to give people guidance through ethical codes – perhaps your organization has such a code. Sometimes new staff are formally trained by colleagues or managers and this provides a set of principles to guide behaviour. The informal socialization will certainly have an impact. This is when the naive new member of staff encounters a discrepancy between what is 'preached' and what is 'practised'. Typically, it may emerge around an aspect of custom such as an informal adjustment of working conditions. The employment contract says that you start work at 9.00 am and finish at 5.00 pm with an hour for lunch. However, colleagues all seem to disappear at 4.00 pm on Friday! Is this unethical behaviour? Perhaps it has been accepted as a variation of the contract – or perhaps not.

Ethical codes

Brigley (1994) commented that 47 per cent of the organizations represented in the Institute of Management survey possessed an ethical code. He found that they were more likely in larger organizations and in public sector organizations. Trends in the United States suggest that such ethical codes are becoming more popular.

Respondents in the survey said that they knew their code well and generally felt that top management enforced the codes. They generally agreed that such codes demonstrated organizations' sense of social responsibility. Few thought that the code was too idealistic and difficult to apply in practice.

Perhaps significantly, the managers who responded to the survey were well educated (70 per cent had a degree or higher qualification as compared to 20 per cent for all UK managers) and tended to be in the more senior managerial grades. This lends strength to a view that ethical codes are likely to be increasingly important in organizations in the UK.

Paul Harris, writing in the *Management Accounting* journal in November 1995, suggests that even though 60 per cent of US businesses have ethical codes these have made little difference to what actually happens. He stresses that the simple existence of a code does not resolve the problem of implementing it.

When companies not only possess a code of ethics but then review and update it, then it can be inferred that it is taken quite seriously. United Biscuits produced an ethics booklet and provided it to staff and shareholders. This was done in 1987. In February 1997, ten years, later the company had reviewed and revised the 1987 booklet. A code of ethics does not stand unaltered with the passage of time.

A code of ethics can be good for business. Companies like The Body Shop and Ben & Jerry's Ice Cream are seen as 'good' by many consumers because of their ethical stance. The Co-Operative Bank advertises itself as an ethical bank whose values dominate its investment policy.

However, there is some doubt about whether 'codes of ethics' can be simply bought in. John Drummond (1995), an expert in this area, comments that ethics are about actions, not words. He helped NatWest develop its code of ethics and this included a 'hotline' for staff with a general guarantee of confidentiality for those who 'whistleblow'. The code encompasses such items as avoiding making disparaging remarks about competitors and not using employment status with the company to influence public officials or customers for personal gain or benefit. Drummond and Bain (1994, p. 204) set out the advantages and disadvantages of ethical codes in Table 3.1.

Staff

A well-known saying is that the biggest lie told in business is 'your cheque is in the post'. Some claim that the second biggest lie is 'we value our staff'.

The obligation between an organization and its employees is one rooted in law. Employment law is well beyond the scope of this book. It is sufficient to note here that much of the relationship between an employer and employee cannot be detailed in a legal document. This is especially the case when you move from routine simple tasks to the more technical and creative responsibility increasingly sought by staff.

There is an interesting question of whether an organization has an obligation to 'find' work for employees. One author did some consultancy work with a local authority which made a commitment to find work for staff. Therefore staff, instead of being made redundant when their job disappeared, were offered redeployment into another part of the organization with some retraining. This was popular with staff at risk but some questioned whether it was fair to the customers of the local authority. The redeployed staff were, in some cases, not as capable as staff who could have been recruited through open competition.

Table 3.1

Reasons for employing ethical codes
1   To clarify management's thoughts on what constitutes unethical behaviour.
2   To help employees think about ethical issues before they are faced with the realities of the situation.
3   To provide employees with the opportunity of refusing compliance with unethical action.
4   To define the limits of what constitutes acceptable or unacceptable behaviour.
5   To provide a mechanism for communicating the managerial philosophy in the realm of ethical behaviour.
6   To assist in the induction and training of employees.

Arguments against ethical codes express the following concerns:
1   Even a detailed list of guidelines cannot be expected to cover all the possible grey areas of potentially unethical practice.
2   Like fair-employment practice statements, codes of ethics are often too generalized to be of specific value.
3   Rarely are codes of ethics prioritized; for example, loyalty to the company and to fellow-employees does not resolve the potential conflict when a colleague is seen to be acting contrary to company interests.
4   As an individual phenomenon, ethical behaviour which has been guided by ethical codes of conduct will only be effective if the codes have been internalized and are truly believed by employees.

Source: Drummond and Bain (1994), p. 204

An important point to make is that the moral obligations between employee and employer are two-way. With the growth of casualization of the workforce employers have taken the opportunity to relinquish certain obligations. Arguably an employer's obligation to a casually employed or agency member of staff is not as great as that towards a long-serving permanent employee. However, the relaxing of obligations is a two-edged sword. Casual or agency staff may feel a lesser moral or ethical responsibility to the organization.

As an example, an education establishment decided to replace permanent portering staff with contracted-in security guards in the evening. This enabled a saving in wage costs to be made. However, students objected when they found that they were being denied access to the library to return books because the security guards had been told to refuse entry to all who did not have a current identity card with them. The portering staff, who knew most of the students, had allowed students to return books even though they did not have a current

ID card with them. The portering staff understood that returning library books was important both to the organization and to its customers, and made the judgement accordingly.

Colleagues

In most organizations of any size there is a some kind of division which leads staff to identify colleagues as opposed to other employees of the organization. Sometimes it is based upon level of responsibility; it may derive from time served or it may be based upon professional training or recognition. Sometimes it can become strongly entrenched as in the legal profession's division between solicitors and barristers.

Should there be a different ethical obligation between colleagues than between employees? A doctor witnesses a porter in a hospital handle a patient rudely and sees that the patient is upset. Is the doctor likely to respond differently if it is another doctor rather than a porter? In the first instance the doctor may reprimand the porter directly or even report the porter to a manager. In the case of two doctors it is less likely that the matter would be reported formally and possibly it may not even be mentioned. One factor is whether there is some kind of common bond of training or professionalism which makes people colleagues. In such a case the measure of acceptability/non-acceptability of behaviour may not be the same as the standard applied by the organization. Musicians in an orchestra or actors in a play may be harsher in their judgements on their colleagues than an organization would be.

On the other hand, in some organizations or occupations there are the equivalent of 'old Spanish customs' which govern behaviour. 'Old Spanish Customs' were particularly common in the pre-Wapping print industry. Print workers would sign up imaginary employees and draw their wages.

There is a danger inherent in the natural feeling of loyalty towards colleagues where ethical issues are concerned. Most occupations have an unwritten taboo which operates against reporting colleagues for unethical behaviour. Rather the expectation is that the guilty individual is discouraged through professional disapproval or social pressure.

In the area of education this is a particularly contentious issue. Most academics in this field have a definite impression of their colleagues. They know who works hard, who is never available for students and who is doing the minimum amount of work to get by. Yet despite the weakness of the trade unions in the higher education sector few academics would choose to stand up and point the finger at (relatively few) non-productive colleagues. There is a feeling that it is 'not the sort of thing a professional academic should do'.

Senior managers

Writing in the *Financial Times* on 22 March 1996 Rob Goffee and John Hunt stress the continuing need for management in the face of the delayering of middle management and the focus upon such concepts as 'vision'. They quote a survey of top managers where the characteristics of most effective top managers were

- Force of personality (33 per cent)
- Competence in the job (26 per cent)
- Good with people (22 per cent)
- Flexibility (10 per cent)
- Ethical beliefs (6 per cent)

The fact that ethical beliefs rated at all is encouraging. However, the rating of it as last would be disappointing to some. Organizational members look to senior managers as role models to indicate desirable, acceptable and unacceptable behaviour. If you read about the horrors of the Holocaust something which is chilling is the cold managerial efficiency with which the victims were rounded up, transported and dispatched. The account of the operation of the death camps given in films such as *Schindler's List* portrays, stripped of ethical considerations, managers struggling with resource constraints. Without an ethical dimension to senior management what is to prevent such further abominations? A key responsibility held by senior managers is often to balance opposing considerations. Perhaps a reduction in the workforce has to be made. The shareholders might probably wish the minimum legally required redundancy to be paid. The manager knows that the workforce would ideally wish for no redundancies but if there are to be any they would want the company to be far more generous than the legal minimum. To which stakeholder should the manager give the most credence? Certainly, resources and company policy will influence the decision. However, there is an ethical dimension as well.

The decision by Ford in early 1997 to make staff redundant in Liverpool was heavily criticized. The company was accused of making the Liverpool workers redundant because they were cheaper to lay off than Ford workers elsewhere in Europe. The management could have simply responded that it was their responsibility to make the decision which minimized the costs and ... so what? Such a response would have not been ethically defensible (assuming it were true).

ETHICAL BEHAVIOUR OUTSIDE THE IMMEDIATE ORGANIZATION

Where are the ethical boundaries of the organization in behavioural terms? There is no simple answer to this question. We asked a group of managers from public sector organizations to categorize a range of behaviours in terms of whether they were ethically acceptable or not. Factors such as talking about their clients in social settings varied in the extent to which they were seen as unacceptable depending upon the type of organization.

Some organizations are very extensive in their definitions of ethical boundaries. Staff at the Government Communication Headquarters at

Cheltenham were denied the right to join a trade union. The reason given was that it might represent a conflict of loyalties given the secrecy of the work. Yet the staff are also expected as part of their work to intercept private communications usually without the knowledge or agreement of the communicating parties. This is justified on the grounds of national interest.

There are stakeholders which are close to the organization and the manager such as customers and suppliers. There are ethical considerations which enter into how you as an employee or manager relate to them. Similarly, if you are a professional then you may well be governed by a code of behaviour particular to your occupation. Legislation also has a bearing upon the way many people make moral or ethical decisions.

Customers

The mottoes 'the customer is always right' and 'give the customer what they want' have a certain cachet to them. Sorell and Hendry (1994) note that the consumer can be seen as victim as well as king. Much of the concern expressed over the ethics of the National Lottery is based upon gullible consumers being conned into spending more than they can afford. The law is there to protect consumers. Organizations such as the Advertising Standards Authority lay stress upon the need for businesses to observe certain principles in trying to sell their products.

Though you may be a manager or an employee you are also a consumer. In some situations you are a powerful consumer. If you are buying fast-moving consumer goods such as audio or video tapes then you can shop around and compare prices. If you buy a tape which is defective then you know this quickly. There is an element of trust but not as significant as the trust you place in the supplier of a less tangible product such as a pension.

There has been considerable concern expressed about the mis-selling of endowment mortgages and personal pensions. This is a product which is very different from audio tapes. The consumer is less informed about the product and relies upon the person selling the product for guidance. They may not realize that the product is wrong until many years later and they may be grossly disadvantaged by that.

It is helpful to put yourself into the frame of mind of your customer and to ask yourself some searching questions:

- If I were buying or using this product or service what standards of advice would I expect?
- How vital is it that I understand the implications of the purchase decision or decision to use the product or service?
- How significant is the nature of the purchase or usage which I, as a consumer, am making?

The exercise of what has been described as 'the golden rule' of treating others as you would have them treat you is always worth bearing in mind.

Suppliers

Much of what has been said about customers is also true of suppliers. Suppliers are often larger players than customers. Thus the agreement to supply may be accompanied by a more formal contract.

A senior government minister came in for considerable adverse criticism when he suggested that companies could save money by delaying payments to suppliers. This illustrated what is possibly a significant difference where suppliers are concerned. If a company goes out of business then it is usually more likely that the suppliers will suffer immediate financial loss than the customers. The lack of customers may well be the cause of the company going out of business, but it will be the suppliers to the company who are left at the end of the queue to be paid after the banks and the Inland Revenue!

Suppliers are sometimes heavily dependent upon particular purchasers. Marks & Spencer is well known for the close and exclusive relationships which they have with their suppliers. This creates a certain ethical obligation upon Marks & Spencer not to casually drop a supplier. Such an act would quite possibly put a supplier at risk of going out of business.

However, it does raise the question of the extent to which a company can or should 'carry' a supplier who is going through a bad patch. In ethical terms the company may be regarded as failing to meet an obligation to shareholders to safeguard resources if it allows a supplier too generous or lax terms of business. Though the figures are important, in many cases the goodwill which has built up over years of doing business is a factor as well.

Professional codes

In some organizations such as hospitals or research laboratories many staff would regard themselves as professionals first and employees or managers second. Professions often lay claim to a particular set of occupational values. Some professions such as medicine, nursing and law are proud of the fact that they can enforce their professional standards to the extent of expelling a member who falls short of the required standard.

The standards exacted by some professional codes are well in excess of what would be required by any normal code of organization ethics. A doctor who has an affair with a patient risks being struck off. Few employees who have an affair with a customer would risk the equivalent (though some organizations would certainly disapprove of it).

The area of medicine is probably most subject to professional codes of conduct. These can run counter to the desire of managers to run the National Health Service in the most efficient way. Writing in the *Observer* on 3 March 1996 Richard Norton-Taylor gave an account of problems in bringing a large National Health Service computer network on line. Doctors', lawyers' and patients' organizations were concerned about the level of confidentiality. The NHS management claimed that the network would save over £2 billion each year by avoiding duplication of services. The British Medical Association claimed the system was insecure because it had been designed for the benefit of bureaucrats. The concerns were such that the various parties sought to introduce legislation to outlaw the use of illicitly obtained medical data.

If you, as a manager or as an employee, work in a setting where there is a significant professional presence then you need to be aware of the likely reaction to proposed changes which challenge or impact on formal code of professional behaviour. Indeed, sometimes the professional code is informal and just as strong.

Legislation and ethics

The requirements of the law and the dictates of conscience are not necessarily the same. Open any national paper on an average day and you will probably find an example of a person behaving in a way which you would question in ethical terms but which is perfectly legal. How often have you witnessed an incident on the street where you have decided not to intervene yet where you were concerned that someone was being mistreated? The law does not require us to be beyond criticism.

However, as we have indicated earlier, there are situations where behaviour is both illegal and also unethical. Discrimination in employment is such an example. The legislation which a manager needs to be aware of in this area would be:

- *The Equal Pay Act 1970 and the Equal Pay (Amendment) Regulations 1983*: These set out to eliminate discrimination in pay and terms of employment between men and women where:
  - Men and women are doing work of a similar nature
  - Jobs have been evaluated as similar
  - Work is of equal value to the organization.

  The last category is significant because of proceedings against the UK government under the Treaty of Rome. It raises the possibility of comparing jobs in terms of their value to the organization.
- *The Sex Discrimination Act 1975*: This stipulates that it is unlawful to treat anyone, on grounds of sex, less favourably than a person of the opposite sex. This includes discrimination on the basis of marital status. *The Race Relations Act* was extended in 1976 and requires employers to treat people from different racial backgrounds equally. This would include colour, race, nationality and ethnic or national origin. For both of these pieces of legislation you need to be aware of the difference between direct discrimination where a person is treated less favourably because of sex, race, etc. and indirect discrimination where the employer imposes a condition which one sex, race, etc. would find it harder to comply with.

ETHICS AND FAIRNESS AND INTEGRITY IN DECISION MAKING

How can you apply fairness and integrity in the decisions which you make as an individual and as a manager? One proverb which is useful to guide you speaks of seeking to experience walking in another person's shoes in order to understand how they feel.

When one of the authors lived in the United States in the 1970s he came to know the father of a friend very well. The man was about to retire after many years as an FBI agent. The author noticed when visiting at Christmas the large number of cards the man had received. Surprisingly, many were from people the FBI agent had arrested and who had subsequently been to prison. How was it that convicted criminals sent the FBI agent who arrested them a Christmas card? The FBI agent explained that in his entire service he had never drawn his gun to make an arrest. When he visited to arrest a person he treated the person with respect. He was polite, he advised the person of his or her legal rights and often would arrange that the person could call their lawyer from their house before leaving. He would suggest the sort of clothing and toiletries the person might need. Afterwards he would contact the person's family to reassure them that they were well and were being well treated. He commented to the author that just because someone had committed a crime did not deprive them of the right to decent and respectful treatment.

More recently one of the authors was talking to a senior manager who had conducted a number of disciplinary hearings with staff whose conduct had fallen short of what the organization expected. The manager said that these hearings were very stressful for the staff concerned. She had arranged that a long-serving and well-respected member of staff was available to spend some time with each person after their disciplinary hearing. She commented that people were often upset and sometimes angry after such hearings. She felt that it was important that there was someone supportive able to offer a sympathetic ear when the person came out of the hearing.

In both these cases we offer examples of people demonstrating an empathy for how the other feels – ' walking in their shoes'.

Taking responsibility for a decision is part of what you get paid for as a manager. We would hope that all the decisions which you make will be the correct ones. In the real and imperfect world in which we all live, however, it is more probable that you will make mistakes. When you do make a mistake then ethically we would argue that you have several obligations:

- First, you have an obligation to learn from the mistake and this means acknowledging it and endeavouring not to repeat it.
- Second, you have an obligation to remedy, as far as is possible, any damage or loss which someone else has suffered as a result.
- Finally, you have an obligation to help and advise others in order that they also can learn from it.

These obligations, we believe, are common sense and most people would not dispute them. Nevertheless, they do not sit well with organizational procedures which instruct staff to 'never admit responsibility for anything to a customer or member of the public'.

ENVIRONMENTAL ISSUES, ETHICS AND MANAGEMENT

At the time of writing (February 1997) a rather unexpected hero is featuring on the pages of the national newspapers. His claim to popular fame is that he obstructed the construction of a road for several days by tunnelling underground in the path of the construction machinery.

The green agenda is important for organizations and managers. Green products are sought by consumers and will become even more important. It is more probable now that you are a member or supporter of an environmental pressure group than you are an active member or supporter of a major political party.

Many years ago in the United States there was a saying that 'what is good for General Motors is good for America'. That saying would now be heavily qualified by environmental concerns. Many Americans are actively considering or pursuing claims against tobacco companies to seek redress for illness caused by their products. Will the next ten or twenty years see similar claims against car and petrol companies for illnesses associated with vehicle pollution?

The environmental agenda for a thoughtful manager cannot simply be a reactive one. You could wait until the popular pressure for internal or external stakeholders mounts up and becomes irresistible and then acquiesce in recycling, use of renewable energy or whatever the demand is. Alternatively, you can seize the initiative and set out either as an individual or as an organization to lead from the front.

The experience of organizations such as The Body Shop suggests that taking a proactive and ethical stand on environmental issues is good for business. But should this be the guiding principle? Suppose that a concern for the environment was not good for your business?

Where organizations fail to take an ethical stand then it is quite conceivable that society in the form of the state may do so. In Denmark you will not find any canned drinks for sale. The government decided that this form of packaging was not environmentally friendly and banned it. Despite efforts to overturn this decision via the EEC eventually all the major drinks companies had to accept the decision. Pepsi, Coca-Cola and all the main beer companies have to package their products in bottles which are recyclable.

Jennings and Wattam (1994) suggest a useful approach in assessing the environmental impact of a possible course of action. They divide the consequences of the course of action into primary – or immediate – impacts. Each of these primary impacts then has secondary consequences and the secondary consequences have tertiary consequences. By following through these you can trace the impact of a possible decision. Table 3.2 illustrates how this might operate for a decision to relocate a factory to a new site instead of refurbishing the current factory.

Table 3.2   Consequences of factory relocation

Activity:	Primary impact	Secondary impact	Tertiary impact
			Local authority takes action to deal with risk
		Old factory gets vandalized	Factory site is sold for houses
	Old factory lies empty		
		Loss of jobs in area of old factory	People find new work
Relocate Factory			
			People move away
	New factory is less polluting	New factory needs less energy	Less environmental cost
			Fewer energy costs
		Some jobs created in area of new factory	
			Some new house building

The question of the environmental impact of managerial and organization decisions may become an important consideration for government and regulators. There is frequently expressed concern over, for example, the growth of out-of-town shopping malls and their impact upon high street shops. Siting shopping malls many miles away from town centres causes greater car usage and is seen by many as eroding the very soul of many town centres.

SUMMARY

Simply reading a chapter of a book such as this does not make you more ethical in your actions as a manager or as a member of staff. Nor will it resolve any problems of unethical behaviour on your part. However, we hope that what you have read will cause you to think more carefully about how ethical issues should be tackled in your work role. 'Doing the right thing' is not always easy. Sometimes the choices are by no means obvious. In particular, speaking out – or whistle-blowing as it is sometimes called – often takes a particular brand of courage.

We believe that ethical decision making is here to stay. Organizations and managers who engage in short-term 'fixes' or who seek to ignore the ethical implications of their actions are likely to regret it.

PREPARING FOR ACTION PLANNING

Remember the checklist of questions identified in the introduction to this book? Try them again to identify your further development needs. We have reproduced those most appropriate to this chapter to help you. You will need to adapt them to the issues discussed.

What would you do if there was a low take-up of the products/services you provide?

How do you currently coordinate your activities in order to develop your product/service provision?

How are organizational performance standards determined and by whom?

How do you ensure that these performance standards are being met?

How do you measure these standards?

How do you deal with any customer complaints?

How do you handle health and safety issues at your workplace?

How do you deal with the requirements of relevant legislation, industry regulation, professional and organizational codes etc.?

Which outside agencies do you currently liaise with?

What actions would you/have you taken with others at times of particular difficulty or change?

How do you liaise with others at off-site locations?

How is information fed back into the decision-making process?

What, if any, interdepartmental group activities do you participate in?

What are the main purposes of these groups?

What are the main working relationships you maintain?

How do you/would you maximize productive relationships and networks?

How do you/would you promote equal opportunities within and between those with whom you relate?

What are the key elements, in your opinion, in promoting effective working relationships?

How would you/do you go about establishing and developing working relationships with others, both internal and external to the organization?

What support would you/do you give to others in their relations with others outside the organization (or department)?

How could these relationships be improved?

What formal and informal actions would you/have you

taken to actively promote effective working relationships and prevent their breakdown?

How do you/would you deal with conflict in your relationships or in the relationships of others arising from:

- Differences of opinion on courses of action?
- Personal animosity?
- Moral/ethical dilemmas (between individuals or individuals and the organization)?
- Racism?
- Sexism?
- Other discriminatory behaviour?
- Non-compliance with organizational rules, norms or values?

Have you taken any steps to improve equality of opportunity in the development of others?

What were the outcomes?

Have there been any specific incidences which have caused you concern for the equality of opportunities in the development of all?

How do you set work objectives (or participate in setting them) for yourself and others?

How do you review and update these objectives?

How do you decide how to allocate work to others?

What would say is your leadership style?

What are the effects of your style on others? For example, are you, do you think, making the most use of the skills available to you (yours and others)?

How does this tie in with the overall work objectives set?

How do you evaluate your own performance against your work objectives?

How do you evaluate the performance of others against their objectives?

What methods do you use to give feedback to others about their performance?

What information do you need to do your job and for what purposes?

Do you have any problems obtaining this information?

To whom do you supply information?

Questions devised by, and adapted from, the Crediting Competence Team at South Bank University and reproduced with permission.

FURTHER READING

Brigley, S.(1994), *Walking on the Tightrope*, IM Research Report.

Connock, S. and Johns, T. (1995), *Ethical Leadership*, IPD, London.

Drummond, J. and Bain, B.(1994), *Managing Business Ethics*, Butterworth-Heinemann, Oxford.

Drummond, John (1995), *Financial Times*, 6 April.

Friedman, M. (1970), 'The social responsibility of business is to increase its profits' in *Free to choose*.

DesJardins, J. R. and McCall, J. J. (1990), *Contemporary issues in Business Ethics*, Wadsworth, Belmont, CA.

Kant, I. (1959), *Foundations of Metaphysics of Morals*, (translated by Beck, L. W.), Bobbs-Merrill, New York.

Matthews, M. C. (1988), *Strategic Intervention in Organizations*, Sage, Beverly Hills, CA.

Mill, J. S. *Utilitarianism* (various editions and commentaries).

Newell, S. (1995), *The Healthy Organization*, Routledge, London.

Sternberg, E. (1994), *Just Business*, Warner, New York.

Sorell, T. and Hendry, T. (1994), *Business Ethics*, Butterworth-Heinemann, Oxford.

4 Focus on results

Managers who focus on results are proactive and take responsibility for getting things done.

INTRODUCING THE RELATIONSHIP BETWEEN THE MCI PERSONAL COMPETENCY MODEL AND TO FOCUS ON RESULTS

The MCI Integrated *Model of Personal Competency* identifies the behaviours and skills necessary for you to develop, before you are able to prove competence in any managerial function. This chapter attempts to deal with the various behaviours and skills necessary for you to apply across all managerial functions, transferring your learning to different occasions, at different times and under varying circumstances (contexts), consistently. The outcomes below, as identified within this section of the model, should be borne in mind while you work through this chapter.

Outcomes required in focusing on results

There are two major sets of behaviour addressed in this chapter, the first of which identifies that when a manager is *planning and prioritizing objectives*, behaviour is developed which shows that he or she:

- Maintains a focus on objectives
- Tackles problems or takes advantage of opportunities as they arise
- Prioritizes objectives and schedules work to make best use of time and resources
- Sets objectives in uncertain and complex situations
- Focuses personal attention on specific details that are critical to the success of a key event.

The second set of behaviours contained in this chapter concentrates on the manager *showing commitment to excellence*. In showing such concern, it is believed by management gurus that the individual manager:

- Actively seeks to do things better
- Uses change as an opportunity for improvement
- Establishes and communicates high expectations of performance, including setting an example to others
- Sets goals that are demanding of self and others
- Monitors quality of work and progress against plans
- Continually strives to identify and minimize barriers to excellence.

INTRODUCTION AND OBJECTIVES

Planning activities are a key part of management work. Planning is linked closely to both setting and prioritizing objectives. After examining these this chapter will look at the most precious commodity available to a manager in undertaking planning and goal setting. That commodity is time.

By the end of this chapter you should know how to :

- Assess how you spend your time
- Be aware of ways in which you can use your time more effectively
- Understand what planning is in organizations
- Appreciate the stages of planning and their importance in management
- Understand how to set objectives
- Prioritize your activities and tasks.

PLANNING IN ORGANIZATIONS

Planning is an activity which frequently gets pushed aside in the hurly-burly of everyday pressures. Nevertheless, it is a key part of effective management. There is a link between the planning level and management level in the planning process. The more senior the manager, the more likely that the planning undertaken will relate to the organization's strategic as opposed to operational objectives. The relationship between the planning level and management level is shown in Figure 4.1.

The differences between planning day-to-day tasks, operational and strategic activities primarily relate to the extent the plans affect the way the organization operates. A salesperson plans the order of visiting customers as a day-to-day activity. The sales manager may plan that the customers in, say, the Birmingham area should be the target of a particular sales drive. The sales director may plan to change the whole sales strategy for the company's products.

It is important to note that the distinctions are sometimes not always clear. Recently there has been press publicity about conditions and practices in certain secure hospitals staffed by prison officers. It was reported that the prison officer staff brought a custodial as opposed to a caring approach to their duties. Clearly, the kind of approach adopted towards patients in these hospitals is at least an operational if not a strategic planning decision. Yet it would appear that it had been decided, possibly by default, by relatively junior staff.

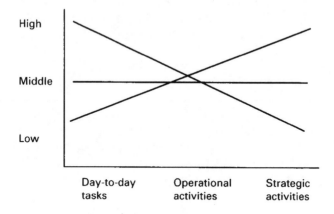

Figure 4.1   Amount of time spent in planning

Planning is important to managers in a number of ways. First, it enables the organization to achieve its objectives. Without the concept of direction which planning requires then organizations are akin to the drunk staggering from lamp post to lamp post. The drunk has little plan beyond the short-term goal of reaching the next pool of light.

Second, planning, as Figure 4.1 shows, is a part of the managerial task irrespective of the level of the manager. Even relatively junior managers plan their activities. The main differences are the time frame and scope. The more senior the manager, the longer the time frame and the greater the scope.

Third, planning is arguably the managerial activity which occurs before other activities. In order to organize resources the manager, at whatever level of seniority, needs to plan. Sometimes the planning can have a macabre aspect to it. During the Falklands War part of the planning before the major battles of Goose Green and Port Stanley involved supplying body bags for burying the dead.

Finally, planning is inextricably linked to effectiveness and efficiency. Cost-effectiveness has to be a key factor. The organizational world is full of examples of plans conceived at a cost far in excess of any possible savings that they could achieve. There is often a fine calculation over how much to invest in planning given the likely return.

During the Second World War a large number of Allied military personnel were captured by the Germans and became prisoners of war. They were housed in well-guarded camps and a number of prisoners sought to escape. Initially a large number of attempts failed and in part this was due to a lack of coordination and planning. In several of the larger camps this led to escape organizations being set up. If a prisoner wished to have the support of the organization he had to present a plan to a committee. The committee would then decide which plans to support.

The success of these escape organizations was considerable despite the fact that they had no formal authority to forbid escape attempts. The plans prisoners had to submit were akin to 'business plans' which bid for the limited resources available (food, tools, 'civilian' clothing, documentation, outside contacts and prisoners' skills).

There is a hierarchy of planning which operates in organizations of any size (Figure 4.2). At the top of the hierarchy is the mission or purpose of the organization. Sometimes it is described as the 'mission statement'. Possibly one of the simplest was that given to NASA (North American Space Administration) after the former USSR was the first to put a man into space. President Kennedy told NASA that they were to beat the Russians in getting to the moon. The clear and straightforward nature of that objective certainly fostered its success. It is possible that the current lack of an objective of such clarity is creating a strategic problem for NASA.

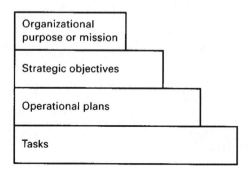

Figure 4.2   Hierarchy of planning

Any well-run organization needs to be able to draw up a planned strategy for achieving the organizational mission. This will commit the resources of the organization and will involve making choices. For example, over the next year (1992-1993) British Aerospace will have to decide whether to sell or retain the Rover Group. Objectives are almost certainly in place to guide the company. These would be at a strategic level. They are likely to be based upon a view of where the company sees its future. What mix of products? What customers? What market sectors or segments should be targeted? It will also be based upon the company's assessment of what is likely to be happening in the economy. Possibly most important of all, the company will have a keen eye on the expectations of its shareholders.

Then there are operational plans which serve to direct the everyday running of the organization. For example, currently there are two large companies, IBM and BT, who are engaged in reducing their workforce. For IBM this represented a major change in the ethos of the company since security of employment had been a key belief held by the company and its employees. IBM planned the workforce reductions in four phases in the UK aimed at careful targeting of particular staff sectors. Extensive counselling was provided and the severance terms were not just presented in terms of cash. Employees were encouraged to set up in business with work contracts with IBM.

For BT the process was less drawn out and it was reported that about 19 500 left in a single day, representing one of the largest one-off workforce reductions in UK industrial history. The incentive offered was primarily financial and the redundancy offer was strongly marketed to staff. The demand for the offer was such that unions described BT's policy as one of compulsory retention, with many people applying being refused redundancy.

The operational plans drawn up by the two organizations led to two quite different outcomes. The human resources plans of both organizations probably included the following planning elements:

1 Recruitment plan
2 Training plan
3 Redevelopment plan
4 Productivity plan
5 Redundancy plan
6 Retention plan

Operational plans create a hierarchy of tasks which need to occur in order to meet the plans' objectives. These tasks often imply a planning activity in order to ensure that they are carried out. Thus if we consider just one of the operational plans above, the redundancy plan, we can list some of the activities which need to take place.

Redundancy plan

- Workforce audit (age, sex, seniority, skills, etc.)
- Consultation
- Nature of redundancy offer
- Costing and budget
- Preparation of redundancy offer
- Communication of redundancy offer
- Decisions and any negotiation/appeal process
- Communication of results
- Implementation of payments/severance.

The above list is only a basic guide. Some items may be directed by company procedures or rules. Some may be the subject of legal requirements. However, if we take just one item, communication of redundancy offer, we can see that it too might break down into a further subgroup of tasks/activities:

- Media of message (verbal, individual letter, poster, leaflet, etc.)?
- Wording?
- Timing?
- Messenger (who delivers the offer?)
- Printing?
- Costing and budget?

Each of these tasks or activities has a planning component. The old saying is applicable that 'for the want of a nail a shoe was lost, for the want of a shoe a horse was lost, for the want of a horse a soldier was lost, for the want of a soldier a battle was lost'. Consider the effect of a postal strike on a redundancy offer which has been communicated by letter to the employees' home address. If the letters have all been sent out it is possible many employees will not receive them until the postal strike is over.

Most organizations will, as part of their planning process, identify possible problems in implementation. They will then take preventative action to reduce the possibility of the problem affecting implementation. In circumstances where the problem is a serious one then there will be a back-up facility or contingency plan. Thus it is probable that the car you drive (or whatever public transport you use) will have a contingency device to ensure that a leak of the brake fluid will not deprive the vehicle of all braking power.

Preventative action is cheaper than contingency plans. It is cheaper to have office equipment regularly serviced than to have a back-up for each item of equipment. Besides, there is always the residual possibility that the 'back-up' may fail to work!

However, there is a trade-off between risk and the cost of a contingency plan. The loss of company records through a fire would generally be very serious. Research suggests that many companies fail to survive such a calamity. Therefore back-ups of computer data and perhaps having a back-up computer facility available are usually worthwhile expenses. The likelihood of the fire occurring is small but the implications of a fire are great. Therefore a company would be quite averse to taking the risk (see Chapter 5).

On the other hand, if a company is contracting with an advertiser for all households in an area to be leafleted about a new product there is a high likelihood that some households may not receive the leaflets. They may not be delivered or may be picked up by other people, etc. The implications of this happening are probably not serious. A contingency plan to send out further leaflets would be costly and inappropriate. Preventative action would be a better way to deal with it perhaps through arranging a check on a sample of households to ensure that leaflets were delivered (and letting the advertiser know you will be doing it). The advertiser, knowing that the company would be checking up, would be careful.

GOAL SETTING AND ANALYSIS

This can be seen as a process which has a number of logical stages. Figure 4.3 shows these. The process begins with establishing objectives. If we look back to the example of the company wishing to circulate product information to households in an area then let us assume the objective was: 'To increase public awareness of Product Z in the area'. This might in turn have led to the following action plans:

1   Advertising in the press
2   Advertising on radio
3   Poster advertising on billboards
4   Leaflet delivery to local households.

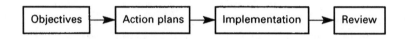

Figure 4.3   The goal-setting process

Implementation would involve the preparation of the advertising copy and placing it in the appropriate medium. The leaflet distribution would probably require a contract with an experienced organization familiar with the area.

Review is the stage when the nature of the original objective becomes crucial. We used the term '*increase public awareness of Product Z*'. How do we review how well our four action plans have done this? We could go out and ask people but how do we know that their awareness afterwards is any greater than it was before?

All goals should be SMART:

Specific
Measurable
Assignable
Realistic
Time related.

The original objective does not lend itself to being SMART. It is not specific (what *is* public awareness and in what area ?). How do you measure an increase in public awareness? It does not specify responsibility for carrying it out. It may not be realistic depending upon what Product Z is (no size of increase is mentioned). No time is specified.

So let us re-examine the objective. This will involve a certain amount of analysis.

Robert Mager in his book, *Goal Analysis*, offers a five-step process for analysing goals which consists of the following:

1   Write down the goal.
2   Write down a list of what achievement of the goal would represent in terms of actions or speech.
3   Review what you have written down. Check for duplications and what Robert Mager described as 'fuzzies'.
4   Write a sentence which describes each item on the list.
5   Check to make sure everything is covered.

If we take Robert Mager's steps to analyse the situation we might come up with the following.

Assuming that the company is profit orientated then what is really at issue is *sales* of Product Z. This does lend itself to specific measurement. Therefore what we might write down as achieving this goal would be:

■   A substantial increase in sales of Product Z over a period of time in an area which can be attributed to advertising.

If we examine this statement we see some words which are clear in their meaning:

■   Increase
■   Sales
■   Product Z

There are some words which Robert Mager might describe as 'fuzzies' such as:

■   substantial
■   period of time
■   in an area
■   can be attributed to advertising

'Fuzzies' are things that are abstractions. They do not lend themselves to general agreement over whether or not they have happened. Thus there would be little problem in gaining general agreement over whether there has been an increase in sales of Product Z. However, whether that increase is substantial or not may be subject to disagreement.

The aim is to identify the 'fuzzies' and, as far as possible, turn them into performance-related statements. Therefore we might do this as follows:

■   substantial = an increase of over 20 per cent
■   period of time = 3 months

- in an area = Corby, Northamptonshire
- can be attributed to advertising = following an advertising campaign in Corby.

Our objective thus becomes:

An increase of over 20 per cent in sales of Product Z over a period of three months in Corby, Northamptonshire following an advertising campaign in Corby.

If Product Z was sold elsewhere we could make the goal relate to an increase in sales in Corby *compared* to average sales elsewhere.

The reworded goal is Specific, Measurable and Time Related. The question of whether it is Realistic is only answerable in terms of the market and the product. If the market is very slow-growing then 20 per cent over 3 months may be very unrealistic. The goal is Assignable in that the sales manager (or whoever) can be tasked with carrying it out.

The objective can then be turned into an action plan or, rather, a series of action plans. Thus the plan to leaflet households might include elements aimed at:

- Identifying suitable leafleting contractors
- Drawing up and agreeing contract specifications
- Soliciting bids for the work
- Awarding the contract
- Monitoring contract performance
- Evaluating the impact and reporting back.

PRIORITIZING OBJECTIVES

Setting priorities is inevitable in any situation where the resources are insufficient to meet all the demands placed upon them. Some managers have no system to work out priorities. They may rely upon the guidance of other managers or staff. They may simply adopt the old engineers' maxim that 'the wheel that squeaks gets the oil' and simply focus effort on those objectives where the clamour for action is the loudest.

However, there are several simple ways to set priorities. If used and communicated these can enable a manager to target resources in a way which puts the manager in the driving seat. It is important to check that the priorities identified by the manager are agreed by the organization as appropriate. Therefore priority setting should be a joint activity between managers and subordinates.

The ABC approach

This represents possibly the simplest method of setting priorities. Let us suppose that you have a list of tasks which may require your attention. You cannot do them all at once. You must find some way of establishing which ones are more urgent. Let us suppose the list runs as follows:

Prepare monthly sales returns
Arrange staff appraisals
Conduct fire drill
Visit Northern Region customers
Draft new sales brochure
Test new product
Negotiate maintenance contract
Review disciplinary code
Recruit clerk
Prepare budget

You could then categorize the list in terms of:

A   Highest priority – cannot wait
B   Next priority
C   Do it if possible after A and B.

It is a simple system which only requires a basic categorization of priorities. The resulting list might look as follows:

Prepare monthly sales returns (A)
Arrange staff appraisals (B)
Conduct fire drill (A)
Visit Northern Region customers (C)
Draft new sales brochure (C)
Test new product (A)
Negotiate maintenance contract (A)
Review disciplinary code (A)
Recruit clerk (B)
Prepare budget (A)

The list is then sorted according to priority:

Prepare monthly sales returns (A)
Conduct fire drill (A)
Test new product (A)
Negotiate maintenance contract (A)
Review disciplinary code (A)
Prepare budget (A)
Arrange staff appraisals (B)
Recruit clerk (B)
Visit Northern Region customers (C)
Draft new sales brochure (C)

The disadvantage is that sometimes it can prove difficult if many (or most) of the tasks are seen as of the highest priority. Then the manager has to use some other criteria to prioritize the A group.

Prioritizing by paired comparison

This is a more sophisticated method which takes more time and thought. Therefore it would not be appropriate for looking at your objectives for the next few weeks. It is useful in considering longer-term objective setting.

Let us consider an example of a training manager in an organization. The manager has established that there is a priority need for training in the following areas:

Equal opportunities
Appraisal
Budgeting
Negotiating
Sales
Assertion.

The problem the manager confronts is how to prioritize these six areas in terms of both managerial time and training resources. The ABC method is seen as insufficiently sensitive since all the areas have high priority.

Paired comparison is a way of developing a priority ranking. The easiest way to do it is to set up a matrix so that each item can be compared with every other item. This is done in Figure 4.4

The manager (or perhaps the management or staff group) then considers the first training item (Equal opportunities). They compare it with each alternative item in turn and decide whether:

Equal opportunities is more important – give it 2 points (and the other item 0 points).
Equal opportunities is less important – give it 0 points (and the other item 2 points).
Equal opportunities is equally important – give it 1 point (and the other item 1 point).

Thus Equal opportunities is seen as equally important as Appraisal but more important than Budgeting in this example.

After you have completed all the paired comparisons then you add up the totals and have a point score for each item:

Equal opportunities (6)
Appraisal (4)
Budgeting (1)
Negotiating (5)

Focus on results 109

	Equal Opportunities	Appraisal	Budgeting	Negotiating	Sales	Assertion
Equal opportunities	X	–	0	–	–	–
Appraisal	–	X	–	–	2	–
Budgeting	2	–	X	2	2	2
Negotiating	–	–	0	X	–	2
Sales	–	0	0	–	X	2
Assertion	–	–	0	0	0	X
Totals	5	4	1	5	6	8

Figure 4.4   Training priorities for an organization

Sales (6)
Assertion (8)

The method is useful in establishing priorities between a number of objectives which all seem equally favoured. If using the alternatives of 2,1 or 0 still lead to deadlock then the alternate choices could be widened (3,2,1,or 0). Alternatively, a forced choice rule could be used to prevent the allocation of 50 per cent of the points to each item. A computerized variety of this method was developed by Jimmy Algie at Brunel University to enable social services departments to rank order their priorities.

MANAGMENT BY OBJECTIVES (MBO)

Management by Objectives has been described as a:

1   Strategy
2   Process of planning and control
3   Process of participation
4   System for getting results
5   Attitude of management
6   Time orientation.

Paul Mali (1986), a leading American expert on MBO, has defined it as:

> a participative system ... in which managers look ahead for improvements, think strategically, set performance stretch objectives at the beginning of a time period, develop action ... plans, and ensure accountability for results at the end of the time period (p. 35).

MBO contrasts with 'traditional' management practices in that it involves the worker in an objective setting. To do this the organizational purpose has to be made clearer. If responsibility is pushed down the hierarchy as far as possible then knowledge and understanding must also be encouraged. The focus moves from effort to accomplishment. Individuals and teams agree targets which are measurable and which are reviewed.

There is a future orientation in planning. The stress is not upon examination of the past but rather upon where things are going in the future. The progress made towards objectives is strongly tied into assessment at time intervals. Time is a vital component not just in MBO but for managerial effectiveness and it is considered at greater length later in this chapter. Strategy and planning have been covered previously and the comments are relevent to MBO.

Participation and MBO

The participation of staff in objective setting is central to MBO. If you have contributed in or, better still, have been responsible for the agreed target then you are far more likely to be committed to achieving it. The 'R' (Realistic) factor in SMART is addressed by getting people to set their own targets rather than imposing ones on them.

You may comment that letting someone set their own target will mean that they set one which is 'too easy' or insufficiently challenging. The evidence is that given encouragement and support people will usually set themselves challenging targets and work hard to accomplish them. Clearly the excuse that the target was 'handed down' is not available when the individual had a major say in setting the goal.

Communication, both verbal and written, is central to achieving participation. Chapters 2 and 3 have given you the basic understanding to enable effective communication.

Getting results through MBO

Earlier in this chapter we discussed how to express goals in the form of measurable desired outcomes. MBO has a similar focus upon measurable results. Organizations which are 'for profit' have a number of obvious result measures (sales, costs, profit margin, gross profit, etc.). These are explained in greater detail in other books in the series.

Even organizations which do not have a tangible 'product' or which are 'not for profit' have result measures which can be used in MBO. A charity might look at the percentage of administrative costs, the effect of fund-raising drives, the speed of response to requests for help and so on. In fact we would argue that anyone working in an organizational context can set objectives which are measurable. There may be an issue around how well the measures reflect the organizational mission. How well does church attendance show that the church is promoting the gospel, for example?

THE CONCEPT OF TIME

There is an oft-repeated story in which a person advises another to invest their money in land. When asked why the response is 'because they are not making any more of it'. Time is a commodity which, for you as an individual, is similar to land. You only have so much of it. Unless science comes up with a magic potion which enables you to work without sleep or beyond the current limits of our biological span you have to confront the reality that the only option you have is to improve on your management of your time.

Thus time is different from many other resources available to the manager. The ways it differs are crucial to understanding its importance.

- It cannot be stored up like a charge in a battery.
- For each person the amount of time available is limited.

Some professionals, such as lawyers, charge for the use of their time and thus have to record it in order to bill the client. Tradespeople such as plumbers or electricians also usually charge an hourly rate.

Do you know what you cost per hour? It may come as a surprise to you. Let us assume that your salary is £18 000 per annum. What you actually cost your employer is more than this. For professional, managerial and administrative staff the 'on-cost' of pension, national insurance contributions, etc. is often about a third of salary. Added on this makes your annual cost £24 000.

Let us say you take three weeks' annual leave and there is another week which is counted out because of statutory holidays. This makes your weekly cost £500. (£24 000/ 48 weeks). Your working week is 36 hours but there is about 6 hours in total spent at lunch to be taken off. This leaves 30 hours. Then you have to allow for other 'dead time' such as tea breaks or waiting for something . Let us say conservatively about another hour per day. So this leaves you 25 hours effective working time per week. You cost your employer £20 per hour.

That does *not* include all the support services (office rent, equipment, company car, electricity, secretarial help) without which you probably could not function. Depending on your office location, position, work and other factors this could *double or even quadruple* your hourly cost.

As an exercise to focus your mind you may wish to calculate your hourly cost to your employer.

The usage and wastage of time

Sir John Harvey-Jones (1988) offers these thoughts on the use of time:

> I suppose the most essential part of this struggle is the management of one's time, and here there are a number of key things that can be done. I have always believed that when I am at work I should work as hard and effectively as I can, all the time that I am there, but that equally, when I am not working, there should be a clear line between the two experiences. In order to cover the sheer amounts of work, of contact, reading and writing and so on, it really is necessary to use every moment of enforced working time to the best effect (p. 288).

Sir John offers various personal suggestions for the use of time. These include being in a position to work when travelling by carrying portable dictaphones and suitable reading matter and visiting people in *their* offices rather than asking them to come and see you. His comments upon the cost-effectiveness of private aircraft and chauffeurs are unlikely to apply to more than a small proportion of managers!

In 1750 Edward Young said 'procrastination is the thief of time'. Procrastination is putting things off to a later day or time. It is not simply resolved by 'knee-jerk' reactions and trying to do everything immediately. Rather, it is a syndrome characterized by a willingness to defer action or a decision which has become a habitual form of behaviour. The question asked by someone 'suffering' from this syndrome is 'Can I put it off?' as opposed to 'Why can't I do it now?'

Problems in use of time

The indicators of time management problems have been described as the following:

- Having to work long hours
- Insufficient time for planning
- Frequent interruptions from people in person
- Frequent telephone interruptions
- Resolving subordinates' problems.

Managers describe the following ways to address these problems:

- Set goals and priorities
- Make time to plan
- Delegate
- Focus time on the key activities.

Research has identified particular kinds of people who are prone to use their own or others' time ineffectively. These are people who are:

1 Recognition seeking
2 Complainers
3 Resentful
4 Spontaneous
5 Fearful
6 Indifferent
7 Over-organized
8 Activity-driven
9 Time-obsessed.

We can consider these types in terms of brief pictures of the behaviours involved.

Recognition seeking

Everyone knows how much work Lee does. Lee is at pains to let them know. Whatever the task, Lee rushes around struggling to make deadlines with the sweat pouring out. However, planning is a low priority. The recognition of the pressure is vital to Lee. People comment on how Lee always takes too much on.

Complainers

Sam is never short of a reason for why the job can't be done. 'The organization is badly set up, the people are incompetent and nothing can be done.' Certainly Sam is not going to sort out the problems. Telling everyone about them takes up all the time available!

Resentful

If you want cooperation and support don't go to Pat. Pat is nursing such a grudge about the organization. The basis of the resentment may be short lived or long standing. The effect is that Pat has no desire to do anything to help the objectives of the organization.

Spontaneous

Beverly hates predictability. Planning and work diaries smack of regimentation. Beverly likes to 'go with the flow' and take each day as it comes. There is little point for staff asking Beverly for deadlines or boundaries.

Fearful

Jo never makes a wrong decision. Jo rarely makes any decision at all. Jo feels that the organization is always blaming people for wrong decisions. All possible risks have to be thoroughly explored and discounted first. This takes a lot of time.

Indifferent

Lesley is a real 'jobsworth'. When asked to do anything Lesley's most likely response is 'It's more than my job's worth'. Lesley is indifferent to whether projects are finished on time. Lesley is bored with the job and the only exciting day is payday.

Over-organized

Nikki is a 'list person'. There is a list for everything and they cover every eventuality. Nikki spends most of the time updating the lists. The one list Nikki doesn't have is a list of things actually achieved.

Activity-driven

Mel is a real dynamo. Mel organizes everyone and is a constant source of energy. However, whether the activities relate to the real world is another matter. Mel would have been great at arranging deck chairs on the sinking *Titanic*.

Time-obsessed

Karel has the biggest diary in the office. It is full of appointments and every minute is fully accounted for. At every meeting Karel becomes anxious as soon as any delay to (Karel's) timetable seems likely to occur. Karel has worked out a faster way to go to the bathroom. It may even save 30 seconds a day. Karel never has enough time for all the things in the big diary!

Do you recognise yourself or a colleague in any of these descriptions of (mythical!) people? If so do not despair for there are certain simple things you can do to manage your time more effectively.

Knowledge essential to good time management

There is an old proverb which says 'know thyself'. This is particularly true of time management. Before you can set about improving your use of time you need to know *how* you currently use it and what attitudes affect how you structure this, your most precious resource. This involves undertaking a certain amount of personal research. Usually this is through completing what is called a 'time log'. A time log is a record of how you spend your work time.

There is no form of time log precisely suitable to everyone. However, the model offered (Figure 4.5) may give you some ideas to use. The principles which should guide the time log are as follows:

- It should be completed over a reasonable length of time. For most people a period of 2 or 3 weeks is suggested. Obviously you need to be aware of whether this time period is 'typical' of your work pattern. A period covering the Christmas and New Year holidays may not be representative of how you spent the rest of the year.
- It should enable you to record the kind of activity quickly and in sufficient detail to analyse how you use your time. Therefore you should develop some kind of list of your activities. Here is a simple form one manager used:
  Outgoing telephone call
  Incoming telephone call
  Meeting (planned)
  Meeting (unplanned)
  Routine paperwork
  Non-routine paperwork
  Travelling
  In recording which activity was happening during each 15 minutes the manager also used an arrow to show whether the activity was
  → = self-initiated
  ← = responding to someone else
  The manager also used a shorthand to show who (if

Activity	9.00	9.15	9.30	9.45	10.00	10.15	10.30	10.45	11.00	11.15	11.30	11.45
Time (15 minute intervals)												
Outgoing telephone call	B→											
Incoming telephone call		F←										
Meeting (planned)			C↓	C↓	C↓							
Meeting (unplanned)												
Routine paperwork						C↓	C↓	C↓				
Non-routine paperwork									B→	B→		
Planning activity											B→	B→

Figure 4.5   Typical time log

anyone) was involved in the activity.

B = Boss
C = Customer
S = Subordinate
A = Admin
F = Finance

■ It should use intervals of short enough duration to pick up activities which 'interrupt' your planned activities. With management students we use intervals of 10 or 15 minutes.

From this you can see that if you record your main activity every 15 minutes over some 100 hours of work (3 weeks) you will end up with 400 pieces of data. Making useful sense of the data is the next step.

As an example Figure 4.5 shows a morning from the time log of the manager. That day the manager came in at 9.00 am; made a phone call to her boss confirming agenda items for a meeting later that day; received a phone call from someone in Finance; held a planned meeting that a customer had asked for; spent time writing up aspects of that meeting; planned for the meeting with her boss which she then went to.

The manager who keeps up the faithful and accurate recording on this basis over a period of 3 weeks will be able to look at the 400 (approx) entries and analyse them according to:

1   Proportion of time spent undertaking various activities
2   Proportion of time spent on self-initiated activities
3   Proportion of time spent on activities associated with different people in the work setting
4   Sequences or patterns of activity
5   Duration of individual activities (or the extent you change from one activity to another).

Now how you draw up a time log is your decision. But the categories of activities which you use must make sense to you. It is often useful to include items to record interruptions to ongoing activities. Otherwise it is easy to lose track of the number of times someone 'drops in' while you are trying to get through your in-tray.

Measuring your use of time is not in itself sufficient. You also need to think about your approach to time management. Do you set priorities and deadlines for yourself and do you review them regularly? This is dealt with elsewhere in this chapter. However, it is an integral part of successful time management.

What about delegation which is also dealt with elsewhere in Chapter 2? How easily are you able to say 'no'? You may wish to reconsider the section on assertiveness in Chapter 2.

How much time do you spend on unnecessary detail? Perhaps you are the sort of person who tries to be accurate to five decimal places when one is quite sufficient?

SOURCES OF IMPROVEMENT IN TIME MANAGEMENT

Routine paperwork

Few managers enjoy handling routine in-tray items. Henry Mintzberg, a well-known writer on managerial work, suggested from his research that often managers desire to be interrupted and fight shy of routine humdrum activity. However, routine paperwork is a 'necessary evil'. In some cases it is essential to accomplishing managerial targets. Paperwork can be categorized as follows:

- Writing
- Reading
- Calculating
- Searching
- Scheduling
- File retrieving
- Delegating
- Proof reading
- Filing

There is an acronym which can be used to describe the possible ways of responding to a piece of paper arriving on your desk. If can be be summarized as 'The four F's':

Follow it up
Forward it
File it
Forget it (i.e. use the 'round filing cabinet' under your desk)

The chosen action is best undertaken immediately. A speedy follow-up almost invariably saves time later on. The more times that you handle the same piece of paper, the less efficient the use of time.

How the *follow-up* happens is often important in the use of your (and others') time. Consider the implications of the following responses to an internal memo.

1 Dictate a reply to your secretary.
2 Draft a reply to be typed up.
3 Write a memo back youself.
4 Write a response on the memo itself and send it back (keeping a photocopy if necessary).
5 Telephone the sender with any information required.

Obviously the circumstances may rule out some of these options. However, the options are listed in order of the *total* time they would probably take (including the time of the person receiving your reply). If you only use the first option then you should review whether this is the most effective use of your time.

Forwarding items for action is a skill in itself. Winston Churchill reportedly distinguished items for quick response by writing on them 'Action today'. You may wish to review Chapters 2 and 3 to see if your skills in delegation are making the most effective use of your time. The use of Post-it type notes can be a useful device if it is not suitable to write upon the paperwork itself. However, there is always the risk of the note becoming detached from the associated document.

Filing information is a task many managers are able to delegate. However, in these days of leaner organizations and computerized information systems a secretary per manager is likely to become a thing of the past. The test of any filing system has to be the extent to which it helps you do your job.

The increasing use of computers offers both benefits and risks. The benefits come from the sophisticated techniques for searching the memory for that memo you recall writing some time in 1991 and the vast storage capacity available compared to 'paper-based' systems. (This whole book can fit on just one computer disk the size of a drinks mat.)The risks come from the possibility of system/disk failure or theft of the actual computer itself. You also need to be sensitive to the provisions of the Data Protection Act! Recent research suggests that many people recall where information is by cues which are not usually incorporated on computer filing systems. They might remember the colour or thickness of the document or where it is geographically (in the top drawer).

Forgetting or getting rid of pieces of information is sometimes the hardest thing for a manager to do. It is often quite surprising how much information you file which, like the clutter in your attic or garden shed, serves no useful purpose. Rather it actively impedes you by slowing up the retrieval of documents which *are* essential.

A piece of advice was offered by a very successful (and paper-averse) manager to one of the authors who, as a manager, inherited a huge paper mountain. It ran roughly as follows: 'I suggest that you put it all in a large cupboard. Throw out anything you haven't had occasion to refer to within 3 months'.

Use of meetings

Meeting and chairing skills are covered elsewhere (Chapter 2). However, your analysis of how you use time may well reveal that you spend a lot of it in scheduled or unscheduled meetings. Meetings cost organizations a lot. So as a manager you should ask:

1   'Is this meeting really necessary?' Perhaps a telephone call or a memo would suffice.
2   'Is there a clear purpose for the meeting?' It does not follow that every meeting has to have a formal agenda. Many meetings (and organizations) are not like that. However, if *you* do not know why you are going to a meeting *and* you are chairing it then we would suggest there is a problem. It

is also hard to prepare for a meeting whose purpose is unclear. A subsidiary question which often helps is 'How will I know if the meeting has been successful?'

3   'What do I need to bring to the meeting?' Sometimes it may be something tangible, such as a report or an item. At other times it may be an opinion or informed comment which you need to think through beforehand.

4   'How much time will the meeting need?' The calculation of how much to fit into an agenda and in what order is the art of a good chair. However, if you are not the chair you can often help by identifying how much time your items will need and how important they are.

5   'What records will be kept?' Meeting minutes do not (usually) need to record matters in great detail. However, they do need to record decisions and actions. If names are attached to actions then it assists the communication of decisions and later follow-up. Records made at the time, even if brief, are usually far more useful than more lengthy records made at a much later date.

Handling interruptions

As we have noted elsewhere, managers are subject to frequent interruption. Sometimes these are 'self-inflicted'. A proper time log will reveal the extent to which you are so affected. There is no lack of good advice for handling interruptions.

1   Avoid people coming to your office. Instead, go and see them and then you control the length of the discussion.

2   If people do interrupt you be firm but polite with them. Go straight to the point rather than engaging in small talk.

3   Stand up and sit in the edge of your desk when someone comes in. This shows you do not wish a long interruption.

4   Offer to call back.

5   Give a clear indication of how much time you have – and stick to it or the word gets around that 'one minute means up to half an hour'.

6   Display a clock prominently where a visitor can see it.

One of the authors used to have two rules which staff all were aware of:

1   If the door was shut then no interruptions.

2   If the door was open then interruptions were OK so long as the duration was agreed to be no more than 5 minutes. Beyond that required an appointment via the manager's secretary. This enabled staff to feel comfortable about

approaching the manager directly. It also provided the manager with the opportunity to both control the length of interruption and to stop all interruptions without the use of 'do not disturb' signs.

Use of the telephone

It is a source of some surprise that telephone skills have not been normally taught to managers until recently. Telephonists, receptionists and secretaries have had training provided yet the manager is a late starter.

Increasingly business is done by distance using the telephone. Managers spend a lot of time 'on the 'phone'. Sometimes there is some kind of perceived status attached to being the one 'receiving' the call. Yet if you can make the call at a time of your choice then *you* control the time, not the recipient.

Therefore analysis of telephone usage can pay dividends in time efficiency. The following guidelines are useful:

1   Plan telephone calls. Treat them as mini-meetings. Time the length of calls using that clock or a watch.
2   Set time aside for making calls in blocks rather than making them in a sporadic fashion.
3   If you are subject to frequent telephone interruptions which disrupt your work then try to have calls 'fielded'. If you have no secretary or receptionist to do this then it is often possible to come to reciprocal arrangements with a colleague.

Use slack time

Sir John Harvey-Jones is a strong advocate of making the best use of travelling or waiting time. He apparently carried several dictaphones and plenty of spare tapes and batteries when travelling. Though you may plan your time well it is inevitable that often circumstances may force you to wait to see someone or you may have to undertake a long trip. Being prepared for such eventualities is a sign of effective time management. Non-essential but important reading can be kept in a folder in order to provide a ready source of material.

In our time calculation of the work cost above we allowed a total of 11 hours each week for breaks and meals. Often this time can be used very effectively for something similar to what the Americans call 'working breakfasts'. If there is someone who you need to talk to informally then rather than scheduling a meeting in one of your offices why not join them for coffee or a walk at lunchtime? Hewlett-Packard and other companies often encourage such informal association. One local authority set up coffee areas throughout the civic centre for staff to meet informally.

Time dualling

This is related to the use of slack time. It involves trying to find a way in which you can use the same time for several purposes. For example, perhaps you have to meet a group of new staff and also you have get some views on how staff feel about the cafeteria for the next management meeting. Why not combine the two?

Use of routine

This last point is in many ways the most important. Managers like to think that they manage by exception and delegate all the routine work. But the reality is that virtually all managers have a substantial amount of their work which is routine – such as the paperwork referred to previously.

The development of work habits which effectively and speedily handle the routine aspects of your job makes a major contibution to both freeing up time and minimizing stress. Some suggestions are:

1   Set aside blocks of time for routine work.
2   Have a simple diary system which your staff and colleagues understand.
3   Try to get routine aspects of your work as habitual as brushing your teeth. Then you might even be able to do other things simultaneously!

EXAMPLES OF OBJECTIVE SETTING AND PRIORISATION DRAWN FROM MANAGERS IN VARIOUS ORGANIZATIONS

Setting objectives

We have performance-related pay and the guidelines say that there should be a quarterly review. We discuss their objectives and have a personal development plan for every member of staff. Every member of staff has their own job description and also a skills matrix which sets out all the skills which are necessary or desirable and staff are encouraged to plan their own career. They are always aware that there is a limited budget in terms of time and money for people to undertake their training.

David Tait, Manager, Woolwich Building Society

Project realignment

The organization had decided to reduce the number of organizational layers and a large number of employees would be affected. Work patterns needed to change to meet a new concept of service delivery. This would involve a different contract for a group of the employees. Staff were concerned and the trade union was resistant to the proposed change. Relatively junior trade union representatives were bypassing normal consultation machinery and going to the director. The project was widely seen as 'stalled' and not progressing. There was a sense of disbelief. The trade union had organized a large meeting to discuss the perceived threat to the current service.

Geri and her colleague took on the task of communicating the project to staff in order to get it moving again. They undertook a 'road show'. This had the aim of giving the same message to the staff. Every member of staff had a personal invitation to attend. The trade unions were invited to be involved without any commitment to its objectives. The road show aimed to take the message of the project out to staff and visual aids (flipcharts) were extensively used. There was a question-and-answer session afterwards. After that staff had an opportunity to discuss the project with the invited trade unions. The road show presenters deliberately withdrew to ensure free discussion took place.

After each session the presenters checked with the managers present and got feedback to inform future presentations.

After the road show a workshop was held to enable managers to share their experiences. There was still a level of anger and managers had wanted the road show to 'lay down the law' to get things moving. People were asked to identify issues and action plans. It enabled managers to share fears about the changes. It also enabled information to be picked up and issues identified. Regular consultation continued afterwards.

Managers said they were unclear about budget issues so training seminars and consultation sessions were set up.

The effectiveness of the road show was assisted in four ways:

- The consistency of the message
- The information was given to large groups of staff over a short time so minimizing the distorting effect of the 'grapevine'
- It was recognized that different groups of staff had different communication needs – hence the workshops for managers
- The balance between supporting staff through change while conveying the reality of the change.

Since the road show staff have shown more willingness to discuss the changes and the new jobs involved. Staff are taking up new duties voluntarily and accepting changes in conditions of work. Staff are undertaking the training necessary for the adjustments. In some areas up to 80 per cent of the staff affected have moved to new contracts. The trade unions have reverted to using the normal communication channels.
Geri Mitchell, Advisor, London Borough of Enfield

Figure 4.6   Example of communication

Goal setting

We are driven by PRP and we set quantifiable objectives for everyone down the line. It isn't MBO like Humble, which advocates bottom-up objective setting. It's very much more top driven. In effect it's a performance management system which is linked to pay. It falls into two categories. There are quantified business objectives which come out of strategic plans. There are qualitative objectives such as personnel ones. They are all deadlined and quantifiable as far as possible and must meet the following criteria:

■   Measurable
■   Achievable

- Relevant
- Controllable

I spend most of my time setting objectives for line managers to achieve on a shorter (sometimes daily) basis. I tend to operate on the basis that people develop plans. The plans need to be clear with itemized action points and deadlines which are clear and acceptable to me. I want to see one sheet of paper with action points – task related.

I believe if you develop a plan which is a decent one and you monitor progress against it then there are only a couple of reasons why it doesn't work. Either the plan was wrong in the first place. Maybe someone didn't fight for a principle or was pressured into something sooner than they could. If so they should bloody well have said so. Or implementation failed somewhere along the line. Perhaps circumstances changed. Were they circumstances we could have foreseen and done something about? Or is it simply that you are not putting into practice what you put on paper?

If you are talking task-orientated things then this is a good way to operate. I find it is very successful. You can be flexible within it if you are very clear with your managers. You say I want a plan. I want it to have bullet points. I put it in my diary system and monitor it. Something arrives on my desk. I can then say I've either got the response which says 'yes, I've done it, it's OK' and I can check the quality and I can delve underneath and go and sample the work and say: 'Oh well, you say you've done it but I don't think much of this' or I can say: 'That was super, I've got some very good feedback on that'. It works very well.
Nigel Wright , Woolwich Building Society

It is a large store in the top fifteen with 180 staff and four sales managers. The pharmacy manager also covers other areas. P found that the junior manager (B) operating the dispensary was ineffective. He was disorganized and struggling. P had to cover the pharmacy to help him cope.

P's impression was that B was disorganized. There was a massive queue and staff didn't seem to know what to do. P felt B clearly needed to improve.

Though B knew what his job entailed, the problems P found hadn't been raised with him. So B needed to have this discussed with him. This P did by:

- Involving other members of the management team in looking at best practice elements to work with
- Looking at reorganizing the layout and customer flow (labelling, dispensing, checking and reception)
- Moving equipment
- Relocating stock
- Most importantly in getting B to see he had a problem with the pharmacist who was poor at managing reception.

They involved the area operations expert who produced a report. B received personal feedback – he was told he was 'too laid back' and did not put theory into practice

B spent some time looking at another (well-run) department. After about 4 weeks B could see the problems and began to look at solutions.

It was important to persuade B that the problems were immediate and needed a quick solution. P used B's appraisal to point this out. P indicated that B was not measuring up against performance criteria. B didn't like hearing this but accepted the criticism.

After this, progress began. The area ops expert made another visit and goals for change were set. Measures for change used were:

- The time P had to spend in the dispensary
- The ops expert report
- Measures of customer flow
- A performance checklist which covered ten different aspects of the work (this latter was completed by B then by P).

Long-term measures were payback in terms of improved customer service and growth in prescription volumes.
A senior manager in a retail organization

Prioritization and goal setting

I run several things at once, like a computer running programs which has several loaded up at one time. For example, if something needs checking out with a management team or involves a committee report then those events have their own time cycle. Something else may be more personal and be more flexible.

Every time I pick up my in-tray at the other end of the office I find a couple of days' work sitting there waiting for me. I manage that by avoiding going down to that end of the office. In terms of my own mail I think I'm fairly good with most letters that come in. Quite a lot of them I ignore or throw away. If I'm in at work just after Christmas and there's not a lot of people around or over the summer when things go quiet I have obsessional phases when I decide to deal with everything. I'm surprised then to find out that quite a lot of memos (sent to me) they've forgotten about.

I do find that a lot of time as a manager is reactive. It's a bit of the job I could do without. About every two months our training unit will have an attack of cockroaches or a solicitor will try and evict us from it. On those sort of things I'll drop everything.

We do have an MBO system. It's called the Business Process. It's meant to be that everyone can point to it and say that's my job there. It got a bit messy in social services because our job is about development – this project and that project. The Business Process is structured in a task analysis kind of way. There is an aim which is called a committee aim which is then broken down into key result areas of which we have about fifteen. Each result area has several action plans and then each action plan has several key tasks. When you get to a key task it is written in such a way as you'd know whether it was down or not. Every year from about February to May people review themselves against key result areas and action plans. For people who can't do that you write a report about what the hell you've been doing. The idea is that everyone should be involved – even social services clients.

The director would cream out headline news and feed it back to the councillors to show whether the committee aim is being met or not. Things are also used internally. We asked to identify areas for cutting back or for growth. These are used in the annual budgeting cycle and in appraisal of managers. I use the review as a way of generating another year's work for the trainers.

Richard Hooper, London Borough of Enfield

I was asked to set up a Quality Assurance (QA) group. I was given a vague outline and was unsure over how to go about it. We were very busy and QA seemed a bit of a luxury. I found it hard to understand what QA about.

I read up a bit about it and then wrote a report which I sent around to staff. I asked for comments and suggestions. There were none. So I held a staff meeting and 'nobbled people' beforehand.

At the area meeting I aimed to put it across in a simple way. I asked for help and ideas. I stressed that only attendance and a contribution to the QA group was required. I told them that the QA group would only run for a limited time with a set number of meetings.

I got names of people who might be interested. I had to sell them the idea. I was aiming for a mixture of staff to get involved in the QA group. Sometimes it involved using someone to find others who might be interested. I was looking for creative people. We split the group for a couple of meetings. I split the group – the only criterion was that there was staff in each group. But in one group there was very little representation.

The main reason was to encourage people to contribute – carers and clients would find it hard to contribute in the larger group. Afterwards people said that the group had affected their attitudes and had enabled them to listen to others.

What has happened to the report?
Standards are being set as a result of this and other reports. Within the office there has been a continuing impact. One of the admin people and one of the OT's are following up on QA. One of the problems is getting information out to people. Managers have a copy and all those taking part; there is a copy on the notice board. People were excited when they got their copy.

I tried to make the report interesting by using sample questionnaires at the end.
Vickie Golding, Area Manager, London Borough of Enfield

LEARNING POINTS

- How does planning affect managers at different levels of seniority?
- Why is planning important in management?
- How do tasks, operational plans, strategic objectives and organizational purpose fit together?
- What is the goal-setting process?
- What is meant by SMART?
- What is a 'fuzzy' as opposed to a performance aspect of a goal?

- How can you prioritize objectives
  - By ABC?
  - By paired comparison?
- What is Management by Objectives (MBO)?
- What characterizes 'time' from most other resources?
- What sort of problems do managers encounter in managing their time?
- What kind of people waste time?
- What do you need to know in order to improve your time management?
- What ways can time management be improved?

PREPARING FOR ACTION PLANNING

Remember the checklist of questions identified in the Introduction to this book? Try them again to identify your further development needs. We have reproduced those most appropriate to this chapter to help you. You will need to adapt them to the issues discussed.

Who/where are your largest customer bases (customers may be internal or external to the organization)?

How do you currently coordinate your activities in order to develop your product/service provision?

How are organizational performance standards determined and by whom?

How do you ensure that these performance standards are being met?

How do you measure these standards, organizationally?

What actions would you/have you taken with others at times of particular difficulty or change?

Which methods do you use to analyse facts and figures for your job purposes?

How do you present these facts and figures to others for decision-making purposes?

How effective are your analytical and mathematical skills in convincing others?

Were the outcomes of these presentations appropriate for the decision-making purposes?

How might you improve your analytical and mathematical skills?

How is information fed back into the decision-making process?

How do you set work objectives (or participate in setting them) for yourself and others?

How do you review and update these objectives?

Identify an objective you have had to meet and specify how you planned the work activities to meet this objective.

How did you decide which method would work best?

How do you decide how to allocate work to others?

How do you evaluate your own performance against your work objectives?

How do you evaluate the performance of others against their objectives?

What methods do you use to give feedback to others about their performance?

Can you pinpoint anything which you consider particularly important when giving feedback?

What information do you need to do your job and for what purposes?

Do you have any problems obtaining this information?

To whom do you supply information?

Do your meetings result in positive action?

Have you attended committees in your current role and prepared action reports for these committees?

Questions devised by, and adapted from, the Crediting Competence Team at South Bank University and reproduced with permission.

ACTION PLANNING

- Identify the planning process in your organization.
- Ascertain where your contribution comes in.
- List the work and non-work objectives which you have over:
  - The next month
  - The next year
  - The next five years
- Try to set them up so they are SMART.
- Use a prioritizing system to identify the ones that are most important.
- Develop action plans to implement them.
- Analyse the way you spend your work time over a period of at least three weeks.
- Identify ways to improve on your time management.
- Turn these into goals which are actionable and measurable and implement them.

FURTHER READING

Adair, John (1988), *How to Manage Your Time*, Talbot Adair.
Mager, Robert (1991), *Goal Analysis*, Kogan Page, London.
Mali, Paul (1986), *MBO Updated*, John Wiley, Chichester.
Treacy, Declan (1991), *Clear Your Desk*, Business Books, London.

5 Influencing others

Managers who are able to influence the behaviour of others plan their approaches and communicate clearly using a variety of techniques.

INTRODUCING THE RELATIONSHIP BETWEEN THE MCI PERSONAL COMPETENCY MODEL AND INFLUENCING OTHERS

The MCI Integrated *Model of Personal Competency* identifies the behaviours and skills necessary for you to develop, before you are able to prove competence in any managerial function. This chapter attempts to deal with the various behaviours and skills necessary for you to apply across all managerial functions, transferring your learning to different occasions, at different times and under varying circumstances (contexts), consistently. The outcomes below, as identified within this section of the model, should be borne in mind while you work through this chapter.

Outcomes required when influencing others effectively

Influencing others effectively requires development of behaviour by the manager (keeping ethical considerations in mind at all times) whereby he or she:

- Develops and uses contacts to trade information and obtain support and the necessary resources
- Creates and prepares strategies for influencing others
- Presents herself or himself positively to others
- Uses a variety of techniques, as appropriate to the audience and circumstances, to influence others
- Understands the culture of the organization and acts to work within it or influence its change or development

INTRODUCTION TO INFLUENCING OTHERS

Influencing other people is not about getting our own way all the time. Influencing is about being assertive, making sure others know what our views and opinions are and *also* ensuring that we make it possible for others to contribute positively to general discussion, problem solving, ideas generation and decision making. Decisions made in isolation of others are less likely to be owned by them, or gain commitment from them.

We therefore need to influence *each others'* thinking and behaviour for constructive and mutually rewarding effects, in order to reach conclusions which produce effective results. In other words, we all have a duty to *influence* the actions taken at work, and share responsibility in the effects of that action.

THE NATURE OF INFLUENCE

In order to influence others we may consider that we have a certain *power* over them. The power we may have, of course, can be negative as well as positive. Power can be a very effective motivator, depending upon its source and purpose.

According to Charles Handy (1985) when defining *power*, it can be said that it relates to the capacity to affect the behaviour of others, or the actual ability to do something. In being a holder of power, managers are able to *influence* the behaviour and performance of others. *Influence* can be the application and the effect of power and authority.

Charles Handy distinguishes between power and influence. He says that the difference lies in the fact that influence is an active process and that power is a resource providing the ability to influence. Recourse to any source of power is likely to provoke different kinds of response in those over whom it is exercised. (See Chapter 1 for a more detailed account of power and its effects.)

METHODS OF INFLUENCE

According to Charles Handy, influence can be overt (seen) or covert (unseen). For example, where individuals are in a negotiating situation it is not difficult for the parties concerned to determine the areas in which influencing attempts are being made. In contrast, however, one might take any other situation where two or more people are involved in discussion. An observer can often identify where the individuals concerned modify their views as a result of the discussion but this frequently happens without the awareness of those being influenced.

Honest influence

Where influence is *overt*, those who mean to influence others will be honest about it, explaining their reasons and providing evidence and supporting information as appropriate. These people are also more likely to be influenced *by* others in the process, accepting that other viewpoints, whether they are ultimately taken on board or not, are likely to provide a more effective conclusion as a result of including these viewpoints in discussions. This approach will build trust and allow mutual support between individuals.

Manipulation

Manipulation is often used by people in order to *get their own way*. They want their own way but do not want it to be obvious to others and therefore adopt a manipulative approach to make people do and say what they want. This is *covert* influence.

Those who perceive their position to be weaker than those they wish to influence sometimes use manipulative approaches; downtrodden housewives (not all housewives), victims of familial pressure and demands; secretaries who may feel they cannot stand up for themselves; those who believe they do not have the authority to attempt honest influencing strategies.

Manipulation can sometimes become a more serious case of emotional blackmail, where the manipulator subtly convinces others to act in ways which fulfil their own needs, and who are usually opposed to what is in the best interests of others. This is not a firm foundation upon which to build positive personal *or* working relationships.

Those concerned with *getting their own way* all the time are still being the *child* in a *parent–child* relationship. It is immature behaviour demonstrating that they have not yet learned that other people's involvement in developing their originally identified wishes or beliefs can, in fact, bring about more positive outcomes for all concerned.

Stealing the ideas of others

There are also times when people like to believe all ideas are their own, without any other influence. Such people hope that other people's ideas which they have adopted, because they appear to be valid after reflection but which they did not wish to acknowledge at the time, are not seen to have been *stolen* from them. This approach, however, relies on others' poor memory! How many times have you heard people say 'it was my idea in the beginning and it received little acknowledgement at the time, but an hour later it came back as the boss's idea with full commitment'?

EXERCISE

What kinds of influencing techniques do you employ? Are they always appropriate? Identify and compare various situations. How might you behave differently in the future?

INDIVIDUAL RESPONSES TO INFLUENCE

There are at least three main responses by people to the influence of others. These responses may or may not be the recognition by them of others' seniority or expertise. Such responses can often be related to the presence or absence of self-confidence, self-reliance and self esteem, depending upon the circumstances. (See Chapter 7 for Self-confidence and Personal Drive.)

- Influence by others is *accepted* by those receiving it because it is in their best interests to do so. It could be, for instance, that those concerned feel they are in no position to influence the process undertaken or the decision being made; that they either have no authority or the relevant expertise, and therefore must obey those who are in a recognized position of responsibility or authority.
- It is possible for recipients to adopt ideas or proposals because they admire or *identify* with the initiator of the influence. For some reason they are overimpressed with the individual concerned and feel they cannot add to what is being presented. They are, in fact, doing an injustice not only to this individual but also to themselves by not contributing and adding to the *quality* of the results.
- Those being influenced may have been so by *adopting* the ideas or proposals as their own. They internalize them so that they become their own possessions. This is, of course, the most positive response, as long as those concerned do not think that the ideas were originated by themselves. This could become another form of manipulation by the person influencing, who will ultimately not be trusted.

EXERTING YOUR INFLUENCE

There will be times when you must ensure your influence is accepted, identified with and/or adopted. The difficulty for you will be to identify when this is necessary; that no further arguments can be introduced and that you must stand firm.

- *When you know your arguments are just*   Do not scale down any requests you make in order to fit others' authority or willingness. It may not, on some occasions, be appropriate to compromise or modify your position, especially in dealing with organizational objectives or procedures such as discipline or grievance.
- *Make allies, not enemies*   If an *excuse* is genuine, it is often useful to enlist the person's assistance in approaching those who can really help, or in assisting the person to identify the means of overcoming difficulties, whether they are perceived or actual problems.
- *In dealing with an ultimatum*   Do not panic and take your time, an ultimatum is seldom appropriate. Test understanding and summarize often (the problem may not turn

out to be as extreme as you at first thought); be firm but flexible, do not gain a reputation as a *soft touch* (you must work out an agreement); widen the debate, employ lateral thinking and influence the thinking of others away from the ultimatum by proving that there may be alternatives to consider.

> **EXERCISE**
>
> Identify a situation where you have recently found it necessary to exert your influence. What were the outcomes? Did you behave appropriately? What might you do differently under similar circumstances in the future?

COMMON INFLUENCING PROBLEMS AND THEIR SOLUTIONS

These problems, and simple rules for overcoming them, are just as successful when dealing with influencing difficulties inside the organization as they are to outside selling situations:

- *Overselling* People often *oversell* their position in order to be heard at all. However, too many reasons put forward or too much emphasis placed upon advocating a particular idea or position will result in others losing interest or simply not believing that being presented.

Recognize the intelligence, reasonableness and logic of others by being realistic about the claims you are making.

- *Diluting benefits* Again too many benefits will dilute interest. Seeking many reasons why someone should *buy* something, or accept claims being made, will make benefits appear multi-purpose with no clear focus and detract from the value of the more legitimate, specific claims.

It is more advisable to make an impact with the most important benefits of your claims, by concentrating on the specific areas for which they are intended and are best at addressing.

- *Irritating remarks* Such words as *be fair, be reasonable, listen to my points, if only you ...* are more often used in the emotional blackmail of those in opposition, or who require more persuasion, and are likely to make others present concentrate on the interpersonal behaviour rather than the purpose of the discussion. Effective relationships are unlikely to be developed in this way.

Be positive and keep to the real benefits of your arguments and issues surrounding them.

■ *Dealing with excuses*   Excuses can often cloud issues and lack of preparation by the person meaning to influence can result in being distracted by those trying to excuse their behaviour or ideas.

As with all organizational activity, adequate preparation is key to encouraging effective behaviour and results. At the same time, it is important not to make people feel threatened by our attitude while they are trying to defend themselves. We must remain calm, helpful and assertive in order to help others identify the problems which are causing their anxieties.

> ### EXERCISE
> Identify a situation where you have recently had problems influencing the behaviour of another. What were the circumstances? What were the outcomes? Did you behave appropriately? What might you do differently under similar circumstances in the future?

COPING WITH AGGRESSION

Do you respond in kind when confronting aggression, because you believe no-one will be listening otherwise? Or do you back off altogether? Either way, you will not influence the aggressor to change their behaviour and nothing will be achieved. The problem will only be unnecessarily prolonged.

You need to respond by stating your own needs, wants, feelings and opinions, directly and honestly. Listen to the other person calmly, test your understanding and be flexible but, above all, the aggressor must have their approach redirected and be allowed to state their position despite the initial aggression. It is most usual for aggression to subside when dealt with positively, and the person does not lose sight of what he or she wants. You will feel very positive towards yourself afterwards.

Acknowledge the aggressive person's determination or anger and state the effect the aggression is having on you, for example feeling nervous or becoming angry in return or whatever it may be.

Make suggestions and direct the conversation towards a goal. It is possible that you will have to go round the cycle a few times before achieving your aim.

Identify a situation where you have recently dealt with aggressive behaviour (your own or someone else's will do). What were the outcomes? What might you do differently under similar circumstances in the future?

THE ORGANIZATION'S CULTURE

While definitions of organizational culture vary considerably, they all point to something which is difficult to define; that it is elusive and intangible, but which has strong influence on all those involved with it. Culture, which may or may not be appropriate to the organization's current purpose, is imposed upon people by people. New members of, or new associates to, an organization often find that they have to conform to the prevailing culture, or the relationship will not gel.

Culture is learned by new members, sometimes by coping with some threat to their individual values by building defence mechanisms, or sometimes through the *positive reinforcement* model where an individual will internalize different values because they work and are accepted by others within the group. This also applies to individual cultures within any one organization, where one group of individuals will exclude other groups and if any new member to that group does not conform, that person is made to feel uncomfortable and is unaccepted by the others.

Charles Handy (1985) identifies four main culture types associated with organizations and expresses these diagrammatically for easy recall:

1   *The power culture* which is entrepreneurial by nature, with one person or a small team of people at the hub of the 'wheel' exerting all the power, control and influence

2   *The role culture* such organizations tend to be bureaucratic by nature, with well-defined jobs within tight structures, specific areas of function, responsibility and accountability (expressed by the 'columns' of the temple in the diagram)

3   *The task culture* a fast-growing and apparently more acceptable culture for *team* and *project* management, where the *manager* will vary from project to project, depending upon expertise and the contributions individuals are able make and/or develop (expressed as a matrix in the diagram, where the dots are different people at different times, or covering the different projects)

4   *The person culture* great fun, but quite a problematic culture, where the individual is the centre of its organization's universe! It operates in isolation of everything else;

only concerned with meeting personal objectives without wider reference

As discussed earlier in this chapter, while it is important to understand the cultures of those organizations and individuals with whom we deal, it is often also important to influence changes as they may be required according to the direction an organization may be taking for its overall development and improvement. This requires strength of character, commitment, self-confidence and personal drive. (Organizational Culture is also discussed in Chapter 9.)

EXERCISE

Study your own organization and/or team (internal or external) in terms of its prevailing culture. What are the difficulties? How might a change in culture meet organizational objectives more effectively (now or in the future as appropriate to you)?

THE USE OF NEGOTIATION

Some people seem to have an in-born ability to get results in conversations and negotiations. This is usually because they have real powers of persuasion as a way of exerting their spheres of influence. Although negotiating is not the same as just getting our own way, we recognize that there are skills needed to increase the benefit to us in any particular situation.

Negotiation is the art of seeking agreement to the maximum advantage of all concerned. This statement bears some analysis. Notice that it says *seeking agreement*. This means that merely trying to bully someone into accepting our position is not negotiation. It is not very effective either. We should not confuse the notion of seeking agreement with the notion of changing someone's mind. It is not necessary to do the latter to achieve the former.

The definition also uses the phrase *maximum advantage*. This is because it may not be necessary to achieve all that is desirable in order to achieve the most important goals. Sometimes an element of compromise on minor issues can secure agreement on the major issues more readily than may be apparent at the beginning. This suggests that we start out with a clear idea of what we want (and the distinction between what we must have, as well as what we would like to have). It also suggests that we use our efforts to find out what the other person also must have, and on what they are willing to compromise.

Fisher and Ury (1984) offer four basic principles for successful negotiating:

1   *Separate the people from the problem.* When self-esteem is threatened, then people react. This in turn can cause a reaction that threatens the other person. The swapping of such emotions and attitudes inhibits proper negotiating. It is important to recognize that the issue that causes the problem is distinct from the people themselves.

2   *Focus on interests, not positions.* Positions are not the same as goals. We can take a position as a point of principle, and let the real issue go. So, for instance, although someone might insist on a colleague being moved to another department (the position taken), the issue might really be to prevent adverse criticism (the interest).

3   *Generate a variety of possibilities before deciding what to do.* Active listening is all-important. Do not accept positions at face value. Focus on possible areas of agreement – not of disagreement.

4   *Base results on objective standards.* These should be quantifiable criteria. They are easiest to understand in the context of financial negotiations. It is always legitimate to ask 'how did you arrive at that figure?' However, objective standards can always be found, whether quantifiable or not.

How to convince people

Tell people when you agree with them
Admit when you are wrong
Do not argue
Put the case, quote the evidence
Use rationality, not emotion
Deal with objections

EXERCISE

Identify a situation where you have recently negotiated with or otherwise convinced people. What were the outcomes? Did you behave appropriately? What might you do differently under similar circumstances in the future?

PREPARING FOR ACTION PLANNING

Do you remember the checklist of questions identified in the Introduction to this book? We have reproduced those which are appropriate for this chapter, which you will need to adapt accordingly.

How effective are the communications methods that you use?

Which outside agencies do you currently liaise with?

Are there any joint working arrangements in your product/service (this may apply across teams, or between organizations)?

What actions would you/have you taken with others at times of particular difficulty or change?

Which methods do you use to analyse facts and figures for your job purposes?

How do you present these facts and figures to others for decision-making purposes?

How effective are your analytical and mathematical skills in convincing others?

Were the outcomes of these presentations appropriate for the decision-making purposes?

How might you improve your analytical and mathematical skills?

How do you liaise with others at off-site locations?

What, if any, interdepartmental group activities do you participate in?

What are the main purposes of these groups?

How do you/would you maximize productive relationships and networks?

How do you/would you promote equal opportunities within and between those with whom you relate?

What do you see as your strengths in establishing good working relationships and which aspects would you want to develop further?

How would you/do you go about establishing and developing working relationships with others, both internal and external to the organization?

How easy/difficult do you find asking support of, or taking problems to others?

How might this be improved?

How easy/difficult do you think others find asking you for support or in bringing their problems to you?

How could it be improved?

What support would you/do you give to others in their relations with others outside the organization (or department)?

How could these relationships be improved?

What formal and informal actions would you/have you taken to actively promote effective working relationships and prevent their breakdown?

How do you/would you deal with conflict in your relationships or in the relationships of others arising from:

- Differences of opinion on courses of action?
- Personal animosity?
- Moral dilemmas (between individuals or individuals and the organization)?
- Racism?
- Sexism?
- Other discriminatory behaviour?
- Non-compliance with organizational rules, norms or values?

What would say is your leadership style?

What are the effects of your style on others?

What methods do you use to give feedback to others?

Can you pinpoint anything which you consider particularly important when giving feedback?

Have you attended committees in your current role and prepared reports for these committees?

Were your conclusions and recommendations acted upon?

Do you find that sometimes when you believe you have influenced people's behaviour, no change occurs?

Why do you think this might be?

Do you use your status in the organization, or some other form of influence associated with your position, in the influencing process?

Are you considered an expert in any way by colleagues and team members? Does this perceived expertise, in your opinion, allow any special influence over others?

Consider your current age as a manager or potential manager. Do you believe this to have any effect in the amount of influence you have over others in the workplace?

Does your age present any barriers when trying to influence others?

Why should this be and what might *you* be able to do about it?

Consider your gender as a manager or potential manager. Do you believe this to have any effect in the amount of influence you have over others in the workplace?

Does your gender present any barriers when trying to influence others?

Why should this be and what might *you* be able to do about it?

Consider any other aspects of yourself as an individual. Do you believe that any of these characteristics have any effect on the amount of influence you have over others in the workplace?

Do any of these aspects of yourself present any barriers when trying to influence others?

Why should this be and what might *you* be able to do about it?

Finally, do you believe you have the necessary qualities to influence the thinking and behaviour of others?

If the answer to this question is *no*, you may need to learn to believe in yourself more.

Questions adapted from those devised by the Crediting Competence Team at South Bank University and reproduced with permission.

ACTION PLANNING

Analyse your own behaviour in terms of strengths (positive outcomes) and weaknesses (negative effects), in dealing with actual work-based occurrences with regards to the various situations discussed in this chapter.

Decide how you might deal with them differently in the future and what are your immediate training requirements and future development needs.

Discuss them with appropriate others and negotiate how you might address them.

FURTHER READING

Handy, Charles B. (1985), *Understanding Organizations*, 3rd edn, Penguin Books, London.

Hannagan, Tim (1995), *Management Concepts and Practices*, Pitman Publishing, London.

Mullins, Laurie J. (1993), *Management and Organizational Behaviour*, Pitman Publishing, London.

Nicholson, John (1992), *How do you Manage?*, BBC Books, London.

Parsloe, Eric (1992), *Coaching, Mentoring and Assessing – A Practical Guide to Developing Competence*, Kogan Page, London.

6 Information management

Managers with information search skills gather many different kinds of information, using a variety of means, develop important working relationships and produce better decisions as a result.

INTRODUCING THE RELATIONSHIP BETWEEN THE MCI PERSONAL COMPETENCY MODEL AND INFORMATION MANAGEMENT

The MCI Integrated *Model of Personal Competency* identifies the behaviours and skills necessary for you to develop, before you are able to prove competence in any managerial function. This chapter attempts to deal with the various behaviours and skills necessary for you to apply across all managerial functions, transferring your learning to different occasions, at different times and under varying circumstances (contexts), consistently. The outcomes below, as identified within this section of the model, should be borne in mind while you work through this chapter.

Outcomes required in information management

In developing this skill, the manager:

- Establishes information networks to search for and gather relevant information
- Actively encourages the free exchange of information
- Makes best use of existing sources of information
- Seeks information from multiple sources
- Challenges the validity and reliability of sources of information
- Pushes for concrete information in ambiguous situations.

The objectives of this chapter are to:

- Recognize the role of communication in marketing

- Know and appreciate the value of various market research techniques
- Recognize the purpose, techniques and the range of activities in acquiring information about products, markets and customer needs and perceptions
- Recognize the function, benefits and processes involved in advertising activity
- Recognize the function, benefits and processes involved in public relations activities
- Practise the skills of active listening to identify needs
- Promote the benefits of a product/service to meet an identified need
- Recognize the function, benefits and processes involved in other means of marketing communications.

INTRODUCTION TO COMMUNICATING OUTSIDE THE ORGANIZATION

Communication is a strategic activity. Not only is it a part of the process of developing goals and objectives, it is also an integral part of incorporating those goals and objectives in terms of profile and branding.

External communications are the processes by which we send the messages about our companies or organizations, and/or its products or services, to potential or actual customers. For some organizations, communicating to the outside world is seen as merely advertising but it is, in fact, a much more complex and broad set of activities.

In the 1990s and beyond there will be many challenges facing organizations of all types and if they do not recognize the significance of these challenges to their own work practices, they are unlikely to survive into the twenty-first century. Some of the challenges already having impact on the economy are:

- Increased market competition
- Rapid technological change
- The 'ageing' of people who work in these organizations, as demographic changes produce a reduction of available young people.

To meet these challenges, organizations are being prompted to invest in people and ensure that valuable human assets are given the best possible chance to maximize potential, just like any other appreciating valuable asset. This investment, it is contended, can only be truly realized through meaningful and relevant training (*Investors in People*, Training Agency, 1990). The justification of this statement will become clear as this chapter unfolds; each section itself describing the complexities involved in understanding, addressing and meeting customer needs in the coming decades.

COMMUNICATING WITH THE CUSTOMER

In the corporate context communication is essentially a sub-discipline of marketing. Marketing has to do with an exchange relationship in which all parties derive satisfaction. The exchange need not be for goods or money. Initially conceived in the commercial world, and still mainly associated with commerce, marketing principles are being adopted in the 'selling' of ideology (political parties), of personnel (employment applications), of a social consciousness (Keep Britain Tidy), of health (anti-smoking) and so on.

The concept is based on the exchange of value for mutual satisfaction, which depends for its success on the correct identification of the buyer's needs by the seller and supplying what the buyer actually needs so that satisfaction occurs. The supplier is also concerned to be satisfied. This may be in terms other than the commercial notion of profit: for example, in the public sector 'the effective, efficient and economic delivery of a service'.

Three elements must be present in order for an organization to claim it is truly marketing oriented:

1 It must be customer oriented – concerned primarily with the needs of customers and to coordinate activities which allow the organization to determine those needs.
2 Its efforts must be integrated to create consistency, avoid duplication, capitalize on individual skills and personal creativity, and, by so doing, create 'synergy' (the value of effects which are more than the sum of the individual parts).
3 Clear objectives must be established with the identification of the performance 'indicators' (outcomes desired to determine relevant organizational activities needed to ensure the successful achievement of these outcomes) which will facilitate the development of appropriate control measurements to monitor performance and progress.

THE MARKETING MIX

The expression 'marketing mix' is a term first coined for the concept of marketing as an integrative function in 1952 by Neil Borden, a US advertising executive and has been used as part of the marketing vocabulary ever since. There are many elements to the marketing mix, but Jerome McCarthy (1960) popularized a four-fold classification of these variables, called the Four P's: Product, Price, Place and Promotion.

Communications are vital to every element of the marketing mix and good communications techniques can be applied to each element of the mix in the following ways:

- *Price and positioning* messages about price competitiveness, value-added benefits, quality and style. Positioning is not what you do with a product or service, but the effects your messages have on the minds of the customers.

- *Products*   consumer information, analysis of benefits, etc.
- *Promotion*   from advertising and sales promotion to packaging and point of sale displays.
- *Place*   the physical distribution of the product or service where they will reach the targeted customer effectively and conveniently.

As with any other communication activity, we need to examine:

WHAT   the message is we are trying to communicate
WHOM   the message is for – the target market
HOW   to reach them – the media to carry the message
WHY   choose the product mix we do? As the environment, the technology and the products change over time, so must the rationale.

IDENTIFYING THE RIGHT 'MESSAGES'

Getting the message across

The variety of messages required to keep a company functioning efficiently in the marketplace is vast. So too is the variety of target audiences and media to carry them. In each case, the purpose is to ensure:

- Recognition
- Quality
- Consistency of the message.

Media campaigns can be very efficient at promoting a single, often simple idea about a company or its products/services. They often concentrate on a USP (Unique Selling Point), with a memorable phrase, or strapline:

'When it positively, definitely, has to be there on time.'

'Probably the best lager in the world.'

To what or whom do these lines refer? The recognition, quality and consistency factors apply in all aspects of a company's communications.

Corporate branding

It is often very important for a company to promote recognition of its own name, as well as its products or services. This is often done with the enhancement of visual recognition techniques such as colour, corporate logos, and so on.

London Underground is recognized, not just in London, or even nation-ally, but the world over, by its very distinctive corporate branding. This is based on the use of its distinct roundel, and the use of its own typeface (called New Johnstone, and a variation of the Gill typeface). Another very strong feature of this recognition comes from the distinctive London Underground map. It is unusual in that it is not a 'real' map, in the normal sense that the distances shown are to scale. It is a topological map, which shows the spatial relation-ships of the lines and stations. It was designed for London Underground in 1933 by Henry Beck, complete with the distinctive colours for the lines that existed then. In substance, it has changed very little since its invention. The roundel, the insignia style and the Underground map are protected very care-fully by London Underground, so as not to dilute the power of their distinctive symbols.

The telephone

The telephone is often the first line of response to customers, or the public at large, for many organizations. But what sort of impression do your customers get from your company/organization?

Try phoning your own organization from outside. What sort of response do you get? Is it prompt, helpful, informative, efficient? It would be a pity to spend millions of pounds on a major media campaign to promote a product/service or company, and have it spoilt because customers are treated badly by your telephonists. Yet this does happen all too often. Malcolm Peel (1987) identifies five steps to help:

1   Get good equipment. Modern technology now enables real sophistication in call storage, diversion and transfer.

2   Give technical training. Obviously this applies to telephon-ists, but all staff should be able to use divert, 'follow me', and other facilities, if they are available.

3   Structure the job right. Good support and guidance for tele-phone operators are essential in helping them to give effec-tive customer service.

4   Establish good discipline. How to deal with various types of enquiry, personal calls, peak time procedures. Are they allowed to take messages for individuals?

5   Behavioural training. If telephonists are the voice of your organization, make sure that it is a voice you would like your customers to hear when they phone. Is the greeting courteous? Does it identify the organization in the proper way? These are all important.

Internal communications

While it may seem odd to consider internal communications in a chapter specifically concerned with external communications, there are occasions when it is impossible to separate the two. It should also be noted that the techniques and standards which should be applied are very similar in both cases. In much of the current literature about the effectiveness of management, and in the growing body of literature that examines successful organizations, a consensus is emerging. It suggests that successful organizations are those that communicate their mission to their own staff, motivate them to perform, and train and empower them to make decisions and to achieve success.

At each stage, communication plays a vital role. Obviously, an important aspect of this is the interpersonal communication that takes place throughout an organization and at every level. This is dealt with in more detail in previous chapters. Corporate communication to staff as a body is in itself like a marketing exercise to a specialized group of internal customers. Such internal corporate communications can be used for many purposes:

- *Information* ensuring everyone receives the information they need in order to fulfil their individual and departmental objectives, based upon the overall corporate mission.
- *Corporate branding* to ensure all 'internal customers' have full understanding of the corporate image and reflect the agreed standards in all their activities.
- *Training* to provide benefits to the organization which will be reflected in: increased profitability; increased turnover; higher quality; improved image/reputation; better ways of meeting client needs and so on.
- *Teambuilding and integration* by defining and promoting cultural values and norms.
- *Motivation* the organization's 'internal customers' will be more highly motivated if they understand and grow to identify with the corporate image.
- *Social bonding* internal messages about corporate image and identity will enhance interpersonal relationships and create a sense of belonging.

ESTABLISHING CUSTOMER NEEDS AND SIMPLE MARKET RESEARCH TECHNIQUES

Market research

If marketing is the process whereby we 'identify, anticipate and satisfy customer requirements profitably', then we need systematic means of undertaking each of these stages. Market research is the process by which we research the nature of customer tastes and preferences, and by which we measure their satisfaction with products and services. It is one of the means of forecasting demand in the marketplace which might be included among the following:

- Buyer intentions
- Sales force assessment
- Trends analysis
- Market research
- Leading indicators
- Comparative studies
- Experimental research

The scope of market research

Market research is generally agreed to give information about the following:

- Buyers' habits
- Demography
- Consumer product/service knowledge
- Opinions/attitudes
- Intentions
- Motives
- Perceptions

It operates in two key dimensions. The first is in acquiring information about current products/services, and their position in the market. The second is in identifying new market opportunities.

Some of the most important techniques

- *Panels*   These are a selected sample of a target population who give interviews and express opinions on a regular basis. A problem with using panels is in assessing the reliability and validity of the information they give. A more specific technique is the retail audit, which is used to establish brand share and volume sales.
- *Qualitative*   This is the acquisition of opinions, reactions and behaviour. It can take many forms and it can be carried out by interview, questionnaire, or by informal means.
- *Media research*   This involves identifying the size and nature of audiences for advertisements in various media. It can also be used to audit the effectiveness of specific advertisements. Researchers look for evidence of 'spontaneous recall', or 'prompted recall' of a product or service.
- *Test marketing*   The various processes by which new products are tried out on customers to gauge reaction. It is used to reduce the chances of expensive failures.

■ *Preference mapping* This is a specific technique for analysing the customer perceptions of the benefits of a product or product range.

Interviews and panels are used to identify significant attributes. These attributes are tested with sample groups to identify priority order, and eliminate unimportant ones. For instance, with training shoes, the key attributes might be price and style. Then a selected sample of customers are asked to rate their ideal product/service in terms of the attributes identified. This rating is quantified so that the responses can be mapped onto a matrix like the one in Figure 6.1. When more than two attributes are identified, the matrix becomes multidimensional. In the final phase, real products/services are rated and compared to the ideal product.

The advantage of this method is that a very clear picture of a product or service can be drawn in terms of customer response. So, if your product is identified as being too expensive, then countering strategies can be drawn up – either to reduce price, or to emphasize value added aspects. This technique works better for well-understood products or services, or ranges thereof, than it does for potential or innovative products or services.

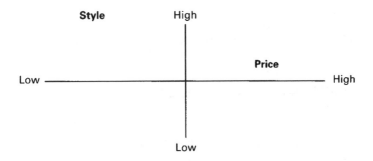

Figure 6.1   Example of customer ratings matrix

Where customers or clients are also citizens with social needs

Some readers of this chapter may feel that marketing is of little relevance to them because they serve a 'market' of an entirely different sort. For instance, those working in parts of the public or voluntary sectors may believe that some of the concepts discussed here are quite irrelevant when addressing, for example, the needs of the elderly in residential care homes. For the purposes of relating some of these theories to such situations, consider the following information obtained from interviews with the two managers quoted in earlier in this book.

Instead of enabling clients to develop their independence within one of the homes, a care assistant was actually leading others into 'disabling' the clients by telling them what to do, how to do it and what not to do, etc. The manager believes it is simply a matter of educating both staff and clients who may believe that providing attention in a continued 'fussing over others and doing things for them' manner is the correct behaviour. According to the manager 'it is difficult to convert to a customer care culture and to break down the 'you do this and fit into our routine' approach, but an important challenge'.

Before the manager joined the care team, residents had no locks on their doors and the doors were also kept permanently wide open so that an 'eye could be kept on them'. When the manager discussed the idea of privacy and locks on residents' doors with the team, an uproar ensued. The general excuse made was that the 'corridor would be dark'. The locks were eventually fitted, but staff and residents alike found the idea very difficult to accept initially.

Clothing was another issue. Care assistants had habitually produced whatever clothes they thought the residents should wear. Now the clients are being asked what they would like to wear and proper discussions and questioning about such issues are replacing the well-intentioned, but inappropriate control of client interests.

The manager believes that staff must continue to identify residents' needs and wishes and work towards those, instead of always telling them what to do. If they continue to concentrate on residents' disabilities, the results will be negative. Therefore they must concentrate on individuals' strengths and abilities for positive outcomes. The negative results, and indeed the disabilities themselves, she says, will then recede into the background.

SIMPLE NEGOTIATION AND SELLING TECHNIQUES

Selling skills

If we consider selling to be 'convincing someone of the advantages of accepting your position', then we can interpret it in a wide way. Some of us will be involved in selling products or services to customers face to face. Many more will have a marketing role. Nearly everyone will be involved in persuading internal customers to 'buy' an idea we are 'selling', whether it be a new project, or a new system. The theory and practice of selling is a personal skill, and it is the communication skill *par excellence*. By putting the theory and practice to good use, everyone can benefit, not just those who have the responsibility for moving products or services to individual customers. It can inform much of our persuasive activity.

Features benefits and positioning

When we sell we are looking to satisfy customers' needs. Clearly the most important element of selling is to find out what those needs are. This is interesting because it contradicts many people's notions of what selling is. They seem to characterize it as talking and persuading. In fact listening is a much more important skill. Again, our active listening skills come to the fore. It is necessary to look more closely at products and services, and what they are in a customer's eyes.

The features of a product or service are the technical or user characteristics that make a product or service interesting. On a video recorder, a seven-day timer is a feature. For a shop, seven-day opening is a feature.

A benefit is the advantage gained by the customer by virtue of the features. So, if we are selling furniture, we might sell the benefit of comfort. For certain types of car we might sell status or speed.

Positioning is about the way that we promote the image of a product/service, a range of products/services, or a brand name.

The most important aspect of this knowledge is that we sell benefits, not features. Most potential customers will not be interested in the finer workings of the epicyclic overdrive capacitor. They will be seeking the answer to the question 'What can it do for me?' This can only be answered if we work to uncover what their needs really are.

Identifying needs

Most people have needs. They are not always expressed explicitly and strongly – particularly at the opening of a sales presentation. Initially, needs are expressed as a dissatisfaction with some aspect of the current situation. The need grows eventually to a stronger and more positive commitment to a particular solution. Research shows that selling is much more efficient when it is directed to a strong explicit need than to a weak and implicit one. A weak implicit need might be: 'Our order processing is not very efficient.' A strong, explicit need might be: 'I need a photocopier that will count copies used by our different departments.'

We return to some practical examples obtained from one of the residential care homes surveyed. As a result of interviewing and finding out their client needs, the management team improved the information and facilities available to residents as follows:

- Brochures available from area doctors' surgeries
- Special transport arrangements in the area
- A suggestion book
- A simplified complaints procedure
- Computerized menus, with large print for the short-sighted
- Regular meetings for clients and relatives
- Various clubs were introduced
- Regular and special outings were arranged
- Pictures for walls were provided
- Public relations activities were introduced
- Summer and Christmas bazaars were introduced
- Open days were arranged

■ Donations were encouraged from residents, families, local services etc. and proper mechanisms installed for thanking them.

(Many things seem so obvious – after they have been discovered!)

If we know we are seeking to encourage customers to tell us their needs, we need to think about how to construct a sales presentation that enables us to do this.

The sales presentation

A one-to-one sales presentation should have structure and purpose, and should have the following phases:

■ *Courtesy/introduction* This involves introducing ourselves and establishing rapport. We have already talked about the importance of good first impressions and nowhere are they more important than here. Look back at the rules for creating a good impression.

■ *Exploration* This phase is really the one where we identify the needs of the customer. It is vital that we give the customer the opportunity to tell us what their needs are – not the other way around. Research shows that successful selling occurs when buyers do more talking than sellers. Where we do talk, we should be actively seeking – not telling at this stage. What we need to do is to talk about the most interesting thing in the world to our customer – themselves! Again, our active listening skills are crucial here.

Once we have explored and identified explicit needs, we move on to the next stage.

■ *Offering solutions* It is only now that we can offer solutions. The solution offered relates directly to the expressed need. The key idea is to match benefits to needs. This will be followed by discussion, objections, reinforcement.

Many books on sales technique talk about buying signals. These are basically the customer 'trying out' the ideas in their minds. They may range from vague interest to a genuine objection. Your job is to pick up these signals, find out their significance and respond accordingly. Once you see a level of commitment developing you should move on to the last phase.

■ *Closing the deal* There are really no rules about closing a deal, although there are many books that give advice, information, techniques and so on. The major objective is to seek a level of commitment. The level of that commitment will depend mainly on the customer and the circumstances.

'Would you like to pay cash or cheque?' is a nice close, but it does not work like that every time. It may be that the maximum commitment a customer can or will give is to see the product/service in action, to use it for a week on trial, or any other commitment up to on-the-spot purchase. The skill is finding the maximum level of commitment that the customer is comfortable with (and has the authority to provide!).

More formal presentations have more formal requirements. The written presentation should:

- Summarize your understanding of the customer's situation and needs
- Describe key features and benefits of the proposed services and how they will meet customer needs
- Summarize costs
- Project your offer as different to and/or better than those of others
- Enable the client to evaluate your services, products and reputation
- Communicate your message in a way that is appealing and intelligible to the decision makers.

The oral presentation should:

- Get and keep the listeners' attention
- Keep them interested in what you have to say
- Spotlight four or five benefits or points of major interest to the customer
- Answer questions and clarify any points necessary.

What you should find out about the customer

You should assemble and evaluate information about:

- Technical, financial and historical information; this may be abstracted from client documentation to ensure accuracy.
- The personnel involved: their main interests; the level of their technical expertise, particularly in relation to your products and services; the interpersonal relationships between them. (You will need to 'pitch' your presentation according to the culture of the organization and the apparent power bases.)

- The state of the relevant industry: whether it is a new industry; if it is expanding or declining; who are the major competitors, etc.
- Major problems currently faced by the organization: a SWOT and STEP analysis is useful here, but at the very least you should discover whether the industry confronts the possibility of takeover; the implications of any major technological advances; important changes which are either pending or being avoided by the organization.
- The reasons the customer wishes to consider your proposal: it may be purely economic; for example, a local authority may be more interested in in-company training provided by an academic institution than a leading consultancy, based purely on the costs involved; whether they are seeking to short-circuit any improvements they should be considering; perhaps your product or service is of higher quality standards than others, and so on.

You should dentify the prospective decision makers and pitch your presentation according to expertise, degree of influence, the role they perform (their information needs will vary accordingly). You should also gain information quickly and effectively. Make full use of published material, knowledge held by colleagues and associates and use questioning techniques appropriate to eliciting free-speaking (open-ended questions) and specific information (closed questions).

Find out what the customer needs and how you can meet the need

- Actively identify needs by responding fully to expressed (recognized) needs and seeking out unrecognized (but real) needs. Needs may be personal, task oriented, or organizational.
- Decide which services could be helpful in meeting needs and assisting in the solution of problems, identify the benefits and link a feature (attributes of the service) to the benefit (what's in it for the customer) it brings.
- Customers do not buy services; they are looking for a bundle of benefits.
- Analyse the strengths and weaknesses of your organization's services; demonstrate the strengths and minimize the weaknesses.
- Demonstrate clearly what your organization can do more effectively than any other.
- Assess the personalities on your team as appropriate counterparts to the customer's team of decision makers.

How to make the sale

- Be effective: the content of your delivery should match the customer's needs and your delivery should demonstrate that you are confident, perceptive, responsive and enthusiastic. You should use humour, listening skills and show ability to think on your feet; provide all information needed for the customer to make a decision; present information with different emphases according to the individuals in your audience.
- Present the right image – personal and professional.
- Communicate with skill (as discussed in other chapters of this book).
- Deal with objections: anticipate them and formulate responses; seek to forestall them; if raised, respond to them by probing the nature of the problem – an apparent objection may be a device to seek further information.
- Find out about your competitors: who they are; where they are; their strengths and weaknesses and which major strengths you will have to compete against in this instance.

If you are unsuccessful!

Failure to obtain an organization's commitment is still a valuable learning experience. Capitalize on the investment put into it:

- Review the whole process.
- Identify precisely what you have learned.
- Identify other opportunities for your services or products.
- Build contacts.

THE VALUE AND USE OF ADVERTISING AND PUBLIC RELATIONS

Advertising

Advertising has been called 'the means of making known in order to sell goods and services'. It is easy to associate advertising with the high-profile, expensive TV campaigns, but advertising can be carried in many different media:

- Press
- TV
- Posters and transport
- Cinema
- Radio
- Direct mail

The choice depends on a number of factors, one of the most important of which is budget. There are, of course, other considerations. Examples would be the difference between trade and consumer advertising, and the amount of information needed to convey the message, or arouse interest. For instance, it would be difficult to describe the features of a high-tech item of equipment in a short TV ad, but it could be used to stimulate interest. Instructions can be provided for potential customers to seek further information.

Marketing tasks that can be performed well by advertising include:

- New product/service launches
- Complementing face-to-face or telephone advertising activities
- Entering new markets
- Inviting enquiries
- Direct selling
- Creating images
- Selling services

Although many small and medium-sized enterprises will devise and execute advertising campaigns for themselves, larger companies will use specialist agencies to do this work for them. People who do this need to know how to get the best from such agencies, and their priorities and methods of working are instructive for the 'do-it-yourself' organizations.

Advertising agencies

Agencies have all the experience, expertise and resources necessary to manage the complex processes involved in any campaign. They are organized into specialist departments which undertake different functional activities. These usually include:

- *Creative Department* These include the thinkers and visualizers, whose job it is to create concepts and ideas from a brief.
- *Media Department* who recommend an appropriate medium for a campaign, and who can also 'buy' the space for the individual advertisements.
- *Production Department* Their job is the writing, design, illustration, photography, film and print, to realize a concept.
- *Account Management* whose job it is to manage the whole process to budget and schedule, and to act as liaison with the client.

Choosing an agency

Of course, there are many ways of choosing an agency. A common method for major accounts is called competitive pitching. In this, a number of agencies are invited to work up creative ideas in response to a written brief. This can work very well for the client, as they can judge the potential effectiveness of a campaign from the ideas proposed.

Not all agencies will expend the time and effort needed for this process. For instance, Bartle, Bogle and Hegarty are famous for declining to do just that. They will produce a credentials briefing, where they provide evidence of success based on completed projects. Only when they are contracted will they throw the full weight of their creative team into a campaign.

The brief

The needs of the client are specified in a document called a brief. Because it is the basis from which the creative team builds the campaign, it must contain all the information they need, and it is vital to get it right. It is quite common for the agency to assist the client in drawing up the brief. Some are expert at turning the vague statements and ideas of the client into a powerful and workable brief. However, it is preferable for the client to control the whole process and better results will be obtained if they can communicate their needs clearly to the agency.

The brief should cover five main areas:

- Objectives and tasks
- Background to company and products/services
- Target markets
- Constraints/issues/interests
- Media

The more clues provided, the more accurate the response is likely to be.

Public relations

The function

Public relations (or PR) is the range of activities that seeks to place messages and ideas about organizations and products or services in the media. Unlike advertising, it does not prepare and control specific adverts, but seeks to gain profile through news and features. However, it is not concerned solely with print media, and it can encompass a huge variety of activities. Among them are:

- Press releases
- Research reports
- Events, such as conferences (including press conferences)
- Personal appearances, e.g. on TV or radio talk shows

- Crisis management
- Information services
- Specific briefings, e.g. for financial journalists
- Sponsorship

Quite often, some of the basic activities are covered by in-house press and publicity departments. Even where there is an internal service, one of its functions may be to brief and contract the outside specialist services of a PR consultancy. As well as having the whole range of expertise necessary to manage a campaign on a day-to-day basis, such agencies also have established contacts with people in the trade or consumer press, and can often place features, or gain exposure for press information beneficial to their clients.

As with advertising agencies, PR consultancies vary in their strengths, and in the services they offer. Some of this information can be obtained from trade directories such as *Hollis*, but a credentials pitch for a number of likely candidates is a better way to get a feel for the strengths of an agency. They differ in a number of ways:

- *Size*   from an individual consultant, up to the large consultancies like Biss Lancaster or the Rowland group
- *Style*   from the traditional to the more youthful and upmarket agencies like Lynne Franks
- *Specialisms*   most agencies are generic, but all have particular specialisms like finance, fashion or leisure.

Although it may seem like a soft spend, with little chance of auditing its own effectiveness, PR should be able to quantitatively justify its activities, like any other area of the business. If you wish to commission a PR consultancy you should expect them to project cost-benefits from the work they do. One of the best measures of their effectiveness is the amount of column inches of advertising space that they have gained on your behalf. This can be costed quite easily.

The brief

As with advertising agencies, PR consultancies work best when they are properly briefed. The same criteria apply, and so the brief should contain:

- Objectives and tasks
- Background to company and products
- Target markets (this could include customers, employees, shareholders, community and all other stakeholders)
- Constraints/issues/interests
- Media

In response to this brief, the consultancy should offer a complete service to manage outgoing information to reach target markets, whether they be trade or consumer, and it should specify the targeted media and the means of reaching them.

Campaigns usually involve a mixture of ongoing press activities, together with specific projects aimed at particular targets. In fact, it should be possible to list activities and target groups separately. Alternatively, they can be shown in a matrix, giving specific details.

In order to draw up a PR programme for a local building project, for example, it would be necessary to start by defining the target groups that need to be reached. These might include:

- Banks/financial institutions
- Department of Environment
- Local planning authorities
- Local politicians
- National pressure groups
- Local residents
- Press
- Local pressure groups
- Professionals

Events and activities might include:

- Information pack
- Visits to site
- Press releases/articles
- Press conferences
- Photographs
- Competition/education
- Exhibitions

These can then be plotted on a two by two matrix, and details added (see Figure 6.2).

OTHER MARKETING COMMUNICATIONS

There are a number of other means of promoting profile, products and services direct to potential customers. These can be broadly classified as marketing communications, and highlighted here are a few of the most important ones.

Direct mail

Direct mail is the sending of information to specified and identified target individuals or businesses. As end-user consumers, we often call it junk mail. Despite some negative connotations to the concept, its wide use testifies to its effectiveness, when it is well done and properly targeted. It usually contains product or service information, together with some sort of inducement to buy. Two of the most popular forms are leaflets and letters.

	Banks	DoE	Local groups	Politicians	National groups	Residents etc.
Information packs						
Visits to site						
Press releases						
Press conferences						
Photographs						
Competitions						
Exhibitions						

Figure 6.2   PR matrix for local building project

As a receiver of junk mail yourself, you will know that the one thing you do not want with unsolicited mail is to work hard to understand its meaning, or to respond to it. Therefore, simplicity, directness and brevity are the key to its success. The most usual mistake is to try to send too many messages, and too much information. Ideally, there should be a single, simple message, whether contained in a letter or a leaflet.

In a letter, you should begin with a sentence that catches the interest and imagination. This should then be followed by the claim, and the justification for that claim. You must then make it clear how people should respond – and make it as easy as possible to do just that (Complete the form, send it off ...). It is not expensive to arrange a Freepost reply facility. This also attracts potential customers, not only because it is easy but because they do not have to pay.

To summarize, an effective formula is:

Did you know? – identify the problem
Look at this – here is the solution
Now do this – how to respond

Technology can help enormously in making direct mail effective. There are three main aspects to this:

1   *Consumer databases*   It is possible to buy names and addresses that correspond to specified criteria such as

income, status, demography, etc. The more constraints you specify, the more you pay for each name.

2   *Wordprocessing/DTP*   These systems can enable you to design and produce quite effective and inexpensive letters or leaflets within your organization.

3   *Mailmerge*   Lists of names and addresses can be supplied or entered into a database, and this can be linked to the word-processor package via a mailmerge package. This customizes each letter for the named individual and can also produce address labels.

Brochures

Brochures and other specialist publications can be a very effective means of influencing potential customers. They can carry not only written information but also photographs or illustrations that show products in a very positive light, and design can be branded which can promote very positive images. In order to achieve these effects, however, professionalism is required. Often, this expertise is available within an organization, but even large companies often sub-contract agencies or freelancers to produce specific projects.

Whether the publication is to be produced internally or externally, it is the brief that is all-important. The brief should reference similar elements to advertising or PR briefs. In addition, it should also be explicit about content, style, the nature and extent of illustration and the format (size, number of colours, etc.).

Video recordings

The potential of video recording is being realized increasingly. Its use can range from sales presentations or product briefings through footage for press and publicity purposes, to in-company newsletters. In terms of execution, many of the comments about brochures also apply. That is, use specialists and brief them properly.

These are well-used and popular forms of marketing communications. But all companies are individual in their needs, and often specific requirements can be satisfied by a different or more imaginative approach, for example:

A major manufacturer of domestic electronic goods had a problem in that it was reliant on the sales staff of the major electrical retailers to promote its products. It needed to educate them in the benefits and features of its products and to encourage them to promote them to customers.

Their solution was to provide a sales training kit. It included:

■   Advice on sales technique

- Market information
- Five reasons for buying their equipment
- Information about how the equipment worked
- Features and benefits of their products
- A script for a face-to-face sales presentation

All this was supplied in filofax format, which was known to be useful and attractive to sales staff.

PREPARING FOR ACTION PLANNING

Remember the checklist of questions identified in the Introduction to this book? Try them again to identify your further development needs. We have reproduced those most appropriate to this chapter to help you. You will need to adapt them to the issues discussed.

How do you find out about your customer's needs?

How do you make customers aware that your products/ services are available?

How effective are the communication mechanisms that you use?

What would you do if there was a low take-up of the products/services you provide?

How do you deal with any customer complaints?

How do you handle health and safety issues at your workplace?

How appropriate is your location for the product/service you provide?

Which outside agencies do you currently liaise with?

Are there any joint working arrangements in your product/service provision (this may apply across teams, or between organizations)?

Who are these and for what purposes do the arrangements exist?

What actions would you/have you taken with others at times of particular difficulty or change?

Which methods do you use to analyse facts and figures for your job purposes?

How do you present these facts and figures to others for decision-making purposes?

How effective are your analytical and mathematical skills in convincing others?

Were the outcomes of these presentations appropriate for the decision-making purposes?

How might you improve your analytical and mathematical skills?

How do you liaise with others at off-site locations?

How is information fed back into the decision-making process?

What, if any, interdepartmental group activities do you participate in?

What are the main purposes of these groups?

What are the main working relationships you maintain?

How do you/would you maximize productive relationships and networks?

What are the key elements, in your opinion, in promoting effective working relationships?

What do you see as your strengths in establishing good working relationships and which aspects would you want to develop further?

How would you/do you go about establishing and developing working relationships with others, both internal and external to the organization?

What formal and informal actions would you/have you taken to actively promote effective working relationships and prevent their breakdown?

What methods do you use to give feedback to others about their performance?

Can you pinpoint anything which you consider particularly important when giving feedback?

How do you address equal opportunities issues into this aspect of your work?

What information do you need to do your job and for what purposes?

Do you have any problems obtaining this information?

To whom do you supply information?

How much time do you spend in:
- Gathering information?
- Analysing information?
- Providing information?

How do go about gathering, analysing and providing information?

Can these methods be improved?

How do you currently store and receive information?

How often do you hold meetings (formal and informal), briefings and group discussions?

For what purposes do you hold meetings etc.?

Do you always have the necessary information in advance of the meetings?

Do you always supply the necessary information in advance of the meetings?

What are the meetings' follow-up processes?
Do your meetings result in positive action?
Have you attended committees in your current role and prepared reports for these committees?

Questions devised by, and adapted from, the Crediting Competence Team at South Bank University and reproduced with permission.

FURTHER READING

Fisher, R. and Ury, W. (1984), *Getting to Yes*, Hutchinson Business Books, London.
Kotler, P. (1984), *Marketing Management: Analysis, Planning and Control*, Prentice Hall, Englewood Cliffs, NJ.
Peel, M. (1987), *Customer Service*, Kogan Page, London.
Training Agency, The Training Research Advisory Consultancy Enterprises Ltd (1990), *Marketing Training*, Pittsburg Press, PA.

7 Self-confidence and personal drive

Managers with self-confidence and personal drive show resilience and determination to succeed in the face of pressure and difficulties.

INTRODUCING THE RELATIONSHIP BETWEEN THE MCI PERSONAL COMPETENCY MODEL AND SELF-CONFIDENCE AND PERSONAL DRIVE

The MCI Integrated *Model of Personal Competency* identifies the behaviours and skills necessary for you to develop, before you are able to prove competence in any managerial function. This chapter attempts to deal with the various behaviours and skills necessary for you to apply across all managerial functions, transferring your learning to different occasions, at different times and under varying circumstances (contexts), consistently. The outcomes below, as identified within this section of the model, should be borne in mind while you work through this chapter.

Outcomes required for self-confidence and personal drive

In demonstrating this behaviour, the manager:

- Takes a leading role in initiating action and making decisions
- Takes personal responsibility for making things happen
- Takes control of situations and events
- Acts in an assured and unhesitating manner when faced with a challenge
- Says no to unreasonable requests
- States his or her own position and views clearly in conflict situations

■   Maintains beliefs, commitment and effort in spite of set-backs or opposition.

INTRODUCTION TO SELF-CONFIDENCE AND PERSONAL DRIVE

Organizations are presented with opportunities for constant change and improvement, requiring shifts in emphasis on skills requirements, external relationships, new methods of service and product development and provision. This constant need for change requires *growth* in ways rather different from the traditional economic term; growth in the new sense refers to growth of a more *personal* nature, contributing to the whole.

If organizations do not respond to and then create these opportunities for themselves, continued success will elude them. This factor alone places heavy responsibility on individual managers to keep two major needs in mind:

1   Managers must continually develop themselves to perform effectively against the current and medium-term organizational developments.
2   Managers must constantly predict future opportunities for organizational development and thereby ascertain their individual development needs accordingly

The responsibilities and accountabilities of individual managers may once have been clear-cut, with obvious lines of authority, clear progression routes and career paths based on those ahead of them in the hierarchy. The responsibility now lies with individual managers to plan their own progression routes and career paths, identifying their own development needs as may be required by the organization. It is also more likely that many managers will find that ultimately these paths may take them across organizations, especially where they identify their own talents and potential as being more appropriate elsewhere.

These constant changes, therefore, require all managers to specifically focus on what their future requirements for self-confidence and personal drive actually mean. More will need to identify the importance of this behaviour because they manage contracts for sponsors external to the organization. Such behaviour requires different applications to that which can be demonstrated within the organization and is often not just a matter of transferring their successes across different circumstances.

Much of our current behaviour has been derived through our experiences with known colleagues, a recognized organizational culture, and existing managerial structures. Every new contract entered into with those external to the organization will require a more flexible view of individual behaviour and interrelationships. At the same time, we must demonstrate the same outcomes detailed at the beginning of this chapter.

In learning to become self-confident and to exhibit personal drive, you will need to analyse your behaviour both in terms of your own activities and while dealing with others, which in turn affects their behaviour towards you and the effectiveness of the job they do. You will also need to use this chapter in association with Chapter 8, which discusses managing stress and managing personal learning and development.

Based on the assumption that you are using Chapters 7 and 8 together, you will understand that your personal skills will depend on your stage of personal development, the amount of managerial experience received and what opportunities you have had for applying the knowledge you are building.

KEEPING ABREAST OF CHANGES

In building your self-confidence and personal drive, it is essential that you maintain and improve your managerial knowledge and understanding of external and internal changes and potential changes which will influence your development needs. You should regularly scan appropriate news reports which can and will directly and indirectly affect the environment within which you manage.

EXERCISE

Identify current or potential changes, or changing situations, influencing your organization and decide how you might personally contribute to developments.

INDIVIDUAL BEHAVIOUR

One of the more traditional attitudes has presented many people, living and working in the UK, with difficulties in promoting their own strengths and good features. Upbringing has determined that such a characteristic would be seen by others as conceited and inappropriate. In general, this attitude has presented two extremes of behaviour in such people, both resulting in the inability to identify and promote strengths and, by definition, in being unable to positively address their weaknesses.

First is *false modesty*; this is where individuals say they are not good at something while, all the time, considering that they really are. Second is *underconfidence*; where individuals really believe that they are weak or lacking in some way, through years of either hiding their strengths because they have grown to believe they are inadequate or genuinely denying that they possess them in the first place. This second attitude can, of course, become a self-fulfilling prophecy; believe that a thing is such and it will inevitably come about!

People who exhibit false modesty are also underconfident, but in a different way. They know they have strengths, along with some weaknesses which they are frightened of showing. Past experience may have taught them that they must not reveal any weaknesses at work, or that they may be penalized in some way. Rather than reveal them and seek support in overcoming them, they have been shocked into denying their existence.

In order to hide any weaknesses then, people exhibiting false modesty will openly deny any strengths at all, knowing that others can see how good they really are. Their intention in exhibiting this behaviour is to confuse others and hope that their weaknesses will be hidden beneath, what they believe, are their obvious strengths.

Other cultures, most notably North American and some European, do not share these problems in the same way. Indeed it is considered a weakness *not* to highlight and promote their strengths, as to do so could limit their career opportunities and personal development. Only by acknowledging their strengths openly, it is believed, will it be possible for individuals to learn the opinions of others. In learning whether or not others agree, they will then be able to confront any differences of opinion, decide for themselves who is right and, most importantly, what can be done about it, or whether anything actually needs to be done. Self-confidence allows us to decide for ourselves and act accordingly.

In learning to deal with our strengths in this way we are also able to confront and deal with our weaknesses. We can *balance our act*, so to speak. We know we cannot be good at everything, that some things come more naturally to us than others. Once we accept this, it is then less personally destructive to accept that we have to learn to overcome our weaknesses, or develop the behaviour we believe will ultimately be more positive and rewarding.

Gender and cultural differences

Little research has yet been carried out on these differences, but managers are becoming more aware of the varying behaviours exhibited by people from different racial, educational and cultural backgrounds. What may be considered by one group to be acceptable and the *right* approach to take could well be considered rude and unacceptable by another.

As managers, we all have a responsibility to get to know and understand those with whom we work. Even differences in people's *perceived* class status and regional background will affect their own and others' behaviour. If we spend more time getting to know about people in the beginning, the less time will be wasted later on as misunderstandings become greater and more serious through ignorance of the more subtle differences. It is these very differences which bring together the many and varied skills and abilities we need for effective work performance.

We should also study the differences between how men and women interrelate: woman to woman; man to man; woman to man; man to woman. There are significant differences between the way men and women interrelate and communicate with and between each other which are further affected by the differences between the racial, cultural, educational backgrounds, as well as people's expectations, their prejudices, stereotypical beliefs, values and so on.

All this might appear to be a very complex and daunting task for the newly appointed manager, but it can be a fascinating challenge which will help alleviate the longer-term frictions and conflicts that will occur if the need to understand the differences is ignored or postponed.

Understanding and leading others

There are many aspects both within the organization and external to it which affect managers' ability to make things happen through their own self-confidence and personal drive. It is therefore important for them to know what these factors are and to understand how they influence their own as well as the behaviour of others.

Simply put, individual factors will have been created by upbringing, family background, class and ethnic culture as well as educational opportunities, all of which will have affected people's beliefs, expectations and values. On top of this, there will be personal work experiences which are taken with them from job to job, whether or not they are appropriate or valid. Individuals are often recruited who will reflect the appropriate culture, while others may be recruited with change in mind. Very often there is no certainty about this, only hope that people will integrate and/or influence the culture positively and promote effective performance overall.

Individual behaviour and customer relations

Everyone would agree that customers (internal and external) are important to any organization. However, not everyone demonstrates an understanding of the intricacies involved in meeting people's needs. In attempting to meet anyone's needs, we have to take into account individual human behaviour and how differences of opinion and attitude can have a bearing on how the organization is *perceived* as being concerned with meeting customers' needs.

Your organization may have an overall strategy to address needs in terms of the product or service provided, but somehow not quite meet those needs in the way the behaviour of individuals affects how activities are planned and carried out. As well as producing a statement of recognised need, the customer will have an expectation of the *way* in which that need should be met, which should also reflect an understanding of the benefits derived from having the need met.

When your organization plans to identify and meet customer requirements, it is in fact also planning to meet its own requirements – meeting objectives and retaining a *competitive edge* for long-term survival. Individual behaviour and commitment of those carrying out the necessary activities is, therefore, crucial to these outcomes.

Think of a situation where you to had to take a leading role in initiating and taking action (preferably at work, but if not any area of your social life will be also be appropriate). Did you also have to control people's behaviour to ensure an effective outcome? If so, how did you achieve this?

ASSERTIVENESS AND HOW TO DEVELOP IT

What is assertiveness?

Assertiveness is about speaking one's mind openly and objectively, without undue emotion. It is the art of clear and direct communication. Being assertive enables you to: express personal feelings to others; be direct and ask for what you want; say *No* clearly and firmly without causing offence when you do not want to follow a certain course of action. It allows you to take responsibility when necessary; say what you mean clearly and confidently and stand up for your rights (Hind, 1989).

The most important distinction which must be made is between assertiveness and aggression. It is much easier for some people to be aggressive, but it is very ineffective. Those for whom aggression is the norm are unable to demonstrate their assertiveness for some reason; it may be that their experience has led them into this behaviour as the result of others not listening to them. It may simply be that they are insufficiently confident in their own abilities or the strength of their arguments and, believing others will not accept their 'reasons' under any circumstances, they have to force their opinions and beliefs onto others.

Aggressors tend to rally support from surrounding colleagues and subordinates; they achieve this either through others' fear of their power or as the result of their perceived past successes. Aggressors' behaviour towards those with opposing views who are not themselves sufficiently assertive will either breed aggression in return or encourage avoidance by those whom they wish to influence or *bully*. Either way, nothing will be achieved and the problems will continue.

Assertiveness is about standing up for our beliefs and interests and at the same time taking into account the beliefs and interests of others. While the display of aggression is a *forcefulness* in conveying our beliefs and interests and *not* listening to others, being assertive is *confidently* and politely communicating thoughts, as well as *listening* to others. Also, assertive people who know their own minds are not afraid of the influence of other people's view and opinions, where the outcomes may prove to be more positive or rewarding in order to achieve individual and organizational objectives.

Making and refusing a request

If we transmit to others the full facts relating to our reasons for making or refusing a request, in most cases people will genuinely understand and do their best to assist us when trying to achieve our objectives. By detailing exactly what our situation is, most people would respond positively, and assertively in return. Agreements are mostly reached when both parties are behaving reasonably and considerately.

As is implied in this statement, the tone of our voice and the inference behind the words we use are important factors in transmitting our views and opinions assertively. Politeness is essential, extreme politeness is not assertiveness and would be seen as insincere and is unlikely to promote the desired response in others. (See also Chapter 2 for ideas relating to *body language, tone and pitch of voice* when communicating with others.)

Coping with refusal

There are bound to be occasions when you are denied your request. If this is genuine you need to accept the reasons positively and compromise accordingly, occasionally requiring a completely different answer, or approach, to the problem. Sometimes a refusal may be made by someone who does not have the authority to refuse that request. Again, there is no need to wield your own authority; a negotiated agreement can be reached and should be attempted before moving on to an alternative solution.

Standing up for your rights

Nervous or timid people sometimes have difficulty in saying 'no', even when it is justified. Such people will often take on more and more work and then everyone is surprised when jobs are not completed on time or to the right standard. Managers must remember this when dealing with others if they appear to never say 'no' regardless of how busy they are. Managers must always be aware of the level of work being carried out by all those involved in activities or projects for which they are responsible, and people's workloads must be reviewed and discussed along with other factors in the progress of work being carried out. The organizational objectives, as well as the control of individual stress levels, depend upon managers' personal skills in achieving them.

Managers can help others to say 'no' appropriately by keeping in touch with how they think they are doing; whether they are overworked or not; by finding out the level of work they may be receiving from other managers and so on. When people are asked frequently about their level of involvement they find it easier to express how they really feel, because they will then become more relaxed and learn that the manager is being fair and reasonable.

The secret in you developing your own *self-confidence and personal drive* lies with your ability in recognizing the need for and providing the *wherewithal* for others to build their skills similarly. This approach will then help build positive working relationships and greater commitment to objectives. (See also Chapter 1 to *manage and obtain the commitment of others.*)

Passive behaviour

People exhibiting passive or compliant behaviour usually have come from a background where other people's expectations are that they should behave in this way. Women from many cultures, for example, have been brought up to be obedient to their fathers, brothers and eventually, their husbands also. It is not too difficult to understand how that then becomes translated into *appropriate* and *acceptable* behaviour at work. The working environment itself often expects particular patterns of behaviour from people of varying backgrounds and particularly between the sexes. Many organizations still hold traditional views about the roles of men and women in society.

Where men will largely be encouraged to be competitive, assertive, performance oriented and demanding, similar behaviour in women is often criticized as being jealous, aggressive, overdemanding and selfish. While many occupations are experiencing changed perspectives in the accepted behaviour of men and women, even the most enlightened organizations have their examples of work roles occupied by women exhibiting the passive, compliant behaviours still frequently expected of them, e.g. typists, administrators, cleaners, junior clerks, factory operators and assemblers, etc. The jobs themselves often attract women, and sometimes older men, interested in part-time or flexible work requiring little commitment beyond the hours actually worked.

Most of the job roles in question are of low status, are poorly paid and are often the first to be lost in times of recession. It is very difficult for people to exhibit assertive characteristics when their very livelihood is constantly under threat.

Giving and receiving criticism

In receiving criticism it can be helpful to seek advice from your critic. In discussing the advice, objectively and positively, it is possible that the initial criticism will become less daunting for both parties and a better approach to future behaviour can be developed between you.

Similarly, in giving criticism, it could prove fruitful for you to start by questioning others about whether they believe the outcomes of their action were what they had anticipated. If they are unhappy with these outcomes it follows naturally that you should then ask them why they believe this to be so. They may not have considered that their own behaviour could have brought about more desired outcomes. Whatever discussions ensue, you should offer advice for future development. Those you are criticizing should be in no doubt that you are giving it but, at the same time, they will need assurance that you are prepared to help them to recognize their failings and how they might improve their behaviour.

Handling disagreements and conflict

Conflict exists everywhere, and often provides the basic context in which we need to negotiate. (See also Chapter 5 for further information on negotiating.)

We bring values, attitudes, beliefs, needs and perceptions to any situation and it is inevitable that these will be opposed by those people who have different ones. This then causes conflict. What is important is how we deal with conflict. We can ignore it, seek solutions, or seek to control it. An important element is whether it adversely affects relations within an organization.

However, we are used to and experienced in dealing with conflicts in our everyday lives; house hunting, buying cars, how to be entertained, etc. It can create emotional reaction – anger, hostility, frustration, pain. We should recognize these and avoid them wherever possible.

There are also some important equal opportunities implications in the way we deal with conflict, and from an interview held recently with a manager of a culturally diverse organization it can be concluded that a lot of ignorance exists regarding the differences of opinion, attitudes and beliefs, with conflicting results. The manager concerned believes there is the need for confrontation to promote awareness and education, but that unless it is handled carefully with extra firmness and precision over the rules governing sensitive issues like equal opportunities, unhealthy conflict and stress will result.

Negotiation, then, is often needed to resolve conflict. Resolving conflict does not mean just *winning*, which implies someone losing. It means satisfying the interests of all concerned. Satisfying interests on both sides of a conflict or negotiation situation is called a *win–win* outcome. It can only be achieved by understanding the needs or interests of all concerned.

Mediating

Mediating in a conflict is a task that often falls to managers and can be fraught with difficulty. It should be dealt with as the facilitation of the agreement-seeking process by a third party (the manager). In mediating successfully you should:

- Acknowledge conflict; if conflict is ignored, it will become difficult to control. Healthy conflict, when it is acknowledged, used and ideas are allowed to develop can lead to positive outcomes. When potential conflict can be identified and deemed unnecessary, it should be *nipped in the bud* and thus avoided.
- Be neutral in relation to people; if you appear to take any one particular side when trying to mediate, you will not be mediating at all, but applying extra pressures to influence the behaviour of the other party. Allow each to have their say and facilitate the parties' agreement for a way forward.

■ Keep to issues; do not allow personalities to be discussed or questioned. The issues surrounding the conflict should be discussed openly and objectively, thus keeping emotions to a minimum. It should be noted that sometimes it is impossible to keep emotion out of situations and those who feel that strongly about the issues should not be dismissed by anyone as irrational because of it.

■ Seek clarification; be sure that everyone really understands what is being said by clarifying understanding and summarizing frequently.

■ Focus on agreement; agreeing a way forward is what you should be trying to achieve. Ensure the parties are positively trying to agree on ways that each can work with.

■ Be facilitator, not judge; a judge states the 'crime' and pronounces the 'sentence' or punishment; a facilitator allows discussion of issues, provides the wherewithal for agreement and allows the parties concerned to reach their own conclusions and decide upon methods for resolving the difficulties.

EXERCISE

Identify any situation with which you have been involved and analyse your and others' behaviour in terms of assertiveness, aggression, handling conflict etc. How positive or negative were the outcomes of this situation and why do you think this?

PREPARING FOR ACTION PLANNING

Remember the checklist of questions identified in the Introduction to this book? Try them again to identify your further development needs. We have reproduced those most appropriate to this chapter to help you. You will need to adapt them to the issues discussed.

What actions would you/have you taken with others at times of particular difficulty or change?

Which methods do you use to analyse facts and figures for your job purposes?

How do you present these facts and figures to others for decision-making purposes?

How effective are your analytical and mathematical skills in convincing others?

Were these outcomes of these presentations appropriate for the decision-making purposes?

How might you improve your analytical and mathematical skills?

What, if any, interdepartmental group activities do you participate in?

What are the main purposes of these groups?

How easy/difficult do you find asking support of or taking problems to others?

How might this be improved?

How easy/difficult do you think others find asking you for support or in bringing their problems to you?

How could it be improved?

What support would you/do you give to others in their relations with others outside the organization (or department)?

How could these relationships be improved?

What formal and informal actions would you/have you taken to actively promote effective working relationships and prevent their breakdown?

How do you/would you deal with conflict in your relationships or in the relationships of others?

Are you, do you think, making the most use of the skills available to you (yours and others)?

How does this tie in with the overall work objectives set?

What information do you need to do your job and for what purposes?

Do you have any problems obtaining this information?

To whom do you supply information?

How do you currently store and receive information?

How often do you hold meetings (formal and informal), briefings and group discussions?

For what purposes do you hold meetings etc.?

Do your meetings always (often, sometimes, rarely) :
- Start on time?
- Finish on time?
- Achieve their objectives?

Do you always have the necessary information in advance of the meetings?

Do you always supply the necessary information in advance of the meetings?

Are you confident about:
- Chairing meetings?
- Contributing to the purpose of meetings?
- Taking minutes?

Would you say your meetings are always
- Well prepared?

■   Well administered?
■   Well controlled?
What are the meetings' follow-up processes?
Do your meetings result in positive action?
Have you attended committees in your current role and
prepared reports for these committees?
Were your conclusions and recommendations (where
appropriate) acted upon?

*Questions devised by, and adapted from, the Crediting Competence Team at
South Bank University and reproduced with permission.*

ACTION PLANNING

Analyse your own behaviour in terms of strengths (positive outcomes) and weaknesses (negative effects), in
dealing with actual work-based occurrences with regards
to the various situations discussed and the outcomes identified at the beginning of this chapter.

Decide how you might deal with them differently in
the future and what are your immediate training requirements and future development needs.

Discuss them with appropriate others and negotiate
how you might address them.

FURTHER READING

Cameron, Sheila and Pearce, Sue (1995), *The Management Studies Handbook*,
Chapters 5, 11 and 12, Pitman Publishing, London.
Davis, Stanley M. (1988), *2001 Management: Managing the Future Now*,
Simon & Schuster, London.
Drucker, Peter F. (1992), *Managing for the Future*, Butterworth-Heinemann,
Oxford.
Handy, Charles B. (1985), *Understanding Organizations*, 3rd edn, Penguin
Books, London.
Honey, P. and Mumford, A. (1990), *The Manual of Learning Opportunities*,
Peter Honey, Maidenhead.
Pedler, M. and Boydell, T. (1985), *Managing Yourself*, Fontana, London.

8 Self-management

Managers skilled in managing themselves show adaptability to the changing world, taking advantage of new ways of doing things.

INTRODUCING THE RELATIONSHIP BETWEEN THE MCI PERSONAL COMPETENCY MODEL AND SELF-MANAGEMENT

The MCI Integrated *Model of Personal Competency* identifies the behaviours and skills necessary for you to develop, before you are able to prove competence in any managerial function. This chapter attempts to deal with the various behaviours and skills necessary for you to apply across all managerial functions, transferring your learning to different occasions, at different times and under varying circumstances (contexts), consistently. The outcomes below, as identified within this section of the model, should be borne in mind while you work through this chapter.

Outcomes required for self-management

There are two major sets of behaviour highlighted in this chapter, the first concentrating on the importance of the individual manager's *Self-control*, whereby he or she focuses on his or her own stress management, and *Managing personal learning and development*. In order to maintain *Self-control* the manager:

- Gives a consistent and stable performance
- Takes action to reduce the causes of stress
- Accepts personal comments or criticism without becoming defensive or offensive
- Remains calm in difficult or uncertain situations
- Handles others' emotions without becoming personally involved in them.

The second behavioural set focuses on *Managing personal learning and development*. In this situation, the manager:

- Takes responsibility for meeting his or her own learning and development needs
- Seeks feedback on performance to identify his or her own strengths and weaknesses
- Learns from his or her own mistakes and those of others
- Changes behaviour where needed as a result of feedback
- Reflects systematically on own performance and modifies behaviour accordingly
- Develops self to meet the competence demand of changing situations
- Transfers learning from one situation to another.

INTRODUCTION TO SELF-MANAGEMENT

This chapter focuses on the personal management of the individual, whereby effective outcomes will result in better relationships with others. As a person with your own unique strengths and development needs, your ultimate choice of techniques to achieve personal competency in *Self-management* will depend very much on how you see yourself now, and where and how you wish to apply the skill in the future. The key to self-management lies within your ability to identify and manage your own stress levels, your time and the functional and behavioural aspects appropriate to your job role.

STRESS AND THE MANAGER

This section sets out to examine the nature of stress and how it might be managed. Stress, or excessive stress and pressure (distress), is a problem for many people as well managers. There are various ways to identify the causes of stress and of taking action in order to reduce it. Some will be explored here; you are invited to analyse the affects of stress in your own working environment and to determine how they might further be reduced.

Since everyone behaves differently, the diagnosis of stress symptoms can seem difficult. It is also a very sensitive issue for many people who might feel to experience and show signs of stress is unprofessional and a serious weakness.

What is even worse is that you might not even know you are suffering from stress. It sometimes requires the intervention of a third party to point out that the behaviours you are exhibiting could be proof that your stress levels have increased.

You must first understand that the weakness lies in denying the potential and reality of stress and not in suffering from it. Once you accept the existence of stress, you can then take measures to reduce its effects.

WHAT IS STRESS

Stress is 'a mismatch between perceived demands and perceived ability to cope. It is the balance between how we view demands and how we think we can cope

with those demands that determines whether we feel no stress, distressed or ...
challenged in a way we feel we can handle' (adapted from Looker and Gregson,
1989, p. 29).

Almost everyone, from all walks of life, has a view about stress. Concern
is expressed about the stress associated with such things as:

Unemployment
Raising a family
Illness
Caring for a dependent relative
Moving house
Death of a relative
Relationship or marital problems

EXERCISE

In order to start you thinking about stress, try to list at
least three different sources of stress (other than those
already listed above) in the everyday life of yourself or a
person familiar to you .

1 _____

2 _____

3 _____

Further? 4_____   5_____   6_____

- The things you have listed may have been associated with
  particular life events or changes – a holiday or someone
  leaving home.
- They may have been environmentally related – 'it's not
  safe to go out at night on my own'.
- Perhaps they were linked to particular people – 'my boss
  causes me stress'.
- They may have touched upon how you (or the person you
  had in mind) *managed* life – 'I can never say *no* to anything so I end up doing too much'.

People express a wide range of views about the causes of stress. The sorts
of comments you hear reveal a great deal about the views of everyday managers
and staff. Cast your mind back using your own work and life experience. Recall
the comments which either you or your friends, family or work colleagues, have
made on the subject.

EXERCISE

Now on a sheet of paper complete the following sentences. There is no right or wrong answer. Photocopy the page to make it easier.

1   I find I get most stressed when .....
2   The last time I felt under stress was because of....
3   The most stressful thing about my particular job is ...
4   The most stressful aspect of working in my organization is .... I think this is because ...
5   Of all the jobs I have had, I think the most stressful to be.....................because...........
6   The sort of person who copes best with stress is ...
7   The sort of person who copes worst with stress is ...
8   What my colleagues find stressful in their work is ...
9   What I find most stressful in my private life is ...
10 The single thing an individual(s) could do in my private life, which would most reduce my stress is ...
11 The single thing my manager could do, which would most reduce my stress is ...
12 The single thing my organization could do which would most reduce my stress is ...
13 The single thing the government could do which would most reduce my stress is ...

The answers which you have given provide a picture of how you, as an individual, see stress in your own life and work. It is a brief and oversimplified picture. It does not intend to provide any indication of *how much* stress you might be under.

You may find it helpful to compare your responses with the multiple cause diagram provided in Figure 8. 1.

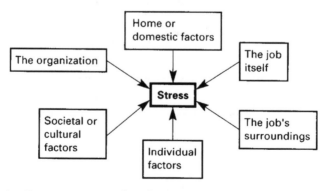

Figure 8.1   Factors associated with stress

Charles Handy (1985) has listed a number of factors associated with the *job* which contribute to stress:

Responsibility for the work of others
Responsibility for innovation
Coordination/liaison roles
Relationship problems with colleagues
Career uncertainty

Cooper *et al.* (1988) further suggests the following sources of work-related stress:

Factors associated with the job
Aspects of the individual's work role
Work-based relationships
Career issues
The structure and climate of the organization

EXERCISE

You may find it helpful at this point to review the answers you wrote to the earlier questions. Can you fit your answers into the categories which have been identified ?

STRESS PERCEPTIONS

Stress as a cause

Stress can be seen as the *cause* of problems. On an individual level we associate stress with a wide range of illnesses such as heart disease, high blood pressure, migraine, asthma, ulcers, etc. Importantly, we also see stress as having an effect upon a person's behaviour. How often have you felt a person's erratic or angry behaviour is down to *stress*?

Stress as the affect of a problem

Stress can also be viewed as the *result* of other problems. Therefore the pressure of modern life, for instance long working hours, the high rate of relationship breakup, etc., are factors which can be seen as the causes of stress.

Stress as a problem in itself

Perhaps stress is a function of how we react to pressure. Some people can cope with incidences of *stress* better than others. Therefore you should look at the actual nature of the stress you and others feel, before developing better coping mechanisms.

Stress can be seen, according to Looker and Gregson (1989), as *good, bad* or *ugly*. It is *good* in the sense that it can be associated with excitement, stimulation, creativity, success, achievement and increased productivity. It is *bad* when it is associated with boredom, frustration, distress, pressure, poor performance, unhappy and disharmonious relationships, failure. It is *ugly* when it is associated with specific health (and sometimes life-threatening) concerns such as ulcers, heart attacks, clinical depression, etc.

Stress is a word which has many meanings. It conjures up a notion of a strain; in the engineering industry, for instance, the word has a technical meaning associated with the amount of pressure a material can resist before deforming. The meaning of stress becomes enriched when applied to people because, unlike concrete, balanced people have some choice over reactions. Unlike the motorway bridge, they can engage in a range of behaviours.

Thus when applied to human behaviour stress is part of an interactive system. People's personalities vary, as do their experiences and motivation, and therefore the same amount of stress applied to different people is likely to have different results.

STRESS AS A PROCESS

Cooper *et al.* (1988) offer a way of looking at stress in terms of a process. They suggest that people generally aim for a steady state in the way they relate to the world. This suggestion is based upon models used in a range of fields (biology, physics and social science) which seek to explain behaviour as aimed at correcting a disturbance. You can see this happening in the way your own body tries to adjust when outside temperature rises or falls. If it is hot your body sweats in order to lose heat. If it is very cold then shivering is an adjustment process to enable the body to increase temperature. Both are *involuntary behaviours* over which you have little control.

Cooper *et al.* suggest that this model can apply to how we react to disturbance in our outside world. They see each person as having a stability range, within which they feel comfortable. When this stability is threatened by an outside force, then the person tries to restore the position to one of comfort. Thus stress can be seen as a feedback cycle (Figure 8.2).

We could suggest that everyone has a certain part of their life which is stable and does not change much over time. Though a person's life may appear chaotic and constantly moving, the argument is that there are *zones of stability* which each person needs and guards jealously.

THE PHYSIOLOGY OF PRESSURE OR THREAT

Pressure or threat has effects upon people in terms of their actual bodily reactions. Some of these are quite noticeable to others. Some of the effects are hormonal. They are natural and in many ways functional. Our ancestors relied upon heightened awareness at times of danger in order to survive. Animals, even domesticated ones, still rely on this. The immediate physiological effects can include:

Enlarging of pupils
Faster breathing
Faster heart rate
Paleness
Sweating
Trembling
Sickness/bowel effects

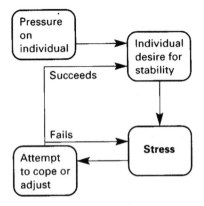

Figure 8.2   The adjustment/coping cycle (adapted from Cooper *et al.*, 1988)

SIGNS OF STRESS AT WORK

In the short term:

1 *Fight instead of flight*   the short, sharp, row. The extreme of this would be taking it out on others
2 *Flight*   going sick, leaving, retiring
3 *Internal flight*   slow down, reduce commitment

In the longer term:

1 Illness or predisposition to illness
2 Absenteeism
3 Indecision
4 Arbitrary decisions
5 Excessive eating/drinking/smoking
6 Theft

7　Workaholism
8　Avoidance or overreaction

EXERCISE

How many of these signs do you recognize in yourself or others in your workplace?

COSTS OF STRESS AT WORK

Stress obviously has a range of costs. One often-quoted figure is that in the UK £5 billion is lost each year as a result of stress affecting people at work. This figure was based upon sickness statistics where the sickness was diagnosed as anxiety or depression. Clearly this figure represents only a part of the stress-related costs. There are other effects of stress which are harder to quantify . But it would be a useful exercise to consider those possible areas of cost.

There are in fact as many costs as your imagination can cope with. If you look at the costs simply in terms of the staff-related costs there are the costs of:

- Covering for people on sick leave as a result of stress
- People leaving *before* they suffer stress-related illness
- Replacing people who leave as a result of stress (or before it becomes obvious)
- Training new people to do the job
- Paying higher salaries and benefits to *compensate* people for stress-related activity
- Costs for people who retire early for stress-related reasons.

In terms of the operations of the organization there are stress-related costs arising from:

- Mistakes being made leading to loss of business efficiency
- Accidents leading to damage to persons, equipment and buildings
- Fines imposed as a result of avoidable industrial accidents
- Disciplining and cautioning staff.

In industrial relations terms there are stress-related costs arising from:

- The residue of ill feeling harboured by stressed staff
- Industrial disputes leading to loss of business
- A lack of commitment to the organization's aims and values.

Indirectly we could attribute a stress-related cost to:

- Actual theft from the employer by staff who feel aggrieved because of the stress they are suffering
- Deliberate negligence, at times verging on sabotage, by staff who feel aggrieved because of the stress they are suffering.

Arguably we could also apportion stress-related costs arising from:

- The cost to the NHS (and thus the tax system) of treating work stress-related illness
- The cost of non-contributory benefits paid as a result of work-related stress
- The loss of tax receipts from people who cease work for stress-related reasons (though these may be part compensated by the tax receipts from people who take their jobs)
- Increases in insurance premiums arising from compensation for stress-related incidents.

We should also not forget to add in the stress-related cost arising from:

- Staff absence which is stress-related but which is not recorded as such in official statistics
- The cost of official investigations of accidents and incidents of theft or sabotage.

ORGANIZATION FACTORS

Some organizations operate in a way which inevitably is stress inducing. Where the organization is strongly sales driven and a manager or employee is only as good as their last achievement, the stress factor can be quite high. You often may hear statements like 'it's a young person's company' to describe such a situation. Advertising agencies can be stressful settings and are characterized by a young staff profile.

The nature of the organization is often a direct result of the nature of its industrial environment. It is evident that the pressure of change and the need to work increasingly more *efficiently* and *effectively*, if seen negatively and with little reward in return, can have an effect upon the level of organizational stress.

As an example of this we offer the situation of a local authority refuse collection service. Prior to the introduction of compulsory competitive tendering the service had employed a proportion of mentally handicapped operatives. After the change the dustcart crews and managers realized the implications of higher performance targets. Suddenly the mentally handicapped operatives were no longer welcome on the crews. One manager explained: 'Contract tendering places the crew under great stress to meet targets. We don't feel it is right to put mentally handicapped people in that situation.'

MANAGEMENT AND STRESS

Moving into management is likely to be associated with a move into a higher stress rating. There are occupations which rate higher than management but management is above average for the stress it incurs.

Many people (perhaps you are one of them) move into management from a background of technical expertise. If so then it is possible that the move will involve a considerable increase in occupational stress.

However, it should not be assumed that the occupation is sufficient to explain the existence of high levels of stress. As earlier models have shown, the sources of stress are numerous. It is not generally possible to put stress down to one particular cause.

WORK ROLE FACTORS

Stress is linked to uncertainty about what the job requires. Stress is also associated with conflicting job demands.

The potential for stress in these two areas is considerable and probably increasing. Why? The world of work and organizations are undergoing faster rates of change. Some organizations have recognised that job descriptions become out of date too quickly. Updating them is seen as a fruitless and increasingly meaningless task. Therefore they are getting rid of job descriptions. Instead, employees will be managed by targets and objectives which are periodically reviewed. But managers used to job descriptions are often inexperienced in managing people by objectives and targets.

In such organizations there is considerable potential for role uncertainty unless the targets and objectives are clearly set. Lines of accountability and authority can become easily blurred.

Both authors have worked in and with organizations where accountability has moved downwards (the terms *decentralization* or *devolution* are often used). A common dilemma in many such situations is that, though the transfer of responsibility has been clearly agreed and communicated, the *head office* perceives that the authority is retained centrally. The managers may then be treated as if they do not have the delegated authority. This can prove very frustrating, especially when key decisions are not acted upon.

There are particular phenomena which can cause uncertainty over job role:

Promotion

Alice was very happy about being promoted. She enjoyed working with her colleagues and saw them as friends. After moving into the supervisor's job she found that light conversation at the lunch table became harder. She didn't feel able to share confidences with her team in the way she had in the past. Her colleagues, on the other hand, seemed to regard her as still *one of the team*. They were quite taken aback when she commented on the need to improve timekeeping. The Alice they knew 'wouldn't say that ...'

A new job

Leslie worked for a commercial manufacturing company. He was used to being set clear targets and was expected to meet them efficiently and without discussion. He moved to work for a voluntary organization and set about his new job in his accustomed fashion. He was surprised when colleagues upbraided him for failing to consult sufficiently and being insufficiently sensitive to the politics of the management committee.

A transfer within the company

Rahni welcomed the opportunity to work with the sales department. She felt that her experience in production had equipped her to move into a sales role. However, when she asked what time people finished work in sales she was surprised to get no clear answer.

A change in procedures

A local authority conducted an audit of the forms in current usage. They found that many of them were duplicating information held on other forms. The senior managers agreed to simplify and reduce the number of forms. The clerical staff found the new forms hard to understand and began photocopying the older versions of the forms. The new forms piled up unused.

A change in the law

The government increasingly requires local authorities to put services out to contract. In order to meet this legislation, local authorities had to set up separate purchasing and contracting departments. People who had worked together harmoniously suddenly began to develop *them and us* attitudes. Distrust and suspicion grew.

COPING STRATEGIES

Some aspects of stress are more controllable than others. If your main source of stress is the nature of the occupation you find yourself in, and if you regard the stress as unacceptable, then you may need to consider an alternative and less stressful occupation .

But for most people stress is an amalgam of many factors of which occupation is but one. Most of these factors can be influenced by you. Some can be controlled by you though you may not realize it.

The way you respond to stress at work may be appropriate or inappropriate. Appropriate responses enable you to cope successfully.

Assertiveness

Assertive behaviour is about recognizing that you and others in any given situation all have *rights*. Let us see how this behaviour operates in a potentially stressful situation (see also Chapter 7).

Your line manager asks you to work late. You do not consider that the request is reasonable because, despite an unexpected backlog of work, you have promised your partner/spouse that you will be home at a specific time due to prior commitments. You might respond by saying:

1   'I promised I'd be home by 7 o'clock, but I suppose I could stay on if I have to.'
2   'You must be joking – no way.'
3   'I appreciate there is a problem, but I can't stay on late tonight.'

The first response is passive. Even though you are indicating a pressure elsewhere, you are showing that you are accepting the right of the other person takes precedence. The second response is aggressive. It is not simply a statement of your own rights but also a denial of the rights of the other person to even suggest that you work late. The third response is assertive. You are acknowledging the other person's right to ask, but are clearly stating that you yourself have a right to your denial.

EXERCISE

Let us try it again only this time apply it to something which you have felt uncomfortable about. Here are several suggestions in case you find it hard to think of a situation:

- You are asked to take on a new job responsibility but you feel that you have not had sufficient training or preparation.
- You are asked to clear up a mess which is not of your making.
- You feel that there is some part of your pay and benefits package which has fallen behind what you regard as the *going rate for your job*.

Find a friend or colleague to assist you. If no-one is available then face a mirror as you say the words which you would use when expressing your concerns.

Then review what you have said. You may find it helpful to write it down. Ask yourself (and your friend or colleague if appropriate) the following questions:

What *right(s)* was I stating for myself?
What *right(s)* was I accepting that the other person had?
How did my tone of voice support or detract from what I said?
How did my facial expression support or detract from what I said?
How did my body posture support or detract from what I said?
(If you had a friend or colleague) How was my message received?

Some experts suggest that it is worth keeping a diary in which you record stressful events, who was associated with them and how you handled them. The purpose of such a diary is not simply to have a factual record but rather to enable you to adopt appropriate (i.e. assertive) behaviour. It is an effective learning aid.

The ability to use assertive behaviour is probably the single most effective strategy available to you. It is something within *your control*. It gives you a means to deal with the various aspects of stress not just in your work but in your life generally. By using assertiveness techniques, you can then move on to apply it to implement such strategies as:

Delegation – upwards, downwards and sideways
Participation – in establishing work objectives
Prioritisation – of tasks
Control over your use of time

Time management

Poor time management can lead to stress and poor performance as well as vice versa. You might be *crying out for help* by claiming that you never have enough time to complete your tasks and meet your objectives. However, situations invariably appear worse than they really are and a positive approach to managing your time can also go a long way to ensuring lower stress levels. (See below for a separate section on managing your time.)

It is a common mistake to believe it is only shy and quiet people who need to develop their assertiveness. However, this is relatively simple and straightforward to achieve compared to the defensive/offensive, aggressive individual. There is a fine line between assertiveness and aggression and it is not easy for this type of person to learn the differences between the two types of behaviour.

Group identification of stress and means of controlling it

Teams or groups of colleagues can work together to:

- Raise stress awareness
- Identify and discuss various negative behaviours
- Identify formal education/training needs
- Regularly review priorities and workload (one to one and group)
- Use counselling as a preventative
- Use counselling as a cure
- Delegate upwards, downwards and sideways
- Participate in establishing objectives
- Exercise control over the use of time
- Give and receive responsibility and authority fairly and appropriately
- Encourage polite interchange and mutual respect – e.g. please, thank you, smile, etc.
- Empathize with others and understand needs
- Encourage and be encouraged to meet challenges
- Exchange ideas and understanding about stress and its causes
- Say 'no' appropriately and encourage others to do the same
- Promote participation and exchange of ideas
- Create a culture of personal responsibility, independence and individual innovation, balanced with openness and safety in seeking and giving help.

LEARNING POINTS

What is stress?
What are the signs of stress?
How can it be seen as a process?
How does it cause costs at work?
What are the physical effects of it in a person?
What are the main factors associated with stress at work
What sorts of occupations have higher stress?
What is it about a job which might make it stressful?

See also Chapter 7.

MANAGING YOUR TIME

Time is probably your most valuable, non-renewable resource. Unfortunately, it can also be the most abused! Time cannot be:

- Turned on or off
- Replaced
- Stored up.

There are only 24 hours in a day, so time is also a *limited* resource.

A key principle in time management is the Pareto principle, commonly known as the 80/20 rule. A nineteenth-century Italian economist, Wilfredo Pareto, observed that the significant items in a group seemed to form the smallest proportion of that group:

20 per cent of a workforce does 80 per cent of the work
20 per cent of a document contains 80 per cent of the relevant information
20 per cent of a company's sales accounts for 80 per cent of its profit.

Applying this rule to time management, 20 per cent of your tasks may produce 80 per cent of your results.

Time management is a process by which you take control of your time and use it to do the things you want, or need, to do. Good time management will improve the quality of your life because you will:

- Achieve more goals
- Become less stressed
- Gain more personal and job satisfaction
- Produce better results – quality rather than quantity
- Have more time to think
- Have more leisure time.

You can improve the way you manage your time if you understand how you use your time at the moment. You will then be able to pinpoint areas where your management of time can be improved and take specific steps to increase your control over your time. You are therefore recommended to:

1 Keep a daily time log
2 Complete time sheets
3 Make lists or notes of what you do, when, and for how long.

See Chapter 4 for more detail about the effects of the expensive resource of time.

Plan and prepare ways of allocating your time and recording actual time spent, which are appropriate to your situation.

When analysing how effectively you use your time, ask yourself:

- Do I spend enough time on planning and scheduling my work?
- Do I make *to do* lists and prioritize tasks?
- Am I doing work which could be done by others? Am I *managing* or *doing* the work?
- Do I need to allocate specific times to specific activities (e.g. Monday mornings for administration)? Are there regular activities which can be planned in?
- Do I leave enough time between activities to allow myself to adjust my role?
- Am I so busy getting low-priority work out of the way that I do not get time for high-priority activities?
- Are there areas which I want to change? What are they? What changes do I want to make?

Personal peak performance time

It is also well known that people vary as to what time of the day they reach their *peak* in terms of performance. We have all heard people say that they are a 'night person' or 'I am at my best in the mornings'. It is useful for you to understand yourself when developing time management skills and maximizing your use of time:

- Think about and identify your energy cycle
- Use your 'peak' time for concentrating on priority tasks
- Use your 'trough' time for doing simple, routine tasks
- For many people, maximum performance time is in the morning
- Also for many, after lunch is a relatively relaxing time (watch people drowse during early afternoon meetings or training sessions!)
- There is often a secondary peak later in the day.

But you can only improve your time management if you really want to. There are several techniques which you can adopt, but they will only work if you are genuinely committed to changing the way you approach your management of time.

HOW PEOPLE LEARN AND WHAT ENABLES PERSONAL CHANGE

In a sense everything that happens, nice or nasty, planned or unplanned, is a learning opportunity. Unfortunately, opportunities do not come neatly packaged and labelled as such. Opportunities tend to reside in the eye of the beholder, more a matter of perception and recognition than of incontrovertible fact. This means that learning opportunities, in common with any other sort of opportunity, are easily missed. A major task, therefore, for trainers and development specialists and managers generally is to get people to recognize and make use of opportunities for learning. The ultimate goal is the complete integration of all kinds of activities and learning (Honey and Mumford, 1990).

Honey and Mumford use the model in Figure 8.3 to show how learning takes place and subsequent change is effected.

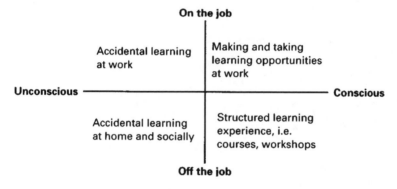

Figure 8.3   Learning opportunities

Most people believe learning from experience to be an accidental, unconscious process. They consider such experiences to be a matter of *serendipity* (discovery by accident) if they happen to consciously realize they have learned something from them.

Learning through competence identification and objective setting can crystallize the meaning of experiential learning and facilitate clear action planning and performance criteria identification.

The advantages of being a learning opportunist

Honey and Mumford go on to say that learning opportunism (i.e. identifying and utilizing learning opportunities) has many potential benefits including:

- Adding an interesting, extra 'learning' dimension to all you do
- Making learning from experience a more conscious and deliberate process
- Making one more purposeful; determined to extract learning even from unremarkable, routine events
- Helping one to learn from successes not just from mistakes
- Making it more likely that one will transfer learning from one specific situation to a broad range of other situations
- Meaning one can articulate what one has learned and communicate it to others
- Provides a recipe both for one's continuous improvement and helping others to improve
- Helps one to keep ahead of, and attuned to, change.

The learning opportunist, say Honey and Mumford, who reaps all these learning benefits finds that, in addition, their overall performance is enhanced.

Work-related experiences likely to provide learning opportunities

Honey and Mumford (1990)

Situations within the organization
Meetings
Managing changes
Tasks – familiar
Social occasions
Tasks – unfamiliar
Foreign travel
Task forces
Acquisitions/mergers
Customer visits
Closing something down
Visits to plant/office

Situations outside the organization
Voluntary organizations
Professional meetings
Domestic life
Sports clubs
Industry committees

Processes
- Coaching
- Mentoring
- Counselling

- Public speaking
- Listening
- Reviewing/auditing
- Modelling
- Clarifying responsibilities
- Problem solving
- Walking the floor
- Observing
- Visioning
- Questioning
- Strategic planning
- Reading
- Diagnosing problems
- Negotiating
- Decision making
- Selling

People

- Bosses
- Peers
- Mentors
- Consultants
- Network contacts
- Subordinates

Once people's minds are focused on the idea that every experience, generating reflection and self-appraisal, becomes an opportunity for development not previously conceived as possible, all experiences take on a new value and are seen as beneficial. It is important to overcome any feelings of self-recrimination, embarrassment or shame over mistakes. The only time there is a need to judge ourselves is when we have wasted the opportunity to learn from such mistakes and then continue to make them!

This process is common to all aspects of life; if we do not learn and develop as a result of experiences, the same mistakes and unfortunate experiences will continue to confront us, and our progress will be arrested. When successes are accepted without understanding their meaning, then the actions taken to create those successes, being accidental, are unlikely to be repeated (see Figure 8.4).

From their Learning Styles exercises, Honey and Mumford identified four preferences in individuals' learning approaches: the *Activist* who prefers to get on with the job and will try anything once; the *Reflector* who spends a lot of time thinking about what has been done and what is to be done; the *Pragmatist* who is happy as long as things make practical sense; and the *Theorist* who likes to analyse situations and behaviour and make philosophical sense of situations, without necessarily needing to prove them empirically.

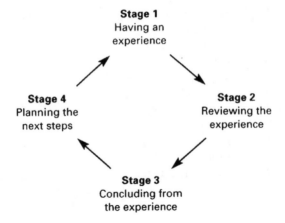

Stage 1
Having an
experience

Stage 4
Planning the
next steps

Stage 2
Reviewing the
experience

Stage 3
Concluding from
the experience

Figure 8.4   The Kolb Learning Cycle

Different learning style preferences lead most people to distort the iterative process of the Learning Cycle by placing a greater emphasis on some stages than on others. Thus Reflector/Theorists tend to linger at Stages 2 and 3, preferring to postpone getting into planning and action, whereas Pragmatist/Activists tend to leap-frog Stages 2 and 3 in their haste to do something! There are, however, other tendencies which become apparent when one examines how people learn from experience.

As the result of Alan Mumford's survey of 144 directors, Honey and Mumford have identified four different approaches to learning with hindsight and with foresight:

1   *The intituitive approach*   involving learning from experience, but not through a conscious process; it is claimed that learning is an inevitable consequence of having experiences.

2   *The incidental approach*   involving learning by chance from activities that jolt an individual into conducting a post mortem; usually when something out of the ordinary has happened or when something has not gone according to plan.

3   *The retrospective approach*   involving learning from experience by looking back over what happened and reaching conclusions about it; especially provoked by mishaps or mistakes – these people are also inclined to draw lessons from routine events and success.

4   *The prospective appraoch*   involving all the Retrospective elements plus planning to learn before an experience; where

future events are treated as opportunities to learn. The *Prospector*:

- Takes responsibility for meeting his or her own learning and development needs
- Seeks feedback on performance to identify his or her own strengths and weaknesses
- Learns from his or her own mistakes and those of others
- Changes behaviour where needed as a result of feedback
- Reflects systematically on own performance and modifies behaviour accordingly
- Develops self to meet the competence demand of changing situations
- Transfers learning from one situation to another.

Create opportunities for your own learning and development

Obtain support in creating learning opportunities

It is often necessary for you to involve other people in your quest for self-development; a key skill which is not always apparent or fully utilized. In fact, to quote Ben Jonson (and many have); 'Very few are wise by their own counsel, or learned by their own teaching. For he that was only taught by himself had a fool for his master.'

The essential fact here is that while we should all take *responsibility* for our own learning, that does not presuppose that we always *know* what it is that we need to learn or develop. We often need mentors, facilitators, tutors or colleagues while learning and developing.

EXERCISE

- Choose a particular situation and *look* for and accept help from others (this is not always easy)
- Identify *who* these people are (they may be inside or outside work)
- Identify *how* they may help you, e.g.:
  - Recognize and use learning opportunities
  - Provide and encourage a learning environment
  - Give you opportunities to review what you are learning and doing
  - Provide constructive feedback
  - Coaching and counselling
  - Sharing and taking risks when seeking and using opportunities

- Joint problem solving, etc.
- Use techniques to make full use of others e.g.: active listening (this involves body language which shows how well you are listening which, in turn, encourages further and deeper communication); observing; questioning; emulating (see Chapter 2)
- Develop and use contacts to exchange information and obtain support and resources
- Create and prepare strategies for influencing others (this is not about winning all the time, but about listening and being heard)
- Always present yourself positively to others
- Use a variety of means to influence others
- Identify and take opportunities when they arise to achieve longer-term aims or needs.

Seek feedback on performance

Feedback is a central part of performance management. It is one of your main tools for maintaining and improving your own performance as well as that of others:

- Measure your own current skills as a manager against appropriate standards and by getting feedback from appropriate others from inside and outside work, etc. as appropriate to your situation
- Identify what it is about feedback from other people that is so important and how it can be used and integrated with your own ideas
- Identify the difference between constructive and destructive feedback
- Identify various types of feedback
- Identify appropriate opportunities when you might receive feedback
- Learn to: enjoy; actively listen to; ask for clarification; seek specific examples; look for ways forward; agree what each will do
- Avoid: defensive reactions; offensive responses
- Compare feedback from others with how well you think you are doing; and improve your future performance as a result

■ Change your behaviour where needed as a result of feedback.

Learning from your own experiences

Learning from both positive and negative experiences is important. When you
have made mistakes, you should try not to make them again, find out what
went wrong and why. When you have achieved positive results try not to take
them for granted, analyse what you did and why it was that you were successful.

Evaluate your experiences

Share your experiences with others and decide what went well, and why, as well
as what did not go well, and why, as a result of your behaviour. Draw from
these experiences for your own future use, by accepting that no-one behaves
appropriately all the time, but that all experiences are valuable. It is helpful to
try to imagine how you might transfer this learning to other situations. Any
behaviour is only truly learned by applying it to various circumstances, involving different people and making some assumptions about how similarly or differently they might respond. It is helpful to evaluate your learning periodically
and identify various situations where the results could be equally valuable. Take
a positive approach to your mistakes, and those of others, to ensure further
learning, rather than to simply take or pass blame.

Develop yourself to meet the demands of changing situations

It is essential that you maintain and improve your behaviour in understanding
and responding to external and internal changes which affect both your routine
and planned activities. You should regularly scan appropriate news reports which
do/will directly and indirectly affect the environment within which you manage.

Keep abreast of developments which constantly occur within the
working environment which are both internal and external to the organization.
You will need to display an understanding of how the different parts of the
organization and its environment fit together and the effects of its culture;
whether it is stable, dynamic and evolving, uncertain. Most importantly, you
will need to identify the resultant behaviour of the people concerned.

PREPARING FOR ACTION PLANNING

Remember the checklist of questions identified in the Introduction to this book?
Try them again to identify your further development needs. We have reproduced those most appropriate to this chapter to help you (and adapted some to
specifically suit you as an individual). You will need to adapt them to the issues
discussed.

How are organizational performance standards determined and by whom?

How do you ensure that these performance standards are being met?

What actions would you/have you taken for your own development and to reduce stress, at times of particular difficulty or change?

How would you identify your own development needs within the job role?

How would you meet the needs you had identified?

How easy/difficult do you find asking support of or taking problems to others?

How might this be improved?

How do you/would you deal with conflict in your relationship with others arising from:

- Differences of opinion on courses of action?
- Personal animosity?
- Moral dilemmas (between yourself and others or yourself and the organization)?
- Racism?
- Sexism?
- Other discriminatory behaviour?
- Non-compliance with organizational rules, norms or values?

How do you determine your training and development needs?

What activities do you use for your development (formal and informal)?

How do you plan these activities?

How do you review your progress and evaluate the outcomes of your own training and development?

Have there been any specific incidences which have caused you concern for the equality of opportunities in your own development?

How have you dealt with this?

How do you set work objectives (or participate in setting them) for yourself?

How do you review and update these objectives?

Identify an objective you have had to meet and specify how you planned your work activities to meet this objective.

How did you decide which method would work best?

How do you decide how and what activities to allocate to yourself?

Did this decision deny opportunities to others?

How might you be fairer in this allocation in the future?

Are you making the most use of your skills and abilities?

Are all your skills and abilities appropriate now, or in the foreseeable future, for the achievement of the overall work objectives set?

How do you evaluate your own performance against your work objectives?

How do you seek feedback on your performance?

How do you take action following such feedback?

Questions devised by, and adapted from, the Crediting Competence Team at South Bank University and reproduced with permission.

ACTION PLANNING

Analyse your own behaviour in terms of strengths (positive outcomes) and weaknesses (negative effects), in dealing with actual work-based occurrences with regards to the various situations discussed in this chapter.

What are the main stress factors for you?

- Individual
- Home/domestic
- Occupation
- Employer
- Work role
- Work setting

How do you plan to manage each of these?

- Over the next month
- Over the next 6 months

How will you measure whether or not you have succeeded?

Have you managed your time effectively?

How might you improve your time management?

How have you managed your personal learning and development overall?

Where you think you have not handled them effectively, decide how you might deal with them differently in the future, what might be your immediate training requirements, and future development needs.

Discuss them with others and negotiate how you might

FURTHER READING

Boak, George (1991), *Developing Managerial Competences: The Management Learning Contract Approach*, Pitman, London.
Honey, P. and Mumford, A. (1990), *The Manual of Learning Opportunities*, Peter Honey, Maidenhead.
MCI (1993), *The Effective Manager – Development Modules*, The National Forum for Management Eduction and Development.
Nicholson, John (1992), *How do you Manage?*, BBC Books, London.
Pedler, M. and Boydell, T. (1985), *Managing Yourself*, Fontana, London.
Pedler, M., Burgoyne, J. and Boydell, T. (1986), *A Manager's Guide to Self-Development*, McGraw Hill, Maidenhead.

9 The strategic perspective

> Managers with a strategic perspective identify the way forward in a complex environment, referring constantly to a longer-term vision for the organization.

INTRODUCING THE RELATIONSHIP BETWEEN THE MCI PERSONAL COMPETENCY MODEL AND A STRATEGIC PERSPECTIVE

The MCI Integrated *Model of Personal Competency* identifies the behaviours and skills necessary for you to develop, before you are able to prove competence in any managerial function. This chapter attempts to deal with the various behaviours and skills necessary for you to apply across all managerial functions, transferring your learning to different occasions, at different times and under varying circumstances (contexts), consistently. The outcomes below, as identified within this section of the model, should be borne in mind while you work through this chapter.

Outcomes required in a strategic perspective

In order to demonstrate effective behaviour here, the manager:

- Displays understanding of how the different parts of the organization and its environment fit together
- Works towards a clearly defined vision of the future
- Clearly relates goals and actions to the strategic aims of the business
- Takes opportunities when they arise to achieve longer-term aims or needs of the organization.

AIMS AND OBJECTIVES

The aim of this chapter is to provide the reader with an understanding of how a manager adopts a strategic perspective in his or her activity. We would identify a strategic perspective as distinguished by a forward-looking orientation. The environment for organizations is increasingly complex and challenging.

Managers can no longer assume that what is true today will hold true for any substantial future time. Management gurus provide new models and some management gurus are quite comfortable with the rapid obsolescence of these models. Indeed one such guru told a manager attending his seminar that the advice in a book he (the guru) had written only a couple of years previously was in effect useless.

Therefore in this chapter we will not seek to offer 'flavour of the month' approaches to strategic thinking. Rather we will introduce you to approaches which we believe possess reasonable durability.

By the end of this chapter and the particular learning exercises we hope that you will be able to:

- Understand how strategy and management are linked together
- Be aware of the nature of organizational mission
- Be able to appreciate the impact of the broader environment upon the organization
- Be able to undertake a simple environmental analysis
- Appreciate the importance of organizational stakeholders to an organization
- Be able to assess the relative importance and influence of organizational stakeholders
- Be able to carry out a straightforward internal analysis of an organization.
- Be able to link strategy to planning and implementation issues.

STRATEGY AND THE MANAGER

It is important at the outset to make a distinction between the kind of planning that is involved throughout an organization and the concept of strategy. We take an organization for which one of the authors worked many years ago. It was a small factory which undertook a range of contract work usually involving minor assembly line work. The workforce were mostly local people who were hourly paid and who worked on shifts.

The manager of the factory saw her role as getting contracts for work and she left the organization of the work to two supervisors who managed the shifts. The factory employed local women and also took on some students (including the author) during the summer holidays.

Quite clearly the supervisors had to plan the workload and this had to be done with some care. The contracts varied in size and in importance. The supervisors were aware of this and also knew the staff. High-value and important contract work was given to more experienced staff, low-value and less critical work to temporary staff.

The owner obviously needed to be informed about the progress of contract work. However, she was also trying to do more than simply 'fill the sausage machine'. She saw the importance of having a range of contracts and avoiding a dependence upon one source of business. In this way she was behaving strategically (though she would have probably called it plain common sense!) What was also interesting was the attitude of some of the workers at the factory. When there was a 'rush job' the workers would often be asked to work extra shifts in the evening. Some of the workers had teenage children and this represented a child-care problem. With the tacit agreement of the supervisors some of these workers sought employment for their teenage children on these shifts. In fact in a few cases the parents actually substituted their teenager for themselves on the extra shifts. Though this practice was questionable it could be argued that it represented 'strategic behaviour' on the part of the workforce. Strategic thinking is not necessarily the preserve of the manager.

Ways of perceiving strategy

For the manager a key element of strategy is thinking. Indeed we would argue that without thought a strategic decision in effect becomes purely reactive. Johnson and Scholes (1993, pp. 5–10) comment that strategic decisions *in organizations* possess the following characteristics:

1   They relate to the scope of an organization's activities
2   They involve matching the activities of the organization to the environment in which it operates
3   They involve matching activities to resources and in particular the resource capacity
4   Strategic decisions have major resource implications
5   They affect the operational decisions which the organization takes
6   The values and expectations of the stakeholders in the organization will have a significant effect
7   A strategic decision is likely to have longer-term implications.

Similarly, Johnson and Scholes suggest that strategy exists at a number of levels in an organization and we could indicate these as follows:

■   *Corporate level*   Here the decisions would focus upon what business to be in; how the organization should be structured and how it should be financed.
■   *Business level*   The focus here is upon competing within a particular market or sector; what sort of products or services should be offered and to which customers.
■   *Operational level*   Here the strategy links the various functions (finance, personnel, IT, etc.) in order to enable them to ensure that the business and corporate strategy is achieved.

In this context we would add the level of the individual. A strategic perspective can be held by an individual. Indeed, many small stock market investors become large stock market investors because they have adopted a strategic perspective on investment which has proven to be more accurate than that held by the large financial institutions.

Perhaps you have decided to pursue a management qualification route independently of the view of your employer. If so then your strategic perspective is individual and possibly at variance of that held by your organization.

What is strategy?

Henry Mintzberg (1994), a well-known writer and author, has had a key influence upon the development of thinking about how strategy is formulated. He suggests that strategic formulation does not take place evenly. Rather there are different patterns of strategic change. The patterns can in some ways be compared to the behaviour of the surface of an ocean. The water in an ocean offers the following kinds of behaviour:

- There are the incremental adjustments represented by the rise and fall of the tide.
- There are aspects which offer continuity such as the deep ocean currents which change little over time.
- There are periods of flux and uncertainty which could be typified by storms which agitate the surface of the sea.
- There are occasional major transformations such as a tidal wave caused by volcanic eruption.

If you apply this model to your own experience as a manager and as an individual you may find it useful to note down examples from your organization and personal life to illustrate each of the ocean movements which have been referred to above. We have done this for one of the authors (Table 9.1).

Table 9.1

Ocean Movement	Organizational example	Personal Example
Tidal changes	Annual workload negotiation	Improving computer skills
Deep ocean current	Move to contract staff	Learning a foreign language
Storms	Major reorganizations	Changing job
Tidal wave	Organizational closure/takeover	Career change

What is perhaps different between the conception of Mintzberg and they way we represent it is that Mintzberg, in talking about strategy, sees the patterns as mutually exclusive. If transformational strategic change is happening then incremental is not. However, if we compare the individual and the organization we can argue that it is quite possible for the individual to be undergoing a different kind of personal strategic change to that of his or her organization. If you compare yourself to your organization then are you similar or dissimilar in your experience of recent and current strategic change?

How strategy relates to behaviour – mission and values

If in the previous section you found that there was a difference between yourself and your organization then how might you account for that difference? Let us suppose that your organization is going through a period of flux (storm) and yet you personally are seeking continuity (deep ocean current). One clue might lie in the actual values or goals that are espoused by yourself and your organization. Possibly the organization has had to make a major strategic change and this has been associated with a reordered set of values. In the public sector many organizations are having to come to terms with 'the contract culture' and meeting performance targets. This has sometimes upset quite deeply held organizational values about public service and 'doing things in the right way'.

When a new set of values supersedes a previously accepted pattern of belief in an organization then it is sometimes linked with a change in 'mission'. Strategic management textbooks talk of organizations having a 'mission statement'. Johnson and Scholes (1993, p. 13) define this as 'an overriding premise in line with the values or expectations of the stakeholders' (of the organization).

One of the authors worked for a time for a major security company. At that time the company had a mission statement emblazoned on all its vehicles. The statement read ' for customers, co-workers and the common good'. The author was initially cynical about whether this statement was representative of a related value system. The company had, at the time, been the subject of press reporting which suggested that it was virtually a 'private army'. However, during the author's training period the message which came across was that the company valued the well-being of staff highly. Security staff were told that their own safety was paramount and that the organization was not looking for 'have-a-go heroes'. At the time the security industry had a very dubious reputation and the author subsequently wondered whether this company's very public espousal of a broad set of values was distinguished.

Problems in behaving strategically

Mintzberg also looked at differences between intended strategies and actual outcomes. He suggests that there are pure forms of strategy which can help understand the way in which strategy is arrived at in organizations.

1   Deliberate strategy: this is defined by two conditions:
   ■   There must have been precise intentions in the organization set out in some detail about what was intended.

- These intentions must have been held in common by the members of the organization.
- Events must have worked out exactly as intended without any surprises.

2   Emergent strategy requires that there must have been no intention to have achieved the actual consequence from the actions taken.

Obviously it is unlikely that many strategic situations would fit in either of these categories. Rather these two represent the two ends of a continuum. They illustrate the problem for the manager in behaving strategically. A former prime minister, Harold Macmillan, summed it up when he commented on what had influenced his actions. He said 'events, dear boy'. Managers do not operate in laboratory conditions. There are many factors which impact upon the likelihood of a deliberate strategy taking place. Many, if not most, of the factors are not within the direct control of the manager.

Hence most managers have to be aware of the need to adapt to changing circumstances and this may mean jettisoning a planned strategy to take advantage of a sudden opportunity. Figure 9.1 illustrates the range of strategic alternatives.

	Dominant theme	Main focus	Principal concepts and techniques	Organizational implications
1950s	Budgetary planning	Financial control	Budgeting and investment appraisal	Financial management as key
1960s	Corporate planning	Planning growth	Market forecasting	Planning department
1970s	Corporate strategy	Portfolio planning	Analyse strategic business units	Integrate strategic and financial control
Late 1970s and early 1980s	Industry and competitor analysis	Choice of industries and markets and positioning	Analysis of industry structure and competitor analysis	Divestment of unattractive business units
Late 1980s and early 1990s	Quest for competitive advantage	Sources of competitive advantage within firm	Resource analysis and organizational competence	Corporate restructuring and business process re-engineering

Figure 9.1   The evolution of strategic management (source: Grant, 1995)

EXAMINING THE ENVIRONMENT

The term 'environment' is much used. Some people associate it with a particular value system or moral code, e.g. 'caring for the environment'. However, in strategic terms 'environment' as used here does not carry any such association. Rather it is used to indicate the context within which the manager and the organization operate. You may hear business commentators speak of a competitive environment, for example. It is perhaps ironic that as politicians extol the value of competition, business leaders may complain that the competition is excessive and seek government aid to enable them to compete or restrictions and tariffs to keep out foreign goods.

The environment, like the weather, is always there. No manager can ignore it. Rather what is needed is some way to understand and evaluate its impact upon the organization and the individual manager.

The nature of environmental analysis

The way in which you approach your environment will depend upon a number of factors. The more senior you are in your organization, the more likely you will look beyond the immediate environment of the organization. The smaller your organization, the more likely it is to be affected by changes in the environment. The more concentrated and focused your organization is in terms of products or services, the more specific your environment is likely to be to those products or services.

Philip Kotler (1980), who has a marketing focus, views the organizational environment as operating at four levels. First, there are the people or organizations within the environment which are crucial to the organization in carrying out its prime function. Thus for a garage these would be the suppliers of petrol and oil, the customers and new car distributors. If the garage needs banking facilities then the bank would be included. If the garage became involved in supplying second-hand cars then the local car auction would also be a key part of the what Kotler call the 'task environment'.

Then there are the other garages which compete with our garage. Nowadays this would include supermarkets who are selling petrol. There are also other suppliers of new and second-hand cars. This constitutes the 'competitive environment'.

Even in a free-enterprise system there are certain rules and regulations. The garage has to comply with these. As a business it has to file accounts and pay taxes. Therefore there is a 'public environment' which has an impact upon the garage.

Finally there is what Kotler calls the 'macro-environment' which involves the more general influences which impact upon the organization. Is the country going through a boom or a recession? Is there a move away from car usage or is it becoming more popular? What about the population itself? Is it getting older/younger, etc.?

Two different techniques to analyse the wider environment

Strategic management courses generally offer managers the following two techniques of environmental appraisal. They are both simple and easy to apply and have much to commend them.

PESTeL analysis

The first technique is usually referred to by an acronym (this is a word made up of the first letters of each part of the technique). The acronyms used are STEP, PEST or PESTeL. The letters mean (PESTeL):

Political
Economic
Sociological
Technological
Legal

- *Political* All organizations and managers are affected to some extent by the political environment. Since 1979 there has been a Conservative government in the UK. This has been associated with some major political changes. The post-war consensus which led one previous Conservative prime minister to observe 'we are all socialists now' has been broken. Yet the 'free-enterprise' ethos of the Thatcher years was associated with an enormous amount of government legislation. At the time of writing (February 1997) there is much speculation about the likely outcome of the forthcoming election. What would an incoming Labour government do? How might it affect your organization?
- *Economic* Most people who are buying their homes or who have borrowed large amounts of money from commercial institutions are keenly aware of the impact of interest rates. One of the authors originally trained as an economist and it is a matter of some distress to observe the relatively minor (and apparently diminishing) role of this subject on many management courses. Who do you know can make the economic (as opposed to emotional) case for or against Economic Monetary Union? What are fiscal and monetary policies and how do they impact upon you and your organization? As a manager – and as a voter – you should be able to appreciate these matters.
- *Sociological* Here most people feel more comfortable. They pick up a broadsheet newspaper or magazine and read about 'Generation X' and the growth of 'portfolio working'. Currently (February 1997) there is considerable discussion around what is described as 'downshifting'.

These all are aspects of societal trends. Some of these trends will almost certainly be highly significant for your organization. It is predicted, for example, that people are increasingly forming smaller households and that therefore there will be a demand for more housing of a more suitable type and size. If you work in an organization associated with construction then this trend is a vital determinant of planning decisions.

■ *Technological* The pace of technical advance is faster now than it has been at any time in our history. In computers it is suggested that the obsolescence of equipment means that the machine you buy today has a product life of some six months. This impacts differently upon organizations. Some organizations are in fact facing a pressure for less rather than more technology. In agriculture, for example, there is a growing demand for organic products which have been produced in a non-intensive way.

■ *Legal* All organizations and managers confront the need to observe the law of the land. When organizations operate in different countries then the legal complexity becomes greater. The delayering of organizations has meant that increasingly managers are expected to know what their legal position is in the workplace.

A PESTeL analysis can become more useful to you as you become more practised in its application. This is a detailed analysis of the external environment looking nationally and internationally as necessary.

■ *Demography* because people make up markets, organizations need to constantly monitor the changes in:
   – Birthrate; which is declining in the UK
   – Population; which is ageing and organizations need to consider policies which address needs appropriately
   – Changes in the family – e.g. single parents; remarriage following divorce; increases in fostering and adoption, etc.
   – Rises in non-family households – more couples are choosing not to have families
   – Geographical shifts in population – these are likely to prove more important in the UK as multinationals move to rural districts
   – Better-educated population – increasing the need to address marketing in the service sectors
   – Changing ethnic and racial population – requiring different cultural needs to be addressed.

- *Economic environment* requiring the analysis of the total purchasing power which includes four main trends:
  - Slowdown of the real-income growth
  - Continued inflationary pressure
  - Low savings and high debt – mortgages, bank loans, etc.
  - Changing consumer expenditure patterns.
- *Physical environment* which requires attention to causes of the erosion of the ozone layer; diminishing rain forests and the general diminution of the world's natural resources including:
  - Impending shortages of certain raw materials
  - Increased cost of energy
  - Increased levels of pollution
  - Strong government intervention in natural-resource management.
- *Technological environment* as one of the most dramatic forces shaping people's destiny, requiring organizations to address:
  - The accelerating pace of technological change
  - Unlimited innovational opportunities
  - Improving research and development
  - Minor improvements rather than major discoveries
  - Increasing regulation of technological change.
- *Political/legal environment* comprising laws, government agencies and pressure groups, requiring organizations to consider the implications of:
  - Substantial legislation regulating British business
  - Increases in government agencies and sub-contracting
  - Growth of public-interest groups.
- *Socio/cultural environment* which are the combined effects of experiences shaping people's beliefs, values, attitudes, norms and behaviour. Organizations need to consider:
  - How persistent are core cultural values in the changing environment?
  - That each culture consists of sub-cultures
  - That secondary cultural values undergo shifts through-time.

The issues within STEP which you use for analysis will vary between organizations and between the circumstances confronting them. Many major organizational changes are made as a result of analysing STEP regularly and thoroughly. The secret to successful application of SWOT and STEP analyses is a manager's ability to communicate the messages effectively to senior management teams.

The author sometimes superimposes the OT part of the SWOT analysis onto STEP. It can be very enlightening and insightful to an innovative manager.

Five forces analysis

Michael Porter (1980) developed a framework for identifying the external environment by assessing the nature of competition within a particular industry or service sector. The five forces which Porter sees as significant are as follows:

- *The intensity of competition within the industry itself*
  Consider your own industry or employment sector and answer the following questions:
  1 Are the various competitors roughly equal in size?
  2 Are there a large number of competitors?
  3 Is the market a mature one (i.e growth prospects are limited)?
  4 Are there high fixed costs?
  5 Are there high barriers to leaving the industry?
  6 Does increasing capacity involve making large investment or purchasing decisions?
  7 Is there a lack of differentiation between your product/ service and that of your competitors?
  8 Do competitors lay great stress upon achieving success?
  The more questions which you answer 'yes' to, the greater the intensity of competition within your industry or employment sector.
- *Threat of new entrants*   Ask yourself the following questions about your industry or employment sector:
  1 Are there significant advantages attached to being a large producer or player?
  2 Do you need a lot of money to enter your industry?
  3 Is it difficult to distribute your industry product or service?
  4 Do existing players have a major cost advantage?
  5 Are existing players likely to retaliate (e.g. by reducing prices) against a new entrant?
  6 Are the current players protected by a legal monopoly or regulatory system?
  7 Is the product or service one which is strongly differentiated (i.e. brand or company name is important)?
  The more questions which you answer 'yes' to, the greater the barriers to new entrants within your industry or employment sector.
- *The power of customers or buyers*   Ask yourself the following questions about your industry or employment sector:
  1 Do your buyers tend to purchase in large quantities?
  2 Are there relatively few buyers?

3   Are there alternatives for buyers to your product or service?

4   Are the buyers' profit margins relatively low?

5   Could the buyers consider making the product or producing the service themselves?

6   Is the product or service fairly standard?

The more questions which you answer 'yes' to, the greater the power which buyers possess.

■ *The power of suppliers*   Ask yourself the following questions about your industry or employment sector:

1   Do you tend to purchase in small quantities?

2   Are there relatively few suppliers?

3   Are there few alternatives to the product or service supplied?

4   Are you as a buyer not particularly important to the supplier?

5   Could the supplier consider selling on the product or service themselves (i.e. cutting out your part of the process)?

6   Is the product or service supplied differentiated?

The more questions which you answer 'yes' to, the greater the power which suppliers possess.

■ *The threat of substitutes*   Ask yourself the following questions about your industry or employment sector:

1   Is there a substitute service or product which represents a real threat to your product or service?

2   Can a buyer switch to such a substitute relatively easily?

3   Would it be difficult to hold on to your buyers by offering product or service improvements?

The more questions which you answer 'yes' to, the greater the threat which substitutes represent.

The development of a 'helicopter' approach

The previous two techniques are only of value if you use them thoughtfully. It is all too easy to only be aware of the immediate forces which impact upon the organization. One of the authors worked some years ago in a college which ran secretarial courses. The staff teaching on these courses were strongly averse to replacing their typewriters with word processors. The reality of the office environment and the spread of IT has in effect rendered the typewriter redundant.

Part of a strategic perspective is developing a 'helicopter' approach to assessing the environment. You need to be able to rise above the trees and see the forest around you. Applying the above two techniques in a careful and wide-ranging fashion will help you do this. It certainly should help you identify the 'typewriters' in your industry.

Using the information

Once you have carried out such an analysis then it is essential to use the information which you have obtained. Perhaps you also need to check that assumptions underlying your analysis are accurate. It is all too easy to overrate skills which you have spent many years acquiring. Possibly new technology has rendered those skills redundant. Often your competitors are a better source of information than your own colleagues. Most managers who attend trade fairs or business exhibitions are open to sharing their opinions about what is happening in your industry.

ASSESSING THE ORGANIZATION

Once you have analysed the environment then the next logical step is to look at the organization. As with the previous example, it is quite feasible to conduct this analysis with you, the manager, as the subject. Indeed these sort of techniques would be familiar to careers and vocational advisors.

The first technique involves looking at the stakeholders. This analysis in some respect can easily bridge across into the environmental analysis depending upon how widely you cast the net. The public discussion about a 'stakeholder society' is an example of casting the net quite widely. Thus, while the traditional view of stakeholders in an organization would only encompass owners, shareholders, managers and employees, a broader view would include the banks, the customers and the suppliers. A still wider view would include the community at large and even the organization's competitors. At that point the stakeholder analysis has in effect become an environmental analysis!

In the context of this chapter we are using the stakeholder analysis in a narrower fashion.

The importance of key stakeholders

Previously we referred to the concept of a 'mission' and 'mission statement'. The key stakeholders are crucial to setting the values and purpose of the organization. Some organizations have only one such stakeholder (or stakeholder group). Some companies, for example, may regard the shareholders as the one crucial group which determines the mission of the organization.

However, it is far more common for organizations to have a significant number of stakeholders. These may, on a simple listing, consist of the following groups:

- Owners/shareholders
- Managers
- Employees
- Customers/clientele
- Suppliers

The groups listed may indeed break down into further sub-categories because of a diversity of views within the group itself. As an example we might break down the stakeholders of a large stock exchange listed company as follows:

- Owners/shareholders
  - Large shareholders (pension funds and unit trusts) some of whom might hold the shares on behalf of others. They would be concerned with the company performance and 'soundness' of the assets
  - Small shareholders who have shares in their own right. They may be very interested in, for example, the chief executive's salary which is probably many times their own income. They may be retired people who depend upon the share dividend for their income.
  - Stock market speculators who may hold the shares (or even simply hold a share option – a right to buy or sell the shares). Their interest would be largely around short-term share price fluctuations.
- Managers
  - Top managers whose remuneration might be strongly linked to the share price because of options to purchase shares at a set price
  - Managers whose pay is performance related
  - Managers whose job security is based upon the success of the company (e.g. contract managers, etc.)
- Employees
  - Employees who have share options and who may be shareholders
  - Employees who are strong trade unionists and who see pay rises as justified by company profits
  - Employees who are on temporary or time-limited contracts
- Customers/clientele
  - Large customers upon whom the company depends for much of their business
  - Small customers who rely upon the company terms of credit to stay in business
  - 'Clients' who need the company products (i.e. users of medicines, etc.)
- Suppliers
  - Large suppliers who depend upon the company for much of their business
  - Suppliers who are owed money by the company
  - Banking and legal suppliers who provide an 'intangible' service.

Stakeholder	Strength	Importance	Main expectations
Current students	• Voice opinions and influence next intake • Limited ability to leave	• Limited power unless expressed collectively	• To be educated • To receive a degree • To have a social life • To have post university prospects
Prospective students	• Able to choose whether to come to university	• Seen as vital and courted assiduously	as above
Parents of students	• Able to influence student • Often power to influence others (polititians etc.)	• Seen as important in influencing student decision	• Quality of education • Career prospect • Reputation
Academic staff	• Knowledge of subject • Tenure (in some cases)	• Dependent on individual academic	• Research opportunity • Professional development • Job security • Academic freedom
Non-academic staff	• Knowledge of systems • Trade Union base	• Limited impact on organization	• Job security
University managers	• Authority of position • Control of budgets	• Key in setting strategic direction	• Career prospects • Control of resources
Employers	• Influence of managers • Provision of endowments • Careers for graduates • Work placements	• Depends on company (some very strong)	• Usable graduates • Useful research
Funding councils	• Ability to award funds • Require statistics • Conduct audits	• Vital to resourcing and academic standing	• Accountability • Efficiency • Reports and figures

Figure 9.2 Stakeholder analysis of a university (source: Blundell and Murdock, 1977)

Simply listing out stakeholders is only part of the exercise. Indeed you can conduct a stakeholder analysis even though you are only an employee. After all, you are yourself a stakeholder!

The main value of the stakeholder analysis for developing a strategic perspective as a manager (or indeed as a prospective manager) is the way in which you develop it further. One way to do this is to 'map' out the stakeholders using further criteria. These criteria might be such factors as:

- How powerful the stakeholder is
- How interested the stakeholder is in using that power.

We have set out in Figure 9.2 an example of such a stakeholder analysis using a university as an example. You will note that there is a significant difference in power possessed by students depending upon whether they are current or prospective students. Currently there is considerable discussion as to whether UK university students should be more easily able to transfer from one university to another (as they can in the United States). If this were to be introduced then enrolled students would possess, as customers, more power to simply take their business elsewhere than they do at present.

Using the SWOT strategic technique

SWOT (Strengths/ Weaknesses/ Opportunities/ Threats) is a standard technique which is familiar to all management students. It is a useful way to bring information together under some simple headings. As a technique it is not simply the preserve of a manager. You may indeed have unconsciously used it in considering a major change in your life. Let us consider the example of a decision on whether or not to sell your current property and buy another.

Few people move house in a careless and unthinking way. It represents a major life change and often involves one of the most significant financial commitments you will ever make. So when you consider doing it you would very probably go through a considerable amount of soul searching and analysis.

One key factor is what factor (or factors) are driving the situation. Perhaps your current accommodation is too small or you do not like the location. You may have had a pay increase or come into some money. These sort of factors represent 'strengths and weaknesses' in your current situation. Hopefully you will be in a position of 'strength' but in this age of uncertainty it is also possible that you are having to trade down in property in order to reduce your mortgage or deal with a reduced income (or both).

As you weigh up your personal situation you will almost certainly also evaluate the options of alternative properties. A prospective property will present 'opportunities' – perhaps to build an extension or to refurbish to your own taste. There may also be possible 'threats' – what are the local authority planning to do with the disused factory down the street? Is the area likely to deteriorate?

In evaluating what to do you therefore may well have carried out, albeit subconsciously, a form of SWOT analysis. It should not be a matter of surprise to management educators that SWOT analysis is almost always the technique of choice that students reach for when they are given a free hand.

Obviously, strengths and weaknesses are relative. Some years ago Lada cars were regarded as relatively unattractive and had a very poor second-hand value. Then with the changes to the former Soviet Union a number of entrepreneurs began to export them back to the former Soviet bloc countries. Soon advertisements appeared in the motoring sections of newspapers seeking Lada cars. A television programme showed how the cars were being loaded onto ships and taken back to Eastern Europe where there were eager customers for both the cars and spare parts. A car which was relatively unattractive to own in the UK suddenly had a good market in its area of origin.

A major responsibility for organizations is to monitor and search the environment for new opportunities. Sometimes motivation of those concerned may be low in times of recession. In fact, difficult times require even more thorough-going searches, because it is at these times that opportunities are more easily missed. It can also be said that the lack of opportunity searching can be one of the causes of recessions in particular industries or even whole economies.

> A company's marketing environment consists of the actors and forces external to the marketing management function of the firm that impinge on the marketing management's ability to develop and maintain successful transactions with its target customers (Kotler, 1984).

The actors referred to by Kotler in his definition of an organization's marketing environment include those operating in the micro-environment and the macro-environment.

There are two basic tools used by managers to analyse and understand the environment in which their organizations operate:

1   Strengths, Weaknesses, Opportunities and Threats (or SWOT) Analysis for the micro-environment and
2   Sociological, Technological, Economic and Political (STEP) Analysis for the macro-environment.

SWOT analysis and the micro-environment

The Strengths and Weaknesses part of SWOT stresses the internal environment and past and present experiences; while the Opportunities and Threats focus on the external environment and potential future experiences. Remember, every threat to an organization also poses an opportunity, or a challenge, although they are not entirely mutually exclusive!

1   The organization; requiring managers to constantly ask-themselves questions like:
 - What are we in business for?
 - Is the original mission still appropriate?
 - How often do we redefine our objectives?
 - Should we be changing direction, e.g. markets, products/services?
 - What are the major strengths and weaknesses of the organization in the past and the present in providing appropriate goods or or services?

2   The organization's suppliers; requiring a constant review of:
 - Relevance of suppliers used
 - Whether the organization is 'supplier led'; what are the choices for alternatives?
 - Whether they continue to supply effectively and efficiently
 - Whether their supplies are and will continue to be appropriate
 - Whether delivery continues to be reliable and timely
 - Would vertical integration (taking them over) be more beneficial to the organization?

3   Marketing intermediaries, e.g.:
 - 'Middlemen' e.g. agents, brokers, wholesalers etc.:
   - Are they necessary?
   - Are they cost-effective and a value to the organization?
   - Are there alternative ways of reselling goods/services?
 - Physical distribution firms; requiring constant review of:
   - Whether customers continue to be reached through their channels
   - Whether their selling pitch is appropriate and accurate
   - Their ability/inclination to promote the organization's products or services
   - Whether they need training/development in promoting the organization's products or services
   - Whether they continue to be needed at all
   - Would vertical integration be appropriate here?
 - Marketing service agencies, e.g. marketing research firms; consulting firms; advertising agencies, etc.:
   - How often are their services reviewed?
   - Are they cost-effective?
   - Do they reach the relevant markets and so on?

- Financial intermediaries, e.g. banks; credit companies; insurance companies, etc.:
    - Does the organization continue to get good deals?
    - When were their services last reviewed?
    - What are the alternatives, etc.?
4 Customers; how does the organization determine:
    - Who they are?
    - Where they are?
    - What their needs are?
    - Does the organization address their needs?
    - Does the organization fulfil their needs?
    and so on.
5 Competitors; does the organization:
    - Carry out regular competitor analyses to determine:
        - Who they are?
        - Where they are?
        - Their strengths and weaknesses?
        - Their major threats to the organization's goods and service?
        - Whether they also analyse the market thoroughly to determine where the opportunities are?
    - Determine what benefits the organization offers to customers that are specific and unique as compared to competitors?
6 Public institutions, e.g. financial; media; government; education; citizen-action. Does the organization understand and address the influences these institutions have nationally in:
    - The ability of the organization to obtain funds?
    - The effects of publicity on the organization – good and bad?
    - What implications the impact of local government policies may have on organizational strategy?
    - The effects of any local initiatives in training and education policies?
    - Public opinion towards the organization's products, services, recruitment and retention, environmental policies and so on.

While not very easy the first time you try it, SWOT analysis is an excellent tool to help managers reflect objectively. The criteria used are largely up to you. You may wish to analyse the management function areas appropriate to your organization or the desired outcomes/impacts which are expected as a result of strategic decision making, whatever you consider most appropriate to your particular area of work. Once you have made the attempt, you will find future exercises will become more sophisticated as you repeat the procedure, and you will become more discerning in the criteria you use and the judgements you make.

Johnson and Scholes (1993, p. 152) indicate that strengths and weaknesses are also closely linked to core competences of an organization and they suggest asking four key questions to establish how important strategically such core competences might be.

1   Who owns these core competences? One argument offered by some organizations to defend a decision not to invest in training is that they will see their investment 'walk out of the door' as the staff are poached by competitors.

2   How long are the competences good for? Currently advertisements for secretarial staff still ask for shorthand skills. However it can be argued that technology (and delayering) is rendering such skills obsolete.

3   To what extent can the competencies be transferred? How much is Richard Branson's name worth without his involvement? The ability of a retailer in washing machines may not transfer to selling personal computers.

4   How easily can the competencies be copied or learnt by a competitor? In February 1997 the motoring organizations expressed concern that certain car manufacturers were producing vehicles which could not be repaired or maintained other than by regular dealers.

The involvement of colleagues

If you refer back to the home purchase example at the beginning of the previous section then ask yourself the following question. 'Would you consult members of your family about the factors involved in the decision?'

For example, if you were moving home because you felt that your children needed more space then would you check that the children shared your interpretation. Perhaps their conception of more space is not simply defined by having more bedrooms. They may prefer to have a 'den' or workshop in the garden or a large loft space.

However, in organizations, just as in many families, the key people are often not involved in the discussion about strategic decisions. *Who* should be involved, *why* should they be involved, *when* should they be involved and *how* should they be involved are the key questions which any effective manager needs to answer.

Who to involve

A trite and simple answer is to say 'everyone who constitutes a stakeholder' in the organization. However, you will get no thanks if you consult everyone in your organization about every single decision which has a strategic implication.

When to involve people

Almost everyone reading this book will have a good example where something described as 'consultation about a change' was simply an information-giving exercise about a decision which had been made and was not subject to any alteration. Where you are seeking to *consult* people about a strategic issue then it is only a valid involvement in the process if you approach them before the decision has been made.

How should people be involved

One of the authors recently supervised a research project which examined the way in which a major change was communicated in a blue-collar part-time workforce. The research identified a strong preference amongst this group of staff for face-to-face communication involving their own line managers. Official documents and 'paper-based forms of communication' were less popular.

In your own personal life, using the example of a housing move, how would you consult your 6-year-old child, your partner or spouse and your solicitor? Quite possibly you would involve them in different ways. The solicitor would prefer paper based communication to ensure a clear record is kept. Your child would probably want to have his or her say based upon physically seeing the possible new home. As a manager you need to be sensitive about the communication preference of different people and groups of staff. For further information we would refer you to Chapter 2 of this book.

Some examples

Consider the following decisions (all of which could be arguably strategic in their implications):

- Whether to move from contract cleaners to resourcing your own cleaning department
- Whether to make the office a no-smoking zone
- How to invest the company pension fund

The first decision obviously affects a number of people but what is most important is obtaining the necessary information about the available options. It is certainly not the sort of thing that many organizations would 'put out to a vote'. Rather the decision would probably be based upon a cost-benefit analysis. However, without seeking the information from appropriate staff and managers it is unlikely that any sort of balanced decision could be made. Given contract notice periods it may be necessary to consult people well in advance of the actual decision date.

The second decision is one which affects all of the people who work in the organization. It also may impact upon people who visit – such as customers or suppliers. Therefore there would need to be a careful and thorough consultation. Even if it was agreed there might need to be special arrangements made for people who are habitual smokers.

The third decision also affects all the people who work in the organization. However, it would be impractical to consult all the staff about specialized and fairly complex investment decisions. The pension fund has trustees who are expected to monitor these on behalf of the staff. Nevertheless, the sad experience of the Mirror Group pensioners demonstrated the importance of the involvement of trustees who focus on the interests of the pension fund membership.

The application to decision making

Strategic thinking is just that – thinking about strategy. Conan Doyle's famous detective, Sherlock Holmes, had a brother called Mycroft. Sherlock Holmes comments that Mycroft possesses the greater intellect but is indifferent to whether any action takes place. He would rather be considered wrong than to invest the energy in proving his case.

Henry Mintzberg (1994) reports a survey in *Fortune* magazine which suggests that less than 10 per cent of strategies are successfully implemented. Other management 'gurus' sees it as much less than this!

One of the authors spent some time in the early 1980s with a group of health service planners. The planners gave an account of how they conscientiously drew up strategic planning documents which then were filed away in cupboards.

This can be contrasted with a more recent (1997) discussion with a colleague who had spent time consulting with a medium-sized company about strategic issues. After a couple of days of intense discussion the colleague produced a full and detailed report for the chief executive. The chief executive requested a much briefer document avoiding the detail. Within a day this had been transformed into succinct decisions which were communicated throughout the organization in terms of time constraints and measurable targets.

The point about taking a strategic perspective is that it has an impact upon the decisions which you take either as an individual or as part of an organization. Sometimes the conscious decision not to act (or react) is as important.

Allegedly when John Major took over from Margaret Thatcher as prime minister he was reported when confronted with an issue as asking 'what if we do nothing?' This was a very significant change from his predecessor. To some this may be perceived as weakness yet we would argue that it is not necessarily the case. The history of his predecessor had the example of the poll tax change where she had determined upon a course of action despite major opposition from cabinet colleagues.

You can, as an individual, assess your career and likely prospects. As a result, you may conclude that your knowledge base is out of date and that your prospects in your current organization are limited and precarious. This should lead you to take decisions over what to do about it. The option of 'what if I do nothing' has a clear (and presumably undesired) consequence in this case?

The consideration of options is addressed in the next chapter (Chapter 10). We would refer you to this chapter.

THE IMPLEMENTATION OF DECISIONS

A key element of the strategic perspective is actually carrying out decisions which emerge from the process of strategic analysis and reflection. As we mentioned previously, many strategies fail in their implementation.

An earlier chapter (Chapter 4) has covered focusing upon results and much of that chapter is highly relevant for implementing strategic decisions. Managers rarely are able to achieve change singlehanded, so winning the active involvement of staff and colleagues is critical.

Often, however, it is very useful to demonstrate that a decision is being implemented through personal example. When Heather Rabbetts was appointed chief executive of the London Borough of Lambeth she took on what had been described as the worst job in local government. Previous chief executives had left in frustration and many saw the organization as almost beyond help. There was no lack of advice about what was wrong – the problem lay in implementing change. Ms Rabbetts identified some areas where it was possible to visibly implement change. One was in ensuring that the broken light bulbs in the public areas of housing estates were replaced. Two staff were given this specific task to complete. It was, on the face of it, a relatively simple and minor task. However, the fact that the chief executive ensured that it was implemented sent out a powerful message within and outside the organization.

The allocation of resources

In many organizations there is a natural inertia. It is demonstrated by the stock answer to the question 'why are we doing this the way that we do?' The stock answer is 'because we have always done it this way'.

When a strategic change occurs in an organization – or in an individual – it is often accompanied by a change in the way that resources are allocated. If you are undertaking some kind of management qualification then it is quite likely that you will have had to decide to reallocate your own personal resources. If you are having to meet the financial cost – at least in part – yourself then you may have had to change your spending or saving pattern. This would be a reallocation of financial resources. You will have had to make a commitment of personal time to the course. This commitment may well involve reducing the time that you spend on other activities – hobbies and sports, for example. You may have had to reschedule work activities or obtain resources such as a computer in order to complete your planned course.

In short, your strategic decision has a resource implication mostly for you but also for your organization. It is a source of interest to us that organizations (particularly in the public sector) are sometimes prepared to give a manager a day off a week for a management course but regard the cost of the course as not within their resources. Twenty per cent of an average manager's salary for one year is easily more than the cost of most management qualification courses. The private sector sometimes views it the other way around. They will pay for the course but expect the manager to take annual leave for at least a part of the time off.

The commitment and use of resources represents one of the most important managerial responsibilities. It sends a powerful message to organizational stakeholders. A strategic decision which is accompanied by a resource decision has a much greater probability of being implemented. Sir John Harvey-Jones, when he visited a major hospital trust during the *Troubleshooter* series on TV, stressed the importance of keeping resourcing promises. Hospital managers had encouraged senior hospital doctors to put forward initiatives to improve services. However, these initiatives had not been resourced in the budget. John Harvey-Jones commented to the new hospital chief executive that when a manager had made a promise then it was essential to deliver upon it.

The use of planning

Earlier in the book we have covered the issues of practical planning activities (Chapter 4). Strategic planning in the sense of a highly structured exercise has been criticized by Henry Mintzberg. He suggests that there are a number of possible uses for planning in terms of adopting a strategic perspective.

First, planning represents 'thinking about the future'. In this respect it is arguable that all managers engage in this so Mintzberg suggests that this does not distinguish planning for the everyday managerial role.

Second, planning can be seen as 'controlling the future'. This, to some extent, is also synonymous with management activity since much of a manager's time is spent on trying to forestall or head off undesirable future possibilities and encourage or enable desirable ones. In short, a good manager engages in 'fire prevention'.

Third, planning can be viewed as 'decision making'. Mintzberg argues that planning as decision making is akin to future thinking because decision making is always undertaken with some view to the future. The more cynical reader may, however, observe that decision making is sometimes undertaken simply to avoid the consequences of the past!

Fourth, planning could be regarded as 'integrated decision making'. This is a more sophisticated view of the manager's role which encompasses making commitments and realizing that individual decisions impact upon each other.

Finally, planning can be described as a formalised procedure to produce an articulated result in the form of an integrated system of decisions. Here the concept of planning is akin to the ideal model of planning envisaged by writers in the 1960s and 1970s. Stages are set out and the parts all fit together like a complex engineering diagram.

Which of these views of strategic planning is best? Arguably it all depends upon the nature of your organization and its environment. There is little point in engaging in long-drawn-out and sophisticated planning procedures where you have a dramatically and rapidly changing environment. Many miners thought that the government's planning document *A Plan for Coal* offered an assurance of the survival of their industry. They were sadly mistaken. On the other hand, there are some aspects of the economy where change is more predictable and longer-term plans can be made. The major utilities such as water are able to plan with a high degree of confidence that the consumer will still desire their product.

Monitoring progress

Some years ago a television documentary followed a number of young managers in various industries. One of the managers was responsible for an 'upmarket' fast-food restaurant. He was asked in the programme what was the secret of successful management. He responded that there were three keys to success and they were 'follow up, follow up and follow up'.

There are some organizations where employees do the right thing and can be simply left alone to get on with the job. Arguably, such an organization should be disposing of most, if not all, its managers.

In the public sector the advent of Compulsory Competitive Tendering (CCT) was seen by some as meaning that staff supervision was no longer needed since the requirements were all set out in the contract. The supervisor no longer had to make sure that the workers were digging holes since the 'hole digging' was contracted out.

However, the old saying 'what gets measured gets done' can be rewritten as 'what gets monitored gets done'. Some activities are more easily monitored than others. One of the authors worked, while a student, for an organization that delivered leaflets. Some of the leaflet deliverers knew that the organization only checked certain streets to ensure that the leaflets had been delivered. High-rise flats and less desirable areas were not checked. So these deliverers would only deliver leaflets to the areas which they knew would be checked and simply dropped the leaflets intended for the other areas into skips. This was at odds with the strategy (and contract) of the leafleting company and its corporate customers. However, because the monitoring was inadequate the delivery workers cut corners.

Leadership and strategy

There is often a view that good leaders are born that way and leadership is not acquired through practice or learnt in the classroom. Certainly leadership is a 'soft skill' and is harder to define than factors such as physical strength. However, people can and do develop leadership ability. The leader in the school playground does not necessarily automatically go on to become a a fast-track manager.

Where strategy is concerned often a particular kind of leadership is required. A famous army general once commented that he saw his officers along two dimensions – the degree of energy and the degree of intelligence. The intelligent and energetic he made into commanders of brigades (large parts of the army) since they would not only carry out orders but would also exercise initiative in how they implemented them. The intelligent and the lazy he kept as staff officers in his headquarters since they could be relied upon to find short-cuts to avoid the expenditure of unnecessary energy. The less intelligent but energetic he entrusted with smaller roles in the field of battle since they could be relied upon to carry out their orders. Finally, the least intelligent and lazy he sought to get rid of.

The example illustrates the point that leadership involves making judgements. These judgements may in some cases be wrong – in fact they almost certainly will be wrong in some cases. Good leaders will recognize this and be honest about their mistakes.

There are two aspects of leadership which are key to success in effecting strategic change.

First, a manager who has won no respect from the workforce is likely to find it almost impossible to achieve major change. Respect is not the same as being liked. Respect is not something that can be conferred like a company car or a new office desk. It has to be earned by the manager. A significant factor in whether respect is earned is whether the manager behaves ethically. Unscrupulous, devious and deceitful behaviour may have a short-term payoff. However, in the longer term it is likely to rebound on the manager. Even in the Mafia the term 'a man of respect' had an implication other than that of a propensity to violence.

Second, a manager must provide an example to others. If the factory has been flooded by a burst pipe then the manager must be willing literally to wade in and lend a hand. In strategic terms this means that where a major change is being sought then the manager must take the initiative and demonstrate the ability to change themselves. This can rebound as a top water company manager found when he advocated, by personal example, being frugal in water usage. Unfortunately the press found that he was going to a relative's house and using their bath.

SUMMARY

This chapter will not, in itself, turn you into a company strategic manager. Hopefully, it will encourage you to think more strategically and where your job involves a strategic perspective you will find useful guidance. At various points we have referred you to other chapters in this book. This chapter cannot be read in isolation. The suggested Further Reading at the end of the chapter is especially important if you wish to explore the techniques further or seek alternative methods.

It is important to stress that 'a strategic perspective' can be held irrespective of position within an organization. The examples we have sought to use have, at times, been independent of whether you hold a management role. Just as a panel of refuse collectors can make more accurate economic predictions than leading business schools, so you can observe and speculate upon what the future might hold and the wisdom of alternative courses of action.

However, if you are a manager then remember that if your role influences the strategic direction of your organization then you bear a particular responsibility to exercise that role as skilfully and conscientiously as you can.

PREPARING FOR ACTION PLANNING

Remember the checklist of questions identified in the Introduction to this book? Try them again to identify your further development needs. We have reproduced those most appropriate to this chapter to help you. You will need to adapt them to the issues discussed.

Who/where are your largest customer bases (customers may be internal or external to the organization)?

How do you find out about your customers' needs?

How do you make customers aware that your products/services are available?

How effective are the communication mechanisms that you use?

What would you do if there was a low take-up of the products/services you provide?

How do you currently coordinate your activities in order to develop your product/service provision?

How are organizational performance standards determined and by whom?

How do you ensure that these performance standards are being met?

How do you measure these standards?

How do you deal with any customer complaints?

How do you handle health and safety issues at your workplace?

How appropriate is your location for the product/service you provide?

Which outside agencies do you currently liaise with?

Are there any joint working arrangements in your product/service provision (this may apply across teams, or between organizations)?

Who are these and for what purposes do the arrangements exist?

What actions would you/have you taken with others at times of particular difficulty or change?

Which methods do you use to analyse facts and figures for your job purposes?

How do you present these facts and figures to others for decision-making purposes?

How effective are your analytical and mathematical skills in convincing others?

Were the outcomes of these presentations appropriate for the decision-making purposes?

How might you improve your analytical and mathematical skills?

How do you liaise with others at off-site locations?

How is information fed back into the decision-making process?

What, if any, interdepartmental group activities do you participate in?

What are the main purposes of these groups?

How would you identify your own development needs within the job role?

How would you meet the needs you had identified?

How do you evaluate your progress?

How do you evaluate your own performance against your work objectives?

How do you evaluate the performance of others against their objectives?

What methods do you use to give feedback to others about their performance?

What information do you need to do your job and for what purposes?

Do you have any problems obtaining this information?

To whom do you supply information?

How much time do you spend in:

- Gathering information?
- Analysing information?
- Providing information?

How do you go about gathering, analysing and providing information?

Can these methods be improved?

How do you currently store and receive information?

Do your meetings result in positive action?

Have you attended committees in your current role and prepared reports for these committees?

Questions devised by, and adapted from, the Crediting Competence Team at South Bank University and reproduced with permission.

FURTHER READING

Johnson, G. and Scholes, K. (1993), *Exploring Corporate Strategy*, Prentice Hall, Englewood Cliffs, NJ.
Kotler, P. (1980), *Marketing Management: Analysis Planning and Control*, Prentice Hall, Englewood Cliffs, NJ.
Mintzberg, H. (1994), *The Rise and Fall of Strategic Planning*, Prentice Hall, Englewood Cliffs, NJ.
Porter, M. E. (1980), *Competitive Strategy: Techniques for Analysing Industries and Competitors*, Free Press, New York.

10 Thinking and decision making

Managers displaying thinking and decision-making skills analyse and make deductions from information in order to form judgements and take decisions.

INTRODUCING THE RELATIONSHIP BETWEEN THE MCI PERSONAL COMPETENCY MODEL AND THINKING AND DECISION MAKING

The MCI Integrated *Model of Personal Competency* identifies the behaviours and skills necessary for you to develop, before you are able to prove competence in any managerial function. This chapter attempts to deal with the various behaviours and skills necessary for you to apply across all managerial functions, transferring your learning to different occasions, at different times and under varying circumstances (contexts), consistently. The outcomes below, as identified within this section of the model, should be borne in mind while you work through this chapter.

Outcomes required in thinking and decision making

There are three major sets of behaviour to this chapter, commencing with the manager's ability in *Analysing*. When analysing the manager:

- Breaks down situations into simple tasks and activities
- Identifies a range of elements in and perspectives on a situation
- Identifies implications, consequences or causal relationships in a situation
- Uses a range of ideas to explain the actions, needs and motives of others.

The second behavioural set focuses on the manager's need for *Conceptualizing* in order to make decisions. In this process, the manager:

- Uses his or her own experience and evidence from others to identify problems and understand situations

- Identifies patterns or meaning from events and data which are not obviously related
- Builds a total and valid picture (or concept) from restricted or incomplete data (which happens to be most of the time).

The third set of behaviours addresses a manager's *Judgement* and *decision-making* abilities. When forming judgements and making decisions, the manager:

- Produces a variety of solutions before taking a decision
- Balances intuition with logic in decision making
- Reconciles and makes use of a variety of perspectives when making sense of a situation
- Produces his or her own ideas from experience and practice
- Takes the experience and practice of others into account
- Takes decisions which are realistic for the situation
- Focuses on facts, problems and solutions when handling an emotional situation (not personalities)
- Takes decisions in uncertain situations, or based on restricted information when necessary.

Thinking, or communicating with oneself, is something we naturally do more unconsciously than consciously. It is such an automatic process that unless we have become aware and educate ourself accordingly, much of our thinking can be wasted. It is the purest form of 'communicating' and does not necessarily involve language. If we are thinking in a structured way, we undoubtedly use our mother-language in order to proceed logically in our thinking. When unstructured thoughts come to us, they can be in the form of pictures, symbols, even quite complicated conundrums at times. We frequently ignore or dismiss them as irrelevant to our present need.

There are times when our random, unstructured thinking is of extreme value; hence the gaining credibility of 'brainstorming' exercises. It is not so easy to brainstorm as some people may believe. We are all concerned, in one way or another, about our individual abilities to do what is right, our credibility in the eyes of others, fear of looking stupid and so on.

We should learn to trust our own thinking more and share random thoughts with others in the workplace. It is a wonderful way of gaining trust and support, because this is a means of refining and developing ideas and issues; allowing the contribution of others to influence our values, beliefs and behaviour. Our own self-guilt often prevents our development of good thinking and communicating with ourselves.

INTRODUCTION

This chapter will introduce you to problem solving and decision making. You may have considerable experience in solving problems and making decisions.

Managers are expected to do this. However, the problem-solving and decision-making methods used may be ineffectual or otherwise inappropriate.

Management writers argue about the relationship between problem solving and decision making. Some claim that problem solving is part of decision making. Others feel the reverse and argue that decision making is part of problem solving. There are those who feel that problem solving and decision making should be seen as similar terms to describe the same process.

Here the view adopted is to see them both as part of a process. The focus of this chapter is on the concept of a problem which has to be identified, understood and solved.

AN OVERVIEW OF PROBLEM SOLVING

Consider a day in the life of Sandy Jones, a manager, in terms of a succession of problems encountered. As you read the problems confronting Sandy consider what your reaction might be.

1   Sandy learns from the news that the train services are delayed, which will create a problem in getting to work for an 8.30 am meeting.
2   On arriving at work Sandy has to cover for the absence of a senior colleague who has been taken ill.
3   Sandy receives a letter from an aggrieved customer complaining about poor service.
4   Sandy's boss discovers that all the managers wish to take holidays in August and asks Sandy to come up with some ideas in response to this.
5   The telephone bills run up by Sandy's section are twice as high as the same time last year. The finance manager calls Sandy about it.

Before reading any further take a sheet of paper and write down your reactions. If you have a colleague or friend to hand, share the problems with them then compare your reactions with theirs.

Some of Sandy's problems might require an immediate solution. Others might be satisfactorily resolved with investigation. Some may not have any obvious solution. Some, on reflection and investigation, may not be problems at all!

It is not the nature of the solutions themselves that you propose which is of interest, as much as whether you actually propose any at all!

Sandy's reaction to the first problem almost certainly would be based upon personal knowledge and experience. Perhaps Sandy has an alternative to using the train. A telephone message could be passed to the person chairing the meeting. Possibly the meeting may be postponed. After all, other people attending the meeting may also be affected by the travel delays.

The second problem would require Sandy to establish what the colleague had scheduled for the day; Sandy would need to find this out from the colleague or those familiar with his or her schedule. Perhaps some of the responsibility could be delegated. If the colleague had a tight schedule then Sandy may well have to rearrange priorities and postpone meetings. Sandy may be quite familiar with the colleague's work and work contacts. Alternatively, the colleague's work may be very unfamiliar to Sandy.

The letter of complaint could require urgent investigation. Much would depend upon the context and the expectations of the organization. If the organization was well used to receiving complaints it may be almost a routine response. On the other hand, the company may be concerned about any complaint because of the quality standards or nature of the product. In such an organization complaints may have the highest priority and be handled at quite a senior level.

The situation of holiday leave is one where there is likely to be different priorities in operation. The managers' interests may differ from that of the organization.

The use of the telephone may not in fact represent a problem. However, in order to establish this Sandy would need to provide information to explain why the bill had gone up. Possibly Sandy's organization does a lot of telephone selling and the usage is a sign of an active salesforce. Alternatively, it could represent a lack of control over resources – or even deliberate abuse of resources by staff making many personal calls.

How did you respond to Sandy's problems? Did you see them in terms of your own particular experience, work setting or work habits? If so then your response could probably have led you to propose 'solutions'. This would not be an uncommon reaction in managers who are 'hands-on' and proactive. It could be said to be more characteristic of an Active or Pragmatist Learning style.

On the other hand, if your reaction was to ask questions to elicit more information then you were possibly reacting in a way less dependent upon your work setting, experience or habits. The reluctance to 'rush to judgement' associated with the desire to acquire more (and more) information can be associated with a more Reflective or Theoretical Learning style.

You may have realized that some of the problems Sandy confronts are more amenable to group discussion than others. Similarly, some have tight time constraints. The first one, for example, requires that Sandy react quite quickly or accept the consequences of 'non-action'. Apologizing after the meeting for failing to attend is less appropriate than communicating reasons for non-attendance in advance.

Some of the problems may not be problems at all. The higher telephone usage may be an inevitable result of staff doing their work effectively. The absent colleague may have had no commitments scheduled for that day.

Some of the problems may not have any obvious solution. There may not be any possibility of building a consensus to accept a solution because those involved have incompatible and opposing priorities. The intention of all managers to take leave at the same time may fall into this category.

Some of the problems could be extremely serious. If the company made very high-value products where failure was seen as having large cost implications then a complaint might be very serious. An aircraft manufacturer, for example, would take extremely seriously a complaint that vital parts of the airplane were failing.

How to categorize problems

There is a wide range of ways to categorize problems. Here are several which you may find helpful in thinking about problems you encounter in your work and home life.

Tudor Rickards (1990) uses the following set of categories:

1 'One right answer problems'

We are all familiar with these. What is 15 per cent of 100 invites the answer '15'. You would justifiably argue with someone proposing a different solution. There is often a considerable element of creativity involved in finding the answer to such problems. The living of crossword puzzle compilers relies on this.

2 Insight problems

Here the answer comes from a new perspective. This involves an element of creative thinking. We have all been there at some time. Anyone who has locked themselves out of their car or house has probably tried to think creatively about how to get in without the key.

The account of Archimedes arriving at an insight in his bath is an example. He was trying to work out how much gold was in a crown. He knew the weight of the crown but was unable to work out the volume. It was necessary to have both the weight and volume of the crown in order to know whether it was pure gold. As he sat down in his bath he realized the water level rose and he could use the displaced water to measure the volume of an object.

3 Wicked problems

The success of the solution requires that it be tried out. Is the reason the light won't work a defective bulb, a blown fuse or the lack of a power supply? One way to find out is to test for each possible cause in turn. It may well be a combination rather than one single cause. More commonly it occurs in organizations when a solution has to be tried out in order to see if it will solve the problem. Restructuring and reorganization are examples of this.

The introduction of water metering on the Isle of Wight is a attempt to try out a possible solution to the various problems of water supply and rationing. The concept of paying for the amount of water you use is seen as something which has to be tried out in practice. The views of experts or the results of consumer surveys would not be regarded as sufficient to support the massive cost implications of changing over a substantial part of the country. There is also the consumer reaction to be considered.

4 Vicious problems

A problem may seem to have a straightforward answer but the human element adds a complication. The presence of outmoded and costly work practices in both the newspaper industry and in the car industry challenged managers for many years. The solutions might have seemed obvious but the industrial relations complications were enormous. There is scope for what Tudor Rickards calls 'lose–lose' behaviours in which those affected by the problems all end up worse off.

The UK coal dispute in the 1980s offers an example where there was from the management perspective a clear need to rationalize the coal industry and make it more competitive. However, the perspective of many of the miners was of a threat to whole communities and a way of life. In hindsight we may well look back and wonder how it got to the stage of such entrenched positions. Surely there must be a more positive way of settling disputes and bringing about necessary change without so much suffering and ill feeling?

5 Fuzzy problems

Here the problem is difficult to solve because straightforward logic cannot be easily applied. An example is the attempt to computerize mail services by using computers to 'read' addresses on envelopes. It works reasonably well with typed envelopes but handwritten addresses pose a major challenge. The machine can process the envelopes far more quickly than the human operator can. Yet the human operator is able to categorize the handwritten addresses.

The way the Post Office resolved this problem was to install a video camera facility which took a picture of each address the machine could not read. The letters were fed through the machine in batches and the human operator fed in the correct code for the letters whose addresses were highlighted on a video screen. The computer remembered the order of the letters in the batch. So the batch of letters could be passed through the machine a second time for the hand-written addresses to be machine coded using the information keyed in by the human operator. While the human operator was keying in the correct information the machine could be processing other batches of letters.

It is worth noting that a problem can occupy more than one category. A fuzzy problem may also be a wicked one for example.

Problems can also be seen as existing along dimensions rather than in seperate categories. Here are some examples of such dimensions:

Straightforward ——————————————— Complex

A straightforward problem usually can be identified because there is sufficient knowledge as to what would constitute a solution and the problem has clear boundaries. The recent concerns about the risks of electrically operated car windows to small children would be an example. The manufacturers are well aware of how to reduce the risk. Some cars already have the necessary safeguards installed. Government legislation to require all manufacturers to do it would constitute a solution.

A complex problem often has no obvious solution and may be unbounded. An example would be the congestion of road traffic in the London area. It is argued that building more roads just leads to more cars followed by more congestion. Improving public transport, on the other hand, is seen as requiring enormous investment and people may even then prefer to use cars. Furthermore, the problem is complicated by the wide range of reasons for travel and the need to move goods and freight. The way the problem is defined can create the complexity. Transport is related to how and where people work. It is hard to put a precise boundary around ' transport' without looking at patterns of change in work generally.

Not technical ——————————————— Highly technical

A non-technical problem is one which is readily understood and solveable by a ' lay person' (i.e. someone who has no particular technical or professional training). We handle such problems all the time in our everyday lives: where to go shopping; when to take a holiday; who to invite to your office leaving party.

Technical problems, on the other hand, require a level of technical or professional training or experience in order to arrive at a solution. When your dentist inspects a cavity in a tooth he or she makes a judgement about whether a filling is suitable or whether a more radical solution is indicated. Similarly, the experienced plumber might know from listening to that worrying groan in your central heating whether your boiler requires a service. When you pay for technical advice you are often paying a premium for the training or experience which enables the person to diagnose the problem.

Hence the oft-quoted account of the service engineer who fixes a domestic appliance by tapping it with a hammer. The customer queries the bill of £30 so the engineer divides the bill into two parts:

£1 for tapping the appliance with a hammer

£29 for the 10 years' knowledge and experience which enabled me to know how hard to tap and where to tap.

Emotionally charged ———————————————— Not emotionally charged

Some problems have a high emotional content. They arouse strong feelings in those involved and sometimes in those not directly involved. Famine relief charities are well aware of the powerful images created by pictures of starving children. The issues associated with adoption of Romanian babies were both complex and highly emotional. Managers often use a shorthand phrase to describe 'emotionally charged' problems. They call them 'people problems'. What is important is to be aware of the limitations of strict logic in their resolution.

There are some problems which have little emotional content. They sometimes involve little personal involvement. The selection of your lunchtime sandwich might be an example. Others may require enormous effort and commitment to resolve. The conduct of scientific research in non-emotive areas would be an example.

Sometimes it can be helpful to use two dimensions to create a box or graph in which to locate problems. This may show, for example, that of a range of technical problems some are highly emotionally charged and thus need to be handled differently. Figure 10.1 represents examples of how four typical office problems could fit into the categories.

	Not emotionally charged	Emotionally charged
Technical	Repair of office equipment	Introduction of new technology
Not technical	Agreement on lunch rota	Staff reorganization

Figure 10.1   Using boxes to categorize problems

The use of simple devices such as this to define and present problems can be of great value to the manager in trying to understand the nature of a problem. They also can serve as a useful communication tool in consulting with staff about workplace problems. Figure 10.1 could be used to show staff that uncertainty and unease over reorganization is in a different category from the lunch rota or getting equipment repaired. All problems can become emotionally charged if badly handled. Thus the agreement over the lunch rota could become an emotional one on account of how it was handled.

CREATIVE THINKING

Creative thinking is the relating of things or ideas that were previously unrelated. People often feel that a problem has a 'single correct answer'. This viewpoint leads to a narrowing down of options. Narrowing down does not promote creativity.

John Rawlinson (1981) distinguishes between analytical and creative thought:

Analytical thought

- Relies on logic
- Aims to come up with only a few answers (or only one answer)
- Is convergent in that it aims to narrow down the range of possibilities
- Is vertical (see below)
- Uses various techniques to close down the range of options (see below).

You will see this exemplified in the problem solving approach of Kepner and Tregoe (1981) later in this chapter.

Creative thought

- Uses imagination
- Seeks many possible answers or ideas
- Is divergent in that it aims to open up the range of possibilities
- Is lateral (see below)
- Uses various techniques to open up the range of options. One of these techniques is brainstorming described later in this chapter.

In practice a combination of both analytical and creative thought is usually required.

What is associated with creativity?

Henry Mintzberg (1973) and others have noted that an understanding of how the brain functions is important to understanding why people seem able to cope with some mental activities but not others. In particular, Mintzberg wonders why it is that top managers often seem impervious to the sophisticated techniques of planning that they have available to them.

The brain is divided into two distinct hemispheres. Oversimplified, you can think of it as an orange split into two halves. Each hemisphere controls movement on the opposite side of the body. Certain functions such as speech are primarily controlled on one side. Stroke victims can suffer major speech impairment as a result of a stroke affecting the left hemisphere of the brain.

Recent research suggests that there is also specialization between the two halves of the brain in respect of thought processes. The left side of the brain thinks in a logical fashion. Hence the fact that speech, a logical ordering of sound, is a left-brain activity. The right side of the brain, however, tends to think more in visual images. Here the way information is handled is more in terms of relationships and the broad picture rather than of a logical sequence.

Therefore certain types of intellectual activity, such as understanding the logic of a mathematical proof, are left-brain focused. Other activities such as the creation of a painting or design of an advertising logo are primarily right brain.

Formal planning activities in management using scientific or logical techniques are left-brain orientated. When you follow the bakery problem using the Kempner–Tregoe technique later in this chapter you will be using the left side of your brain. However, practising managers often operate intuitively. This usually comes from experience. They recognize that problems are rarely amenable to strict logic and that we live in an imperfect world. Hence the need to use the right brain in managerial activity.

Mintzberg (1973) illustrates the 'right-brain tendencies' of managers from the following findings of his research.

- Managers tend to favour verbal over written communication. This is because it enables a whole picture to be formed. The tone of voice and type of expression adds to the image.
- Much of the analysis managers undertake is not of hard numerical data but rather of fuzzy and more opinionated information. The organization grapevine is a source which managers are prone to use as much, if not more, than anyone else.
- Managers often find it hard to pass information down to people. Yet in order to delegate work this has to be done. A possible explanation is that managers rely on the right side of the brain but the source of the information is logical and held on the left side.
- Managers work in short bursts of activity encompassing considerable variety. Longer-paced orderly and logically planned activities tend to be the exception.
- There are a number of managerial roles Mintzberg identifies. He regards as the most important 'leader', 'liaison', and 'disturbance handler'. These roles are often based upon experience and intuition rather than the application of logically based research findings.

- When managers engage in decision making there are parts of the process which often involve the use of intuition. The manager uses the right side of the brain in the diagnosis of what is going wrong and in designing customized solutions.
- There are aspects of the decision process where unpredictable factors have an impact. Issues such as the timing of a decision and the 'right atmosphere' for a change are often subject to intuitive but rather logical thought processes.
- When managers come to make a choice between options the method most used by managers is judgement. The application of rational analysis is less frequently used. The implication is that intuition and 'right-brain thinking' plays a significant role.
- Managers confront not the stable and predictable world that planning would wish to cater for. Rather they have to deal with an unpredictable and turbulent environment. The strict application of logical thought is in itself not sufficient for a manager to survive.
- Mintzberg suggests that strategic vision in organizations is often located within one person.

Barriers to creative thought

The potential value in creative thinking in managers can be stifled because of obstacles, which are often self-imposed. We have limits to our thinking which arise from constraints we consciously or unconsciously impose upon ourselves. This is the person who searches for a lost object in the knowledge that he or she is looking in the wrong place but hopelessly tied to a different kind of logic. Hence the classic and oft-told story of the person looking for a dropped key under a street light when they dropped the key in the shadows. The reason for looking under the street light is that 'it is easier to see what you are looking for'.

This has been observed in managers who have found a particular solution to have worked in a past situation and therefore tend to cling to it even when it is less appropriate to the problem in hand. The effect is to limit the managers' search to particular areas.

As an example consider the following:

$$1 + 0 =$$

Most people would react immediately with '1'. However, thinking creatively the option of '10' is also possible. If the inclination to view 1 and 0 as numbers is resisted and + is viewed creatively the possibility of 'In and Out' occurs. If 1 and 0 are simply seen as geometric shapes then a wide variety of ways to combine them become apparent making a variety of both familar and unfamilar shapes (tree, child's top, eye with eyelid, etc.).

Patterns

We often use particular patterns as a way of forming our thought process. Though useful, these patterns can impede creativity. As an example consider the following:

1,4,7,11,14,17, ...

Which of the following is next in sequence: 21 or 41? Many people opt for '21' by seeing the sequence as a mathematical progression. However, if the pattern is seen in terms of numbers made up only of straight lines then the next number in the sequence is 41 (only straight lines).

Consider the next letter in the following sequence:

FGH ...

I or J?

Conformity

There is a natural tendency to avoid 'standing out from the crowd'. This can be an obstruction to creativity. A famous industrial manager, Alfred Sloan, had convened a meeting of his managers to review some proposals which had been made. He asked if any of the managers had problems about the proposals and received a reply that none had. Whereupon he adjourned the meeting until such time as the managers had found some problems with the proposals.

Not challenging the obvious

The perception of a problem is often based upon an assumption that has to be challenged in order for a creative solution to emerge.

During the Second World War Barnes Wallis invented a number of new and highly effective bombs. One assumption which he challenged was that you had to hit the target in order to destroy it. Some of the fortifications in question were believed impregnable to direct hits. Wallis conceived of destroying them by near misses which would undermine the foundations.

Jump to judgement

There is often a willingness to rush to a solution before the various dimensions of the problem have been fully explored. In effect it involves 'closing off' the options at too early a stage.

The concern about meeting the needs of elderly people, for example, led to the rapid expansion of facilities such as residential homes, nursing homes and day centres. It was assumed that such provision would be the answer to the problem. Experience has shown that the needs of elderly people must be met by a range of resources and that indeed often it is the families of elderly people who need the resource as much as the elderly person.

Looking a fool

It is only natural to avoid potential embarrassment. The fear of seeming foolish often stifles creativity. The technique of classic brainstorming outlined later relies upon the suspension of judgement as to the wisdom or foolishness of the generated ideas.

VERTICAL AND LATERAL THINKING

Edward de Bono developed the concept of Lateral Thinking and contrasted it with Vertical Thinking. He maintains that traditional education focuses upon the development of vertical thought processes. It is important to note that though they are two different and distinct types of thought process it does not necessarily follow that they always lead to different outcomes. De Bono views both as important in problem solving. He distinguishes between Lateral and Vertical thinking in the ways shown in Figure 10.2.

Lateral thinking	Vertical thinking
Seeks changes	Seeks judgement
Looks for difference	Looks for yes/no answers
Uses information to provoke new ideas	Uses information to analyse what works or doesn't
Uses intuitive leaps	Proceeds in logical steps
Welcomes distraction	Focuses on what is relevant
Follows unlikely avenues	Follows the most likely avenue
Open ended: no promise of a result	Closed: promises at least a minimal outcome

Figure 10.2   Lateral versus vertical thinking

Thus an example from De Bono's own younger days happened when on an initiative exercise he was in a group of people tasked with using ropes and bits of wood to get across a water-filled hole. De Bono is reported to have suggested that the problem be solved by moving the hole.

Lateral and Vertical thought is an extremely important concept to understand in problem solving. Let us consider some examples.

You are going on holiday with your caravan and you arrive at Dover Harbour late at night to catch the early morning ferry. You have no alarm clock and know that you need to sleep. How will you wake up in time to catch the ferry?

A logical (Vertical) approach would probably focus upon the possibility of obtaining an alarm clock or securing the help of someone to wake you up in time. The steps would be considered in logical sequence. Try local shops and supermarkets, service stations, etc. Failing that, you could see if a local hotel might agree to wake you up for a fee.

Lateral thinking would open up a range of other possibilities. One solution would be to scatter bread on the caravan roof so that birds would come and feed in the early morning. Why not park illegally so that you would be moved by the 'authorities'? Perhaps you could 'make' an alarm clock by using what you have. A canister dripping water onto another which when it becomes just so full will fall over, making a noise. What businesses are likely to open up early and generate sufficient noise to awaken you ... perhaps the local dairy? Why park near the docks anyway? Why not drive out and park near a farm so that the farm animals will wake you up?

Special techniques to promote lateral thinking

1 Awareness
This is awareness of current ideas and what characterizes them. De Bono Suggests that the following aspects of current ideas are useful in gaining this understanding.

2 Dominant ideas
These can determine how the problem or issue is viewed. Different people may hold different dominant ideas about the same issue. Attitude to trade union recognition may vary but is often shaped by dominant ideas about the role of trade unions in society, etc.

3 Assumptions or tethering factors
Here people often have operating assumptions about the problem. De Bono uses the example that people assume that the longer you park your car, the less it should cost per hour. However, if traffic congestion is caused by parked rather than moving traffic then perhaps the per hour rate should increase, the longer you park your car.

CONVERGENT AND DIVERGENT PROBLEM-SOLVING STRATEGIES

Problems can generally be divided into two categories. On the one hand, there is a problem which shows itself because something that was expected to occur has not happened as expected. Another way of expressing this is as a deviation from some standard or expected result. The nature of the problem can be described in terms of this deviation.

Then there are problems where something prevents what you want to happen from taking place. There is an obstacle in the way which has to be overcome. Typically it is associated with a desire to make some kind of change. Here the need is often to generate ideas and options. Thus the recently issued (July 1992) Customer Charter for London Underground states:

> We aim to run **460** trains each peak period. Our target is to run not less than **97.5** per cent of them at the busiest times. Last year we averaged **96.4** per cent. We will show our performance line by line on a poster at every station.

From this we can infer the following expected results:

1 There is a target of 460 trains each peak period
2 There is a target of 449 trains during the busiest part of the peak period (97.5 per cent of 460)
3 There is a target of showing the performance of each tube line on a poster at every underground station.

These targets may represent desired changes (if they are targets which are not currently being met). If they are not currently capable of being met then they represent the second kind of problem. There may be obstacles such as insufficient trains, staffing problems or lack of space for posters at some stations.

Given the targets are currently being met, if one or more of these results fails to occur then it could be regarded as a 'deviation' from the expected. As such it will be amenable to a structured problem-solving approach.

There are a variety of models to guide a manager on how to solve both kinds of problems. John Adair has run courses on managerial decision making and problem solving. On these courses he asked managers what they actually did. From this John Adair suggests the following five stages which managers follow in problem solving or in making a decision:

1 *Define the objective*: This involves recognizing that a problem exists which requires some kind of solution or decision.
2 *Collect information*: Here the manager gathers facts, opinions, etc. Some may need to be checked. It may also involve establishing the cause or causes of a problem. Time available and other resource constraints will be noted.
3 *Develop options*: The manager uses a range of devices to identify possible solutions. This may be as simple as just listing the options. Colleagues and people affected may need to be consulted.
4 *Evaluate and decide*: The manager uses various devices to decide upon the most appropriate option. This will involve some kind of selection criteria.
5 *Implement*: The chosen option is then acted upon. The progress of the solution is monitored and reviewed.

There is a sixth stage which should usually take place but which is often missed out.

6 Learning and feedback

A post mortem may be conducted to ascertain whether the option was worth doing. This can be a source of learning for the future.

Adair suggests that this five-point plan can serve as a general model of how managers behave. It has strong validity and the virtue of simplicity.

Let us see how it might operate in everyday life. Most of us will have to move home at some stage. If we live with other people then it is a problem which affects more than just the individual. The way the process might operate is as follows.

First, you recognize that there is a problem over your current accommodation. Let us assume that you feel that it has become too small for your needs. You are aware that there is simply not enough space for your family and its possessions. Cupboards bulge and spill their contents. The bicycles rust outside because there is insufficient space indoors. The children need separate bedrooms. You realize that there is a problem and that you need to make a decision to resolve it.

The next stage is (in most households) to consult with partners to confirm the nature of the problem. Perhaps the cupboards are bulging because they are full of junk and a big 'clear-out' is all that is needed. The bikes may not be used at all. Do the children really need separate bedrooms? You also consider the implications of when you might wish to move. How urgent is the problem? Can you wait six months or even longer? The sensitive matter of money also rears up. Can you afford a higher mortgage or higher rent for a larger property? If so, how much? Where might you be able to move to? Moving away from your current area may not be easy.

After gathering information you then consider what options are available. The option of moving to a larger property may be available. Alternatively, you may consider it possible to extend your current property. If the issue is lack of storage for what you have you may consider building a shed or moving the car out of the garage. On a more radical note, you might consider having a major clear-out of everything not essential to your current needs. Perhaps the children could move into the large bedroom and the bedroom could be partitioned to give separate living space for each child.

The options might then be considered. Some may immediately appear as impractical. The garden may be so small that a shed would overwhelm it. Perhaps the large bedroom is impractical for a partition. Here something will almost certainly become apparent. Moving may be favoured but not outside the area. The reasons why particular options are favoured or discounted have as much to do with subjective (emotional) reasons as objective (factual) ones. The partitioning of the bedroom may be feasible in practical terms but it does not resolve the emotional desire for a 'separate bedroom'. The wish to move locally may seem irrational given that other areas have more facilities but you like the local shops and feel comfortable. Eventually you will decide and that decision will bring implementation issues.

Assuming you have decided to move then there is the selling of your current property. If it is rented you negotiate with the landlord about leaving dates and return of any damages deposit. You have to locate a new property and secure it. Then you have to make arrangements to move and have gas, electricity and telephone connected. Probably you will end up with a checklist of tasks and dates by which things need to be done.

Does this seem familiar to you? Problem solving and decision making can and do affect people in their everyday life. The principles are not so very different when it comes to putting them into practice in management.

Convergent problem solving

Kepner and Tregoe (1981) divide problem solving and decision making into two separate phases. They developed a technique for structured problem solving which has been very widely taught around the world. Kepner Tregoe has a profitable consultancy, operating in many countries based upon this problem-solving process. In the year ending 1990 they earned £2.9 million in fees in the UK.

Kepner and Tregoe's approach involves separating problem solving and decision making into two cycles. Each cycle has seven stages. The essence of the technique is that it is based upon a rational approach to problem solving. A problem is seen as a deviation from an expected outcome.

The stages for the problem-solving cycle are as follows:

- A description of the *deviation* from the expected
- An *is/is not* series of statements
- *Distinctive* features which characterize the 'Is statements'
- Whether each distinctive feature represents a *change*
- Once all distinctions and changes have been identified to look for possible *causes*
- Each cause is then *tested* to see if it explains the deviation in terms of the distinctions and is/is not statements
- Finally the most probable cause is *verified* by testing it out in the work environment where possible.

These stages can be remembered by the phrase.

DiD Close Circuit TV (DIDCCTV)

Let us see how this technique can operate in practice. We will use an example from a large bakery.

The Bakery Problem

The bakery took in the raw ingredients and manufactured bread. The dough was mixed on-site by machine from the ingredients. The loaves were then formed by machine and placed on large trays to be baked in several ovens. After they had been baked in the oven the loaves were removed and the trays placed upon trolleys and left to cool. Once the loaves had cooled they were then taken to slicing and wrapping machines where they were sliced and wrapped according to customer requirements. The loaves were then put back on trolleys and wheeled through to the van-loading bays. They were then loaded onto the company's vans. The vans delivered the loaves to a wide range of customers. Most of the customers were supermarkets and small shops who sold the bread directly to the individual customer.

The bakery ran on well-established lines. There were clear demarcation lines between management and bakery operatives. The operatives ran the machinery, handled the bread and loaded the vans. There was overall supervision by chargehands in the bakehouse and in the slice/wrap and loading areas. The chargehands adopted a free and easy attitude to supervision since the work was routine. More senior managers made occasional visits to the factory floor and when this happened operatives made a show of working hard.

However, management became concerned about quality issues. Customers would bring back loaves of bread because they had found a cigarette end embedded in the loaf between two slices of bread. In each case a manager saw the customer and an offer of compensation was made. Some customers were angry, others simply amazed at their find.

The company was understandably very concerned about these incidents. Quite aside from the customer relations impact there was the food hygiene concern. There were obvious health and safety implications.

The problem is one amenable to structured problem solving using a schema such as Kepner–Tregoe. The way it would be handled would be as follows:

Stage One: The deviation statement

Kepner and Tregoe see the problem as falling into several categories each of which needs to be explored.

Identity
What we are trying to explain
Location
Where the problem is observed
Timing
When the problem occurs

Magnitude
How serious the problem is.

The principle is ask questions based upon the maxim taught to new journalists:

Why questions: i.e. Why is it a problem?
What questions: i.e. What is the nature of the problem?
Where questions: i.e. Where does the problem occur?
When questions: i.e. When does the problem occur?
How questions: How often does it occur?

The result of applying this to the bakery problem would be as follows:

1 Identity: Some loaves are contaminated by foreign matter; namely cigarette ends.
2 Location: The problem is observed by customers when unwrapping sliced bread
3 Timing: It is an infrequent occurrence which has recently been noticed.
4 Magnitude: The problem is potentially very serious for a food manufacturer.

Stage Two: Specification of what the problem IS and IS NOT

Here the concept is one of comparison. The aim is to compare where the problem *is* to where the problem could be but *is not*. Hence the application of Kepner and Tregoe to the bakery problem might look as in Figure 10.3.

	'Is'	'Could be but is not'
Identity	Sliced bread	Unsliced bread or rolls
	Wrapped bread	Unwrapped bread
	Cigarette ends	Other items (such as coins)
Location	Customer observed	Noticed by retailers or own staff
Timing	Infrequent	Frequent
	Irregular	Regular
	Recent origin	Long standing
Magnitude	Serious	Minor
	Only few loaves	More loaves

Figure 10.3   The bakery problem (1)

Stage Three: What is distinctive about the 'IS' data

With the availability of '*is not*' comparisons can be made to provide clues as to what distinguishes the '*is*' data (Figure 10.4).

	'Is'	What is distinctive
Identity	Sliced bread	Goes through a slicing machine
	Wrapped bread	Goes through a wrapping machine
	Cigarette ends	Implies a human cause
Location	Customer observed	Disturbed wrapping paper or disfigured bread would be noticed on dispatch or delivery to retailers
Timing	Infrequent	Likely to be a chance happening
	Irregular	rather than deliberate sabotage
	Recent origin	The slicing machines are due for major servicing
Magnitude	Serious	Smoking while working is a sackable offence but many staff are heavy smokers
	Only few loaves	Chance happening

Figure 10.4   The bakery problem (2)

Stage Four: Study distinctions to determine if a change has occurred

Here the aim is to ascertain whether anything has been altered or changed in respect of any of the distinctions that have been identified. Where there is such a change then it can give a clue to the possible cause (Figure 10.5).

	What is distinctive	Change
Identity	Goes through a slicing machine	No changes in
	Goes through a wrapping machine	machines
	Implies a human cause	
Location	Disturbed wrapping paper or disfigured bread would be noticed on dispatch or delivery to retailers	No delivery changes
Timing	Likely to be a chance happening rather than deliberate sabotage	
	One of the slicing machines is overdue for major servicing	Frequent machine stoppages
Magnitude	Smoking while working is a sackable offence but recent staff recruited are heavy smokers	Smokers recruited
	Chance happening	

Figure 10.5   The bakery problem (3)

Stage Five: Generate possible causes

Here the list of distinctions and changes is used to generate possible explanations for the cause. It is important to recognize that it may be more than one cause which may be the explanation for the problem.

■ The problem clearly can be seen to affect only certain types of bread. That is the bread that has passed through one of the slicing and wrapping machines. This implies that the cause should be sought there rather than in the dough-preparation or oven stages. To introduce cigarette ends into the bread after it has been wrapped would involve a high probability of disturbing the wrapper so that it would be noticed by the loader, delivery driver or retailer. Therefore that also suggests that the cause should be sought in a prior stage of the production process.

■ The problem clearly has a human agency since cigarette ends are not part of the production process! Given the employment of smokers, it is probable that a number of the machine operators smoke. The cigarette ends could also have been put in the bread by the customers who complained in order to secure compensation.

■ The strong stricture against smoking while working – especially while working machinery – would mean that anyone doing so would be careful not to get caught. Dropping cigarette ends on the floor would amount to self-incriminatation.

■ Perhaps one or more of the machine operators has been smoking adjacent to the machine and has discarded the cigarette end into the machine where it would not be noticed by a passing supervisor.

■ The most likely machine for this to apply to is the one overdue for a major service. The frequent stoppages may mean that one operative has been smoking while the other has been trying to fix the fault.

Stage Six: Test each possible cause against the specification

The location of the problem with the slicing and wrapping machines matches the specification.

■ The recent recruitment of heavy smokers onto the staff would account for the recency.

■ The overdue maintenance of one of the machines might also account for idle staff smoking near the machine.

■ The possibility of customers putting the cigarette ends into the bread themselves would not explain why it happened only to bread that had gone through the slicing and wrapping machines.

Stage Seven: Verification of the most probable cause

In this case the company could transfer non-smokers onto the slicing and wrapping machines for a trial period to see if the incidents ceased. They could also effect the major service on the one machine so that people were not tempted to stand idle by it.

Authors' note

In the actual case from which this was drawn the approach taken was to issue a further warning to staff about smoking on the factory floor. Further incidents of spoiled loaves occurred. The supervisor then endeavoured to track down the guilty party by asking for cigarettes from each of the machine operators and comparing them with those found in the loaves. The 'guilty operative', quite aware of the supervisor's intent, changed his brand of cigarettes.

Divergent problem-solving techniques

Here the objective is to 'open up the possibilities'. Methods for being woken up for the Dover ferry could be putting birdseed on the roof, parking illegally or across a factory gate.

There are some general principles which usefully apply to such techniques:

1 Suspend judgement – get the ideas out *before* evaluating them.
2 Get as many ideas as possible.
3 Risky ideas are OK – after all, thought is not a crime.
4 Seek to join ideas together to build new ones.
5 Creative thinking is hard mental exercise – take breaks and don't try to push yourself or others into long stints at it.

The first question is whether you are 'alone' or working with a group. If you are alone it is still possible to think creatively! Most artists work that way. Let us briefly outline a couple of techniques to enhance creativity when 'on your own'. It should be stressed that these techniques are quite capable of being used in teams as well.

1 Checklists

Here you use a list of items which might help to clarify aspects of the problem or generate a range of possible solutions. It is often used when inventing new products or services. The four 'P's' in marketing (Product, Price, Place and Promotion) is a basic checklist which can be used to generate ideas.

Another list was developed by Eberle (1990) under the acronym of SCAMPER:

Substitute
Combine
Adapt
Magnify (or minimize)
Put to other uses
Eliminate
Reverse

The use of checklists has the advantage of simplicity but the disadvantage that they generate ideas in the particular direction associated with the item on the checklist. Would a checklist have given rise to the 'invention' of a product like Polo Mints where the key product characteristic is a hole in the middle?

2 Problem division

It may be that the problem can be divided into two or more dimensions and that each of these can be divided into categories which can be compared. As an example, consider problems in communication within an organization. Figure 10.6 shows how this might be considered along two dimensions. The 3 × 3 matrix gives nine possible areas to generate improvements in communication within the organization. Obviously, further dimensions could also be added (Seniority, Department, Location are possibilities). These would give rise to far more possible areas to consider.

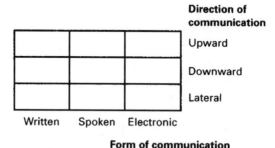

Figure 10.6   Communication problem in an organization

3 The use of analogies

An analogy is an observation which links one item to another in some kind of compared relationship. So you may be concerned with quality of recruitment in your organization. You would generate analogies drawing on the concept of quality. A list of analogies might be the following:

- Finish of product
- Attention to detail
- Amount of thought
- Checked carefully
- Assurance that it has been produced to the best of one's ability
- Won't let me down
- Don't mind paying extra for it
- Five-star hotel
- Reliability
- Focus on design
- Time spent in conceptual stage
- Conscientious about work and standards
- Caring for customer

The analogies are then considered and ones which seem applicable can be, in turn, developed further. Perhaps the analogy of caring for the customer seems useful. Maybe that can be developed into the conception of regarding potential staff as customers. This could give rise such ideas as:

- Personalized letters
- Better reception arrangements
- Interviews arranged at their convenience
- Providing lunch to interviewees
- Demonstrating the company's products to interviewees
- A senior manager greeting potential recruits.

4 Brainstorming

If you are working with a group then you may find it helpful to use brain-storming as an idea-generating device. This is a technique developed over fifty years ago by Alex Osbourne. It is widely practised and has taken a number of forms. The principles which underlie it have already been identified above as applying to divergent problem-solving techniques. The avoidance of early judgement and aiming for as many ideas as possible are central.

The general form taken in a brainstorming sessions is as follows:

- Identify the problem and have it written down in question form. *How can we ensure quality recruitment?*
  It is important to have the problem couched as a ' how' style question.
- Bring together a group of the right size and composition (ideally between five and twelve people). They should have been given the problem statement beforehand.
- Outline the format of the session (sequence of events and time frame).

- Outline the rules of brainstorming:
  - No criticism of other people's ideas
  - All ideas are OK – the wilder, the better
  - The aim is maximum numbers of ideas
  - 'Hitch-hiking' onto or amending other people's ideas is great.
- Sometimes (especially with a new group) it helps to conduct a warm-up. One of the leaders takes off a shoe and asks the group to think of uses for just one shoe. This warm-up need only take 5-10 minutes.
- Display the problem statement for all to see.
- When the brainstorming session starts one person writes down all the ideas as they are offered.
  The session should aim at about 25–40 minutes' duration.
- A sub-group of an odd number (say five) then evaluates the ideas generated and picks the best.
- The selected ideas are reported back to the main group.

It is important to remember that brainstorming itself is about producing ideas, *not* evaluating them. The leader must be careful to facilitate the production of as many ideas as possible.

Brainstorming promotes 'wild and offbeat' ideas. When people of different seniority are involved this can inhibit free-ranging ideas. The more junior staff are often reluctant to suggest things which more senior people may disparage. More senior people may feel that suggesting apparently foolish things might cause them to 'lose face'. Brainstorming is best used:

- When the problem in question can be stated in fairly simple terms
- When the leader (manager) feels comfortable about using it
- When those involved are of a similar seniority (or seniority is not an issue).

5 Card writing

Where the group is not comfortable or suitable for brainstorming then a writing technique to generate ideas can be used. People write ideas on cards (which can be anonymous). The cards are circulated or displayed and other group members then develop further ideas from them or seek to improve on the ideas.

The principle of having a clear and simple problem statement applies here as with brainstorming. It is also important to brief the group and give time for discussion of the statement to ensure it is understood.

The process thus involves the following stages:

- Problem statement
- Group briefing and discussion
- Idea generation
- Ideas evaluation (often by seeking to 'group' ideas in some logical way by moving cards around on a table or pinboard)

Using techniques to deal with complex data

A high level of numeracy is not usually needed to resolve managerial problems but what is often required is an ability to deal with a large amount of information. There are several considerations to bear in mind when dealing with large amounts of data:

First, it is worth considering the value to be gained by summarizing the information in order to get a general picture. Therefore when the newspapers report that inflation has been 5 per cent in the past year they are giving an overall picture based upon the average rise in prices of a range of items. You accept this and recognize that it does not mean that a specific item (the newspaper, for example) has gone up in price by 5 per cent. Think of the difficulty you would have getting an overall picture of inflation if the newspaper instead just listed the individual price rise of every item you might buy and left it to you to get a picture.

Second, it is useful to bear in mind that in a large set of data usually a relatively small number of the items of information account for a large part of the total amount of information. Therefore, returning to the inflation example, you would perhaps be less troubled by a price rise in caviar than you would by a rise in the mortgage interest rate. The reason for this is that (for the vast majority of people) far more of their income is spent on mortgage repayments than on caviar. An economist called Pareto noted this effect and coined what he described as the 80:20 rule. According to this rule about 80 per cent of the problem can be accounted for by about 20 per cent of the possible causes (see earlier).

Let us consider a fairly typical problem confronting a manager. Figure 10.7 is a list of forty members of staff and beside each person is the number of days on which they have been absent from work in the past year.

Let us assume that the manager is concerned about absence from work and wishes to quantify the problem. One way would be simply to start at the top of the list with Adams and ascertain reasons for Adams' absences. Then you proceed alphabetically down the list to Wilson, identifying in each case what reasons for absence exist and whether they can be tackled.

There is an advantage that there is certainly a clear methodology behind it and if you had to break off from the task you could return to where you left off. It is also 'easy' in the sense that you are not setting yourself the task of rearranging the data.

Can you think of any reasons why this strategy may not be the most appropriate?

Name	Days absent in past year
Adams	0
Akran	0
Ahmed	2
Bolt	9
Boston	65
Buck	1
Carson	5
Chung	10
Churchill	180
Comfort	1
Crawford	1
Crosby	2
Cummings	7
Davis	10
Duncker	50
Dunnett	2
Fallon	50
Field	2
Fulmer	4
Gesch	6
Gordon	45
Hamilton	7
Hicks	55
Jenson	9
Kempner	5
Khalid	5
Maguire	2
McIlroy	4
Miller	4
Osborne	10
Prince	25
Simons	5
Summers	8
Taylor	120
Timpson	2
Torvill	4
Van Oss	6
Vickers	6
Williams	9
Wilson	12

Figure 10.7   A staff sickness problem (1)

Summarize the data

Another method may be to endeavour to summarize the data in order to get an idea of what the 'average' amount of absence was. The total of days absent for the forty staff is 750. If you divide 750 by 40 you get an average of nearly 19 days absent per member of staff. You could then pick out those members of staff who had more than the average amount of absence and look into the reasons for it. This method has an advantage in that it enables you to focus initially upon the staff who account for most of the absence. If necessary, you could then go on to look at the absence of the rest of the staff.

However, the average is affected by small number of staff with very high absence. You do not get a picture of the absence pattern for the rest of the staff.

Use the 80/20 rule

However, it is also possible to analyse the problem in more detail and look at the proportion of absence accounted for by the 'worst 10 per cent or 20 per cent' of staff (Figure 10.8).

As you can see from the breakdown the 'top' 20 per cent of the staff account for 80 per cent of the absence. This illustrates Pareto's 80/20 rule (introduced in Chapter 8). It may possibly be one of the most simple and effective rules for a manager in effective analysis of data.

The best way to illustrate it practically for yourself is to try it out. You can try it out on a number of everyday matters. What about looking at your monthly household expenses? Keep the supermarket till receipts and look at your monthly outgoings (mortgage, loan repayments, utilities, etc.). See what proportion of the total is accounted for by the most expensive items. It probably won't work out to be exactly 80 per cent of the bill is found in only 20 per cent of the items but you may be surprised.

Experienced managers use Pareto even though they may never have heard his name. When the board (or the director) says 10 per cent cuts are required the responsible manager knows that it is the larger budgets which are the ones most likely to give the basis for meeting it. Hence in health authorities or in education expenditure cuts of any consequence will involve looking at staff, since staff salaries constitute such a high proportion of the budget. When a 10 per cent increase in sales is required the sales manager knows most of it is likely to be secured from focusing sales efforts at the top 20 per cent of customers.

There is the old management dictum that 80 per cent of the work is done by 20 per cent of the employees. If you are one of those 20 per cent perhaps you can understand why it is that your manager keeps coming to you for that little bit extra.

Use a diagram to illustrate possible cause

Diagrams can be extremely useful in understanding the nature of a problem. If we consider the staff sickness example then we might identify a range of

Name of staff	Days absent	Subtotal	% of absence
Adams	0		
Akran	0		
Buck	1		
Comfort	1	2	0.3
Crawford	1		
Crosby	2		
Dunnett	2		
Timpson	2	7	0.9
Maguire	2		
Ahmed	2		
Field	2		
McIlroy	4	10	1.3
Miller	4		
Torvill	4		
Fulmer	4		
Kempner	5	17	2.3
Carson	5		
Khalid	5		
Simons	5		
Van Oss	6	21	2.8
Vickers	6		
Gesch	6		
Cummings	7		
Hamilton	7	26	3.5
Summers	8		
Williams	9		
Jenson	9		
Bolt	9	35	4.7
Chung	10		
Davis	10		
Osborne	10		
Wilson	12	42	5.6
Prince	25		
Gordon	45		
Duncker	50		
Fallon	50	170	22.7
Hicks	55		
Boston	65		
Taylor	120		
Churchill	180	420	56.0
Total days absent		750	100
Average days absent		18.8	

Figure 10.8   A staff sickness problem (2)

possible causes or factors associated with it. These could be simply listed. However, they could also be shown on a diagram such as Figure 10.9. This sort of causal diagram is often known as a 'fishbone diagram' for obvious reasons. The advantage of using this format of representation is that it enables you to add and amend information in a way that is not so easy when you have a conventional form of notes.

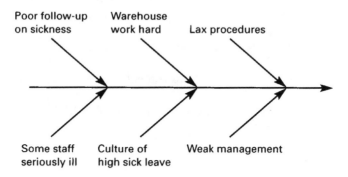

Figure 10.9   A staff sickness problem (3)

Another form of diagram which is often of considerable value in understanding why something has happened (or has failed to happen) is a 'force field diagram'. This depicts the opposing pressures involved in a situation. Returning again to the staff sickness problem, Figure 10.10 shows the forces involved.

Factors promoting high staff sickness

Weak management	Culture of high sickness	Poor procedures	Lax follow up	Physical work hard

| Management concern | | Ceiling on sick pay | Threat of loss of job | Peer group pressure |

Factors promoting low staff sickness

Figure 10.10   A staff sickness problem (4)

Elsewhere in this book (Chapter 2) there are examples of the use of diagrams to facilitate presentation of information.

Characteristics of group process

You will have noticed that problem solving (and decision making) is often a group activity. To function effectively in groups a manager needs to understand something about the process and life of groups.

One simple way to understand group process is to think in terms of the difference between task and maintenance roles. In most groups both these roles appear. Without a task focus the group often fails to achieve its purpose. If there is no maintenance focus then the group may prove to be a fraught and unpleasant experience for those involved.

Task roles
- Concern with content
- Get the job done
- Appearance of being 'tough'
- Related to rationale for group

Maintenance roles
- Give cohesion
- Awareness of individual emotional needs
- Related to the emotional life of the group

These two roles complement each other. Task roles are necessary to get the job done. Maintenance roles promote communication and cooperation.

Group Process

A well-known and tested model of group process is the following:

Forming $\rightarrow$ Storming $\rightarrow$ Norming $\rightarrow$ Performing $\rightarrow$ Ending

Forming
Anxiety, dependence on leader, search for 'code of conduct', testing out behaviour – 'what shall we do'?
Storming
Conflict, rebel against leader, resist task ('it's impossible'), test leadership, work out implications of task.
Norming
Group cohesion emerges, resistance reduces, mutual support appears, resolve to complete task ('we can do it').
Performing
Performance of task, flexible and functional roles, energy high, solutions emerge ('we're getting there').
Ending
Discussion moves away from task, members disengage, often desire to continue and not stop.

A failure to recognize the need to go through these stages can impede the successful operation of a group. Frequently the manager (group leader) displays impatience and tries to 'press on' to the performing part of the process. However, the group needs to go through the earlier stages in order to engage successfully in the performing stage.

Ending is also an issue sometimes for project groups. Having dealt with the particular problem which brought them together the group is often reluctant to disband. Effective problem-solving groups usually have a definite and limited life cycle.

Roles in groups

It is helpful for you as a manager to be aware of different roles which people might play in groups. There is not the scope here to go into a great deal of detail. However, the following role descriptions are useful:

The initiator
Starts things off – usually falls to person who brought group together. Also important in changing group direction – giving new impetus.

The clarifier
Draws out the precise meaning of individual contributions in relation to the group task. Encourages people to be specific and puts generalizations in more concrete terms.

The information giver
May have the information to hand or offers to locate it. May be technical or 'understanding' information. May be superficial or profound but is always relevant to the group task.

The questioner
Asks the fundamental questions about group task. These help define nature of task and challenge assumptions being made. Questioner helps group take a step back.

The summarizer
Pulls the contributions together. Does not add further information but allows a check on progress. Sometimes formalized (minute taker) but may be informal. Provides breathing space and allows for reflection, thus separating out stages of the group's work.

The supporter
Demonstrates warmth between individuals by supporting contributions or by later including them. Support may be non-verbal.

The joker
Obvious – provides light relief and lets off steam. Can be destructive to individual or group but can also be positive and creative.

Sharing experience
Makes personal statements about general issue relating to the group task. Allows group to move to deeper level. Prevents 'over-professionalism' of group.

Process observer
Appears when group is stuck. Reflects on reason for blockage. 'Why are we going around in circles?'

Sometimes as a manager you are able to select the group you would like to assist you; sometimes the team is already there. Considerable research has been done to assist the manager in identifying the characteristics of an effective team.

Meredith Belbin (1991) has conducted such research for many years and as a result he considers that the 'perfect team' is one which includes people able to undertake certain crucial roles. These are described below.

Belbin's eight team roles

1 The Coordinator
The chairperson or enabler. He or she need not be brilliant or creative, but would rather be called disciplined, focused and balenced. The Coordinator talks and listens well, is a good judge of people and things; a person who works through others.

2 The Shaper
Highly strung, outgoing and dominant. He or she is the task leader and in the absence of the chairperson would leap into that role even though he or she might not do it very well. The Shaper's strength lies in the drive and passion for the task but he or she can be over-sensitive, irritable and impatient. He or she is needed as a spur to action.

3 The Plant
Unlike the Shaper, the plant is introverted but is intellectually dominant. He or she is the source of original ideas and proposals, being the most imaginative as well as the most intelligent member of the team. The Plant can, however, be careless of details and may resent criticism. He or she needs to be drawn out or he or she will switch off.

4 The Monitor–Evaluator
The Monitor–Evaluator is also intelligent but it is an analytic rather than a creative intelligence. His or her contribution is the careful dissection of ideas and the ability to see the flaw in an argument. He or she is often less involved than the others, tucked away with the data, aloof from the team, but always necessary as a quality check. The Monitor–Evaluator is dependable but can be tactless and cold.

5 The Resource Investigator
This is the popular member of the team, extrovert, sociable and relaxed. He or she brings new contacts, ideas and developments to the group, the salesperson, diplomat or liaison officer. The Resource Investigator is not especially original or a driver and needs the team to pick up on their contribution.

7 The Specialist
The person who possesses the particular knowledge or skill. Often a solitary 'boffin' type who functions best alone. Contributions made often represent the necessary breakthrough which overcomes an obstacle which has been holding up the team.

8 The Team Worker
Holds the team together by being supportive to others, by listening, encouraging, harmonizing and understanding. Likeable and popular but uncompetitive, he or she is the sort of person you do not notice when there but miss when absent.

9 The Completer–Finisher
Without which the team might never meet its deadline. This is the person who checks the details, worries about schedules and chivvies the others with a sense of urgency. His or her relentless follow-through is important but not always popular.

Note: in teams a person may perform more than one role. The full set of roles is most important where rapid change is involved. More stable groups can get by without the full set of roles.

Examples of problem solving drawn from managers in various organizations.

At the start of a project we set up a controls workshop. We get together a representative from each area. We have a brainstorming session. We think about all the things which could go wrong. We then group like-minded comments together under Key Risk Areas. We then have a benchmark for where controls should be placed. We've found it to be quick and effective.

In all the workshops which we have had the majority of people have been complimentary that areas were identified that they had never considered, that it gave them an opportunity to see the system from a different perspective. It has shown people from branches that if they did not do certain things correctly then there would be problems.

Flowcharts are helpful as a way of sequencing events and you can use them to establish control points. You write a report over a number of pages and people sometimes have problems following the sequence of events. Whereas if you put things down in a flow chart then people can follow the logic of what's happening.

David Tait, Manager, Woolwich Building Society

We've just gone through a merger with Town & Country Building Society. We had a fairly major exercise in systems conversions and coordination. It went extremely well through meticulous planning. We had a problem on a part of the system of day two of the merger. It was a part of the system which enabled us to get account numbers. The system went down. It took us three days to get it resolved. In the end someone came up with something which wasn't obvious but enabled us to get around it.

There were a number of interested parties in the problem. What happened was that we were in communication with the interested parties. But when I said 'have you got the people around a table?' the answer was 'no'. There had been some one-to-one meetings but otherwise it had all been telephone conversations. They needed to look at the paper reports and see why there was a problem with the account numbers. They had spent two and a half days trying unsuccessfully to sort it out. There had been misunderstandings. We got the people together and the problem was solved in half an hour. The solution was to use a slightly different system environment which would produce the information.

The lesson is common sense – some problems you can solve at arm's length but some you can't, especially when they are multi-disciplinary and there is no collective responsibility.
Nigel Wright, Manager, Woolwich Building Society

I find brainstorming is pretty endemic. The other day at a meeting about joint assessment for community care it was suggested that we did brainstorming and everyone seemed to know how to do it. I was quite surprised how widespread it is.

It depends on whether you are working on a group or on your own. A lot of what I do is working in teams. So chairing skills become important. It's about shutting up noisy people and bringing out quiet people. It's more the manager as a facilitator of a group, which means sometimes taking a dilemma to a group without any real idea of how things might turn out. It's different when you're taking something to a group where the solution is quite clear and you're trying to sell something to them.

If a group is not coming up with a solution the first question is will I notice it? Maybe someone else will and point it out. So I'd bring whatever process is going on to a halt. I'd look for a way out – maybe summarizing or asking other people for a way out.

As an example, there was a project-implementation group where we were at a stage where we knew what we were aiming for and we were trying to work out a critical path. We were looking at setting up National Vocational Qualifications. We got as far as describing what kind of assessor training we might need. But then we had some real blocks and we got lost.

> We were trying to sort out the difference between what we were as a project group and as a group trying to implement it. I felt that I had lost the chair of the meeting a few times. It was like a free-for-all. I was getting confused over my chairing.
>
> Richard Hooper, Training Manager, London Borough of Enfield Social Services Department

LEARNING POINTS

- What ways can you categorize problems at work?
- What is the difference between analytical and creative thought?
- What is the difference between 'left- and right-brain thinking' ?
- What are the barriers to creative thought?
- What is 'vertical and lateral thinking'?
- What is divergent and convergent problem solving?
- What are the stages in problem solving which John Adair suggests managers use?
- What is:
  Kepner Tregoe Problem Analysis?
  Checklisting?
  Problem Division?
  Use of analogies?
  Brainstorming?
  Card Writing?
- What are the following techniques to deal with complex data?
  Summarizing
  80/20 rule
  Diagrams
- What are the differences between task and maintenance roles in groups?
- What are the stages in group process?
- What are the key roles group members hold?

PREPARING FOR ACTION PLANNING

Remember the checklist of questions identified in the Introduction to this book? Try them again to identify your further development needs. We have reproduced those most appropriate to this chapter to help you. You will need to adapt them to the issues discussed.

SUMMARY

What actions would you/have you taken with others at times of particular difficulty or change?

Which methods do you use to analyse facts and figures for your job purposes?

How do you present these facts and figures to others for decision-making purposes?

How effective are your analytical and mathematical skills in convincing others?

Were the outcomes of these presentations appropriate for the decision-making purposes?

How might you improve your analytical and mathematical skills?

How do you liaise with others at off-site locations?

How is information fed back into the decision-making process?

How could it be improved?

What information do you need to do your job and for what purposes?

Do you have any problems obtaining this information?

To whom do you supply information?

How much time do you spend in:
- Gathering information?
- Analysing information?
- Providing information?

How do you go about gathering, analysing and providing information?

Can these methods be improved?

How do you currently store and receive information?

Do you always have the necessary information in advance of meetings?

Do you always supply the necessary information in advance of meetings?

What are the meetings' follow-up processes?

Do your meetings result in positive action?

Have you attended committees in your current role and prepared reports for these committees?

Have the results of your reports been acted upon?

If they have not, why do you think this was?

Questions devised by, and adapted from, the Crediting Competence Team at South Bank University and reproduced with permission.

ACTION PLANNING

- Identify at least two different work problems.
- Describe them using at least five different dimensions.
- Draw a diagram comparing them on each dimension.
- Identify what problem-solving techniques would be appropriate (whether you would need the involvement of others).
- Use the techniques to try to solve the problems.
- Identify further opportunities to practise problem solving.

FURTHER READING

Cooke, S. and Slack, S.(1991), *Making Management Decisions*, Prentice Hall, Englewood Cliffs, NJ.

Eberle, R. (1990), *SCAMPER: Games for Imagination Development*, DOK Press, Buffalo, NY

Fletcher, W. (1990), *Creative People*, Hutchinson Business Books, London.

Kepner, Charles H. and Tregoe, Benjamin (1981), *The New Rational Manager*, Princeton University Press, Princeton, NJ

Margerison, Charles J. (1974), *Managerial Problem Solving*, McGraw-Hill, New York.

Mintzberg, H. (1973), *The Nature of Managerial Work*, Harper & Row, New York.

Rawlinson, J. G. (1981), *Creative thinking and Brainstorming*, Gower, Aldershot

Rickards, Tudor (1990), *Creativity and Problem Solving at Work*, Gower, Aldershot.

Bibliography

Adair, John (1985), *Effective Decision Making*, Pan London.

Belbin, R. M. (1991), *Management Teams*, 2nd edn, Heinemann, London.

Brigley, S.(1994), *Walking on the Tightrope*, IM Research Report.

Connock, S. and Johns, T. (1995), *Ethical Leadership*, IPD, London.

Cooper, Gary L., Cooper, Rachel D. and Eaker, Lynn, H. (1988), *Living with Stress*, Penguin Books, NJ.

Drummond, J. and Bain, B.(1994), *Managing Business Ethics*, Butterworth-Heinemann, Oxford.

Drummond, John (1995), *Financial Times*, 6 April.

Fisher, R. and Ury, W. (1984), *Getting to Yes*, Hutchinson Business Books, London.

Friedman, M. (1962), 'The social responsibility of business is to increase its profits'.

Grant, R. (1995), *Strategic Management*, Oxford, Blackwells.

Handy, Charles B. (1985), *Understanding Organizations*, 3rd edn, Penguin Books, London.

Hardy, W. G. (1990), *Effective Business Writing*, BIM, London.

Harvey-Jones, Sir John (1988), *Making It Happen*, Fontana, London.

Hind, David (1989), *Transferable Personal Skills: A Student Guide*, Business Education Publishing, Tyne & Wear.

Janis, I. L. (1972) *Victims of Group Think*.

DesJardins, J. R. and McCall, J. J. (1990), *Contemporary issues in Business Ethics*, Wadsworth, Belmont, CA.

Jennings, D. and Wattam, S. (1997) *Decision Making*, London, Pitman.

Johnson, G. and Scholes, K. (1993), *Exploring Corporate Strategy*, Prentice Hall, Englewood Cliffs, NJ.

Kant, I. (1959), *Foundations of Metaphysics of Morals*, (translated by Beck, L. W.), Bobbs-Merrill, New York.

Kotler, P. (1980), *Marketing Management: Analysis Planning and Control*, Prentice Hall, Englewood Cliffs, NJ.

Looker, Terry and Gregson, Olga (1989), *Stresswise*, Hodder & Stoughton Educational, London.

McCarthy, Jerome (1960), *Basic Marketing: A Managerial Approach*, Irwin, Homewood, IL.

Matthews, M. C. (1988), *Strategic Intervention in Organizations*, Sage, Beverly Hills, CA.

Mill, J. S. *Utilitarianism* (various editions and commentaries).

Mintzberg, H. (1994), *The Rise and Fall of Strategic Planning*, Prentice Hall, Englewood Cliffs, NJ.

Newell, S. (1995), *The Healthy Organization*, Routledge, London.

Open University (1990), *The Effective Manager*, Open Business School Certificate, B784.

Peel, Malcolm (1988), *How to Make Meetings Work*, Kogan Page, London.

Porter, M. E. (1980), *Competitive Strategy: Techniques for Analysing Industries and Competitors*, Free Press, New York.

Sorell, T. and Hendry, T. (1994), *Business Ethics*, Butterworth-Heinemann, Oxford.

Sternberg, E. (1994), *Just Business*, Warner, New York.

Tannenbaum, R. and Schmidt, W. H. (1958), 'How to choose a leadership pattern', *Harvard Business Review*, March–April, 55–101.

Training Agency (1990), *Investors in People*.

Index